Praise for *Leisu...*

"If you are contemplating retirement or know anyone who is doing so, I urge you to read *Leisureville*. You will not find a better written, more entertaining or more insightful account of the myriad implications of the segregation of our society by age and income."
—*Daily Kos*

"Blechman's primary interest is not in the eerily false perfection of such places, but rather in the American psychology of segregation, radical individualism and the fears underlying the dreams of their residents. . . . [*Leisureville* is] part exurban exposé, part postmodern Roald Dahl parable."
—*The Forward*

"A sharp take on care- and child-free 'Active Adult' communities, where golf carts have replaced the automobile, downtowns are make-believe, the days are filled with sunshine and restrictive covenants enforce conformity."
—*Kirkus Reviews*

"Engaging . . . [Blechman] confronts the troubling trend toward isolation and escapism."
—*Publishers Weekly*

"As more and more Baby Boomers retire, the growing phenomenon of retirement communities will continue to expand throughout the country. . . . This lively book reveals why older Americans are flocking to these geritopias and what happens to our social fabric when they opt to live in gated leisurevilles where no children are allowed."
—*Tucson Citizen*

"By using what social scientists call the participant-observer approach, Blechman gives readers a great sense of what it's like to live in developments for senior citizens. . . . Most of the book is not, however, an outlet for the author's social analysis. . . . The majority of the book provides Blechman a great outlet to display his storytelling and descriptive skills."
—*Eureka Reporter*

"Read it."
—*The News-Press* (Florida)

Leisureville

Also by Andrew D. Blechman

Pigeons:
The Fascinating Saga of the World's Most
Revered and Reviled Bird

LEISUREVILLE

Adventures in a World Without Children

Andrew D. Blechman

Grove Press
New York

Published simultaneously in Canada
Printed in the United States of America

ISBN: 978-0-8021-4418-8

Grove Press
an imprint of Grove/Atlantic, Inc.
841 Broadway
New York, NY 10003

Distributed by Publishers Group West

www.groveatlantic.com

09 10 11 12   10 9 8 7 6 5 4 3 2 1

For Erika and Lillie

PETER: Forget them, Wendy. Forget them all. Come
with me where you'll never, never have to worry about grown-up
things again.

WENDY: Never is an awfully long time.

—*Peter Pan*

Contents

Leisureville

1

For Sale

IT WAS A TYPICALLY COLD, BLEAK FEBRUARY MORNING WHEN I LOOKED out the kitchen window and spotted a sign across the street on Dave and Betsy Anderson's front lawn: "For Sale." This came as a complete surprise; I had assumed the Andersons—cheerful acquaintances and active members of our small-town community—were neighborhood lifers. Hadn't they just retired? Weren't they still in Florida celebrating their new freedom with a snowbird vacation?

People like the Andersons don't just pick up and leave, do they? And why would they want to go? We live in a small, traditional New England town, one that people pay good money to visit. Tourists travel from hours away to take in our bucolic vistas, marvel at our historic architecture, dine in our sophisticated restaurants, and partake in our enviable number of cultural offerings. It's a charming place to live, like something out of a Norman Rockwell painting. In fact, Norman Rockwell once lived here.

Although we lived across the street from one another for about two years, the Andersons and I weren't particularly close. We didn't barbecue together in the summer, or sit around the fireplace in the winter sipping cocoa. In fact, I don't think I ever invited them inside my home. But we were friendly. When I left town for a few weeks of family vacation the summer before, it was Dave who mowed my lawn, unsolicited. "I had the mower running anyway, so I figured what the heck," he modestly explained.

Dave and I frequently toured each other's yard, comparing notes about gardening and lawn care. His was immaculate, the lawn cut at a perfect ninety-degree angle to the house "to soften the edges" of his rectangular home. If a leaf fell, Dave was out there lickety-split with his leaf blower and preposterously large headphones. The shrubs were trimmed into perfect ovals, circles, and cones. Dave even tied a rope around his large pine tree and drew a tidy circle with it to mark the boundary between an acceptable accumulation of pine needles and a green lawn.

My yard, by comparison, was a far more haphazard work in progress. Dave started to take pity on me, stopping by to give occasional fatherly pep talks. "Been a rough year for crabgrass," he remarked to me one summer day. "I've seen it all over town. Must be the hot weather." Despite my best efforts, huge, gnarly clumps of it had thundered across my lawn. I found his words somewhat soothing (It's not just me!) until I glanced across the street at his dense, verdant turf.

Over the course of these two summers, I also got to know Betsy. Whether Dave was methodically detailing his van or organizing his garage so that every tool had a proper perch, he moved with precision. But Betsy was a firecracker. She drove a candy-apple-red Mazda Miata, and waved energetically whenever our eyes met across the street. She was the one who loudly cheered me on as I shakily rode my new skateboard down our street. I appreciated her for that.

We were at different stages in our lives and seemingly had little in common. As the Andersons pondered retirement, my wife and I celebrated the birth of our first child. And the Andersons obsessively played one sport we had little interest in learning: golf. But this disparity of ages was one reason we had purchased a house in this particular neighborhood. The generational span seemed to add stability and was somehow endearing.

Besides, I just plain *liked* the Andersons. They were great neighbors: cheerful, low-maintenance, and reassuringly normal. That is why the sudden appearance of the "For Sale" sign threw me for a loop.

The Andersons didn't return until early April, during another frosty spring. I ran into Dave a few days later, while I was out shoveling my driveway yet again. I asked him about the sign and he said something about moving to "sunny Florida." Frankly, with my boots and mittens full of wet snow, I didn't blame him, and I wished him the best of luck selling his house.

"But aren't you a little sad to be going?" I asked.

Dave puffed on his pipe. His face was one big warm smile, childlike in its intensity. "Nope."

Given the glut of houses on the market—three on our street alone—the Andersons' didn't sell right away, and so we spent another summer trading war stories about landscaping. One day Dave found me knee-deep in my shrubs, drenched in sweat, bugs swarming around my face, and my infant daughter perched on my back crying hysterically.

"How's it going?" he asked.

I had spent the morning overseeding my lawn in an unpredictable wind, and most of the seed was now in the street. Then I stepped on the sprinkler and broke it.

"Oh, not bad," I managed. "And you?" I got up and tried to shake his hand, but I was too busy swatting at bugs.

"You know, they make a product that you spread on your lawn that takes care of all these gnats and flies," he suggested, offering me the use of his lawn spreader.

"What does the lawn have to do with all these bugs?" I asked, perplexed.

"Well, that's where they come from, where they live. Haven't you noticed?"

The conversation soon turned to Dave's imminent move. I still felt a little let down by his decision to move away so abruptly. Didn't he feel at least some regret? Weren't he and Betsy going to miss strolling into town for dinner and waving to old friends along the way?

"We never intended to leave the neighborhood, Andrew," he explained. "As you know, I'm not someone who makes rash decisions. But then we discovered The Villages. It's not so much that we're leaving here as we're being drawn to another place. Our hearts are now in The Villages."

The Villages? The name was so bland it didn't even register. All I could picture was a collection of English hamlets in the Cotswolds bound together by narrow lanes and walking trails. But I thought Dave had said they were moving to Florida.

Over the course of the summer, Dave cleared up my confusion. At first, his descriptions of The Villages were so outrageous, so over the top, that I figured he must have been pulling my leg. Then he started bringing me clippings from The Villages' own newspaper. As I sat and read them, I was filled with a sense of comic wonder mixed with a growing alarm.

The Andersons were moving to the largest gated retirement community in the world. It spanned three counties, two zip codes, and more than 20,000 acres. The Villages itself, Dave explained, was subdivided into dozens of separate gated communities, each its own distinct entity, yet fully integrated into a greater whole that shared two manufactured downtowns, a financial district, and several shopping centers, and all of it connected by nearly 100 miles of golf cart trails.

I had trouble imaging the enormousness of the place. I didn't have any reference points with which to compare such a phenomenon. Was it a town, or a subdivision, or something like a college campus? And if it was as big as Dave described, then how could residents travel everywhere on golf carts? Dave described golf cart tunnels, golf cart bridges, and even golf cart tailgates. And these were no dinky caddie replacements. According to Dave, some of them cost upwards of $25,000 and were souped up to look like Hummers, Mercedes sedans, and hot rods.

The roads are especially designed for golf cart traffic, Dave told me, because residents drive the carts everywhere: to supermarkets, hardware stores, movie theaters, and even churches. With one charge, a resident can drive about forty miles, which, Dave explains to me, "is enough to go anywhere you'd want to go."

According to the Andersons, The Villages provides its 75,000 residents (it is building homes for 35,000 more) with anything their hearts could possibly desire, mostly sealed inside gates: countless recreation centers staffed with full-time directors; dozens of pools; hundreds of hobby and affinity clubs; two spotless, crime-free village centers with friendly, affordable restaurants; and three dozen golf courses—one for each day of the month—with plans for many more.

More important, The Villages provides residents with something else they apparently crave—a world without children. An individual must be at least fifty-five years old to purchase a home in The Villages, and no one under nineteen may live there—period. Children may visit, but their stays are strictly limited to a total of thirty days a year, and the developer reserves the right to periodically request that residents verify their age. As a new father, I found this rule particularly perplexing, although I hesitated to say as much.

I asked Dave, a schoolteacher for thirty years, if he felt uncomfortable living in a community without children, and I was surprised when he answered that he was actually looking forward to it. "I was tired of trying to imagine what a thirteen-year-old girl in my classroom was going through," Dave said. "I'm not thirteen, and I'm not a girl. I want to spend time with people who are retired like me."

When I asked about diversity, Betsy said that she didn't much care for it. Dave explained that diversity to him is more about interests and background than about age or racial demographics. "There are very few blacks—although I did play golf with a nice man—and I don't think I've seen any Orientals, but there's still so much stimulus there. Diversity exists if you want to find it. There are hundreds and hundreds of clubs to join, and if you don't find one that suits your interests, they'll help you start one."

Orientals? I hadn't heard that word since the 1970s, when chop suey was considered an exotic menu item. It never occurred to me how culturally out of sync I was with my neighbors. Although Dave and Betsy were young retirees (fifty-five and sixty-two, respectively), we were clearly of two different generations.

"Life in The Villages is really too much to describe," Betsy added. "It's simply unforgettable. For me, it was love at first sight." She patted her heart for emphasis. "I can only equate it to the movie *The Stepford Wives*. Everyone had a smile on their face like it's too good to be true. But it really is."

"I was real worried about Elizabeth when it was time to go," Dave said. "I was worried she would just crumble when we left to come back up here. The place really touched her heart."

"There are a lot of people just like us," Betsy continued. "I was very comfortable there. It's where I want to be. It has everything I could possibly want."

I was struck by how many of Dave's newspaper clippings described the residents' unusual leisure pursuits, including their fascination with gaining entry into the *Guinness Book of World Records*. In the eight months Dave had his house up for sale, his compatriots down south qualified for the big book twice: first for the world's largest simultaneous electric slide (1,200 boogying seniors), and next for the world's longest golf cart parade (nearly 3,500 low-speed vehicles).

As amusing as these descriptions of daily life in The Villages were, they left me feeling dismayed, even annoyed. Were the Andersons really going to drop out of our community, move to Florida, and sequester themselves in a gated geritopia? Dave and Betsy had volunteered on the EMS squad, and Betsy also volunteered at the senior center and our local hospice. By all accounts, they were solid citizens with many more years of significant community involvement ahead of them.

And frankly, our community needed the Andersons. There were whispers that the town intended to pave over our little neighborhood park with a 20,000-square-foot fire station. Other sites were being considered for the station, but because the town owned the property it would be cheaper to build it there. The Andersons were a known quantity around town. They were respected and presumably knew how to navigate town hall and the surprisingly acrimonious politics of small-town New England. And now they were leaving—running off to a planned community where such headaches in all probability didn't exist. Rather than lead, they had chosen to secede.

As Betsy described The Villages' accommodations for the terminally ill, it was clear that she had no intention of ever returning to our community. "The rooms overlook a golf course!" she said. "The Villages has even made dying a little more pleasant!"

After spending so much time discussing retirement living with the Andersons, I decided to take a peek at one of the few places in our town that I'd never bothered to visit: the senior center. I found it to be a rather glum-looking building, resembling an oversize ranch house, with small windows. One look at the activities offered, and it was plain to see that they paled by comparison with the hundreds of activities going on at The Villages: just a lunch "excursion" to a local Chinese restaurant, an art class, and a weekly bridge game. A flyer on the bulletin board advertised a free seniors' seminar titled "I Don't Want to Go to a Nursing Home!"

Money budgeted for seniors' activities and services represented less than half of one percent of our town's annual expenditures. Meanwhile our school system devoured fifty-five percent of the town budget, and residents had recently approved a $20 million bond issue to build two new schools.

This lopsided arrangement isn't lost on Dave. "Pretty soon, Andrew, your daughter will be school-age and your greatest concern will be the school system," he told me one day as I struggled to install a tree swing in my backyard. "You'll want your tax dollars to go there. But our needs are different and we're in competition for a finite amount of resources. It's not a negative thing; it just exists. At The Villages, there's not that same competition. It's not a matter of funding a senior center or a preschool program, because at The Villages we spend our dollars on ourselves."

By September, the little ranch house across the street had found a buyer. The Andersons spent the month packing up their belongings, while I planted crocuses in preparation for winter. The Andersons were positively ebullient on moving day. "The Villages puts everything we had here in a different light," Dave told me, while waving good-bye to our mailman, Kevin. "Sure, we had a lovely home, a nice neighborhood, some status in the community, and some good friends. But none of that measured up to the two months we spent in The Villages."

Betsy mechanically surveyed her empty home as if she were giving a hotel room a quick once-over before checking out. "It's called 'new beginnings,'" she said. Dave asked me if I wanted his winter boots. "I won't be needing them anymore," he said.

As the days grew shorter, the leaves turned fiery red and the sky a brilliant autumnal blue, I soldiered on in the garden while my wife pushed our daughter in her new tree swing. It would be several weeks before the new neighbors moved in, and I couldn't help looking across the street at Dave's leaf-strewn yard and empty house. It fell to me to organize the neighborhood against paving over our park, and I reluctantly accepted the challenge. I soon found myself flushed with purpose, sitting at the computer writing editorials and waiting outside our local co-op grocery store in a bitter wind for signatures on a petition.

A few months later, I received an e-mail from Dave. "The Villages' mystique has not dimmed," he wrote. "It was the right move at the right time for the right people. We've asked ourselves many times if we have any regrets. The answer is always the same, 'No.' He went on to invite me down to see the place for myself. "Maybe you'll want to write a book about it."

I'd already started taking notes, awkwardly following the Andersons around and writing down everything they said, like an ethnologist recording an oral history. Their move fascinated me— and kept me up at night. How could two bright individuals be drawn to something as seemingly ridiculous as The Villages? And by the looks of it, they were clearly not alone. Something was afoot; I could feel it. I suspected that the Andersons were in the vanguard of a significant cultural shift. I took Dave up on his offer.

As the day of my departure for Florida neared, it occurred to me that I had never visited a retirement community before, and so I had no idea what to pack. How does one dress for golf and bingo? I certainly didn't want to cause the Andersons any embarrassment. With gritted teeth, I resolved to purchase a pair of casual loafers, argyle socks, and a sweater vest.

2

Where's Beaver?

THE VILLAGES IS LOCATED ROUGHLY IN THE CENTER OF FLORIDA, about an hour north of Orlando International Airport, where I touch down feeling like a dork in my new argyle socks and loafers, and surrounded by giggling children running around in mouse ears. Given my travel budget, I rent an old beater, which is spray-painted black and is missing hubcaps, and whose odometer registers a quarter-million miles. The car shudders and misfires as I drive north along a relatively lonesome patch of the Florida Turnpike, which to my surprise cuts through rolling pastureland instead of swamps. This is Florida's "high country," home to the state's cattle industry, which is slowly disappearing as ranchers sell their sprawling properties to housing developers and land speculators.

The sides of the road sprout billboards advertising retirement communities. Photos of seniors playing golf and relaxing in pools are plastered with slogans such as "Life is lovelier," "On top of the world," and "Live the life you've been waiting your whole life for!" Interspersed are signs advertising the central Florida of old: hot-boiled peanuts, deerskin moccasins, and 'gator meat.

I don't see any advertisements for The Villages, but I do see state highway signs that guide me there via an off-ramp and a few small towns filled with vacant storefronts and roadside citrus vendors. I know I am getting close when the loamy soil and piney solitude segue into a construction site that stretches as far as the eye can see. A billboard displays a joyful phrase not often seen these days: "The Villages welcomes Wal-Mart!"

A short distance farther I spot the top of a beige water tower painted with The Villages' omnipresent logo—its name written in a looping 1970s-era faux-Spanish script. The construction is soon replaced with lush fairways speckled with golfers. I turn on the radio and tune in to WVLG AM640, The Villages' own radio station.

"It's a beautiful day in The Villages," the DJ announces. "Aren't we lucky to live here? OK, folks, here is a favorite I know you're going to love. The Candy Man Can. C'mon, let's sing it together." I listen in resigned silence to Sammy Davis Jr. and his effervescent lyrics about dew-sprinkled sunrises, feeling slightly claustrophobic and uneasy about living in a gated retirement community for the next month. Can someone under forty and as restless as I am survive an extended stay without going stir-crazy? Can I relate to people who play golf all day and play pinochle at night? Will they inundate me with Henny Youngman one-liners and stories about the Brooklyn Dodgers until I cry uncle?

It doesn't take long before I am hopelessly lost. Every direction is filled with nearly identical rooftops, curvy streets, gates, and flawless golf courses. A little while later the pleasantly landscaped, meandering boulevard I am driving down ends abruptly at a pockmarked county road. Across the way, the green grass and lush golf courses are noticeably absent, replaced with a narrow sandy road surrounded by a scraggly pine forest. Once upon a time, these inscrutable forests were home to fiercely independent subsistence farmers, called Crackers, who delighted in squirrel meat and rarely traveled except to move deeper into the pines. I watch as a towering pickup truck with a Confederate flag turns onto an unpaved road and briefly loses its footing in a patch of deep sand.

I make a U-turn and continue to drive around aimlessly until I spot an arrow pointing toward Spanish Springs, one of The Villages' two manufactured downtowns. A sign beside the road cautions against speeding, noting that The Villages is a "golf cart community." The road is more of a parkway, four lanes across with a handsome palm-studded median. What at first appear to be unusually wide sidewalks turn out to be roads specifically designed for golf carts, which whiz silently along them. I see another sign reminding visitors, "It's a beautiful day in The Villages."

A few miles later, I drive by a hospital, an assisted care facility, and a large Catholic church. I go through another roundabout, cross an ornate bridge, pass something built to look like the crumbling ruins of a Spanish fort, and suddenly I'm in the "town" of Spanish Springs. I spot Betsy outside a Starbucks standing beside her shiny red Miata, dressed attractively in pale pink slacks and a white cardigan, and sporting a nice tan. She greets me with a relaxed smile and a friendly hug, and insists on buying me a very welcome cup of iced coffee. It's comforting to see a familiar face from back home.

"Isn't it nice?" she asks. "People call it 'Disney for adults,' and I'm beginning to understand why. I just can't believe I'm here. I've met people that have been here for five years and they're still pinching themselves. It's like being on a permanent vacation."

Surrounding us is an imitation Spanish colonial town spiced up with a few Wild West accents. There's a central square with splashing fountains, a mission-like building at one end, a stucco church at another, and across the way a saloon in the style of the old West with wrought iron balconies. According to The Villages' mythology, Ponce de León passed through this area, just missing these waters—the fountain of youth he so desperately sought. The streets around the town square are lined with buildings that appear to be about 150 years old. There are faded advertisements on their facades for a gunsmith, an assayer, and a telegraph office. I feel as if I'm on a movie set, which strikes me as an uncomfortable place to live.

Betsy and I take our coffee to the central square, and sit on a bench beside the fountain of youth, which is strewn with lucky coins. The sun is shining, but it's not hot. We catch up on neighborhood gossip, the miserable New England weather, and the uncertain fate of our neighborhood park. Betsy is left pondering her incredible luck. "If we were still living up north, those problems would be our problems," she says with a sigh. Although not meant unkindly, her comment stings. But she's got a point; her life promises to be a lot more carefree down here than it was back home.

We mosey around the square and then head to the western-motif saloon, Katie Belle's, which is for residents and their guests only. Outside, a historical marker explains the building's colorful past. "Katie Belle Van Patten was the wife of Jacksonville business-man John Decker Van Patten, who, along with a number of other investors, built the luxurious hotel in 1851. . . ."

The plaque looks so authentic that I have to remind myself I am standing on what was pastureland a mere decade ago. Inside the saloon the walls are covered in dark wood, and heavy draperies hang from several large windows. An enormous Tiffany-style skylight catches my eye, as do two dozen line dancers keeping time to a coun-try and western tune. Many of the stools along the bar are filled with retirees holding draft beers. I look at my watch. It's just past two in the afternoon. "Line dancing is very popular here because you can do it without a partner," Betsy explains. "They say the only prob-lem with being a widow in The Villages is that you're so busy you forget you *are* one."

Although I've sat for a beer at an American Legion Post be-fore, I've never been to a bar solely reserved for senior citizens. The first thing I notice is that no one is what I would call particularly beautiful, at least not to my age-biased eyes. But they all look as if they're having a good time.

Ever the host, Betsy suggests I drop my luggage off at their house and join them for dinner. "They call it 'Florida's Friendliest Hometown'—and that's just what it is," she says as she gets into her Miata. "Everyone's so friendly because everyone is so happy. So make yourself comfortable at our house and enjoy your stay."

I decide to first take a walk around alone to get my bearings, and perhaps acclimate, before popping over to the Andersons' house later in the afternoon. Although "hometown" is a relative term given that everyone here was born someplace else, damned if, as I look around, everyone I make eye contact with doesn't greet me with a big friendly grin.

I retreat to Starbucks to catch my breath; the coffee shop with its generic interior design feels like a portal back to the real world. I pick up a *New York Times* and scan the headlines. I'm oddly comforted by the fact that there's been continued violence in the Middle East.

Back outside, I walk down the street to a little room with a large display window—the main WVLG broadcast studio. A DJ with a large potbelly and a graying chinstrap beard talks into a microphone while pressing colored buttons on an extensive control board. An outdoor speaker hangs from the building. The DJ repeats the mantra that I will hear so often during my stay: "It's a beautiful day in The Villages!" Then it's a Lesley Gore classic: "Sunshine, Lollipops, and Rainbows."

The studio is attached to the chamber of commerce. Inside, I look at a rack of brochures, but I note that all the information pertains exclusively to activities within The Villages. I purchase a map for five dollars. It is large and double-sided and depicts only streets inside The Villages. Anything outside the community—even something just across the street—is represented by a white void. Curiously, there is a large white empty space in the center of the map as well.

I ask the woman at the desk about the big white space, but she doesn't know why it's there; nor does she know why there are no brochures for any businesses outside The Villages. Typically, a chamber of commerce displays information from a much wider area. "I guess there just isn't space for more brochures," she says, adding, "People ask us the darnedest things." When I ask to use her phone, I notice that The Villages' sales office is the first number listed on her speed dial.

From Spanish Springs, I drive for what feels like a good twenty minutes until I finally approach the Andersons' village. I'm a bit concerned because much of the muffler seems to have fallen off on the drive up from Orlando, and the engine is leaking a lot of oil.

The Andersons' village is clean and new, with rows of tidy ranch homes ending in quiet culs-de-sac. Lawn sprinklers effortlessly turn on and then off in near unison. The lawns are perfectly edged, and try as I might, I can't find a single weed. The driveways are so clean they looked scrubbed, and in fact some are.

The neighborhood is so immaculate that it resembles a set from *Leave It to Beaver*, but Wally and the Beaver are nowhere to be seen. There are no bicycles or baseball mitts littering the yards; no school buses; no swing sets; no children playing street hockey. For that matter, there are no children. There aren't even any young couples holding hands. Aside from the droning of a distant lawn mower, the neighborhood is ghostly silent.

Children aren't the only demographic missing. Despite its Spanish-theme architecture, the community is about ninety-seven percent white. The lack of diversity has led to embarrassing mistakes: the Village of Santo Domingo was originally spelled "Santa Domingo." It wasn't until a Hispanic couple moved into the community, I'm told, that anybody noticed the error.

I noisily pull up to the Andersons' home and cringe at the thought of my car leaking oil on Dave's spotless driveway. I hesitantly park on the street, well aware that parking there overnight is against the rules. It's a quandary: do I stain Dave's driveway, or do I flout the rules that I suspect he conscientiously and happily obeys? I choose the latter, figuring that if I arrive home late at night and leave early in the morning, nobody will be the wiser.

Betsy greets me at the door with another big smile and a peck on the cheek. I'm surprised at how much bigger the Andersons' new home is. The ceilings are high, and the space is airy. The house is so clean it's as if the air itself has been sanitized. I feel like Oscar Madison landing in Zurich, and worry that I might somehow scuff a surface or otherwise make a mess. But after a long, sweaty day of travel, it's a relief to be in such tidy surroundings.

Betsy shows me to the guest room, where I notice shiny plastic beads hanging from a corner of a mirror. "Did you go to New Orleans for Mardi Gras?" I ask.

"No need," Betsy says. "They do Mardi Gras here. And it's wonderful. So much fun."

Betsy tells me to make myself right at home and to please feel free to rummage through the refrigerator as often as I like. Between my bedroom, the kitchen, and a pleasant screened-in porch, or lanai, there is a danger zone: an open living room with a plush white carpet and similarly untouched white furniture. There is one rule: I am not to walk across this carpet with my shoes on. Given that I'm wearing sandals and my feet are often dirty as well, I spend the next few weeks avoiding the room altogether. I notice that Dave does too, except when he dims the light up and down for me above a prized possession hanging on the wall—a print by Thomas Kinkade, an evangelical oil painter with an unusually devoted following, whose trademark is Painter of Light. The iridescent streetscape changes with each motion of the dimmer switch.

There are many framed photos around the house as well, but they are mainly of themselves, or of younger couples from back home—friends they like to refer to as "adopted family." Dave has two adult children with his first wife, but he has an uneasy relationship with them, and it clearly saddens him to talk about it. Betsy doesn't have children. There's just one photo that I can find of Dave's kids, but it's dated, possibly taken before the divorce.

Dave comes home and greets me with an easy smile. Dressed in khaki shorts, a yellow polo shirt, and loafers, he's the picture of leisure. "The only thing I worry about these days is my daily golf game," he says. "It's a totally different way of life."

"It's fun," Betsy says. "Just plain fun. And why not have a good time? We're retired and we have enough money to live here. We've worked hard for this."

"Some folks say we're insulated from everything on the outside," Dave continues. "That bothers some people, but it doesn't bother me. With the Internet, we have access to what's going on in the world. We can choose to be impacted by the news and get involved, or not."

Dave pours me a glass of chilled white zinfandel. "People are happy here," he continues. "Can't say we've run into too many sad people. Have you seen anybody moping around? And not all of them even live in The Villages. That seems to be the whole concept of The Villages—they've created a secure and comfortable zone that other people can share even though they can't afford to live here or if they're the wrong age to participate. They allow the melting pot to occur. You can visit it downtown and then play golf or go home. That's The Villages' way."

"Even the supermarket employees are pleasant to deal with," Betsy says. "There's never any rush at the checkout like back home. They ask you how you are, what you're making for dinner. People are polite. The employees can't do enough for you—and they have a rule against tipping. It's a whole different world down here. We're not used to this sort of kindness."

I ask about the house's previous owners, who put a lot of energy into the place by upgrading the cabinetry and tile. According to Dave, the husband was driven crazy by The Villages' policies and business practices.

"He felt controlled, and nickeled and dimed," Dave tells me. "That's why he installed a satellite dish even though The Villages offers cable. He wanted control over what channels he could select. He rented a post office box outside The Villages so he wouldn't have to buy a key to use the same mailboxes the rest of us use. It seems everything about The Villages started to rub him the wrong way. For instance, the walls come white. He wanted dark beige. He thought beige and white paint should cost the same. But they charged him extra for the tinted paint and didn't refund him for the original white paint. I think that finally drove him out."

"Thank God," Betsy exclaims. "Some people wouldn't be happy if you handed them the world on a platter. I mean, c'mon, look at all this place has to offer."

"So I guess there *are* some unhappy people here, but they move out," Dave says with a shrug. "Some people are just naturally unhappy. They get so wrapped up in local politics; they feel the need to delve into the negatives. Sure, their intention is to improve things, but still: who cares if the monthly amenities fee is $129 or $134?"

I hear the gentle musical blend of WVLG in the background. "None of that acid rock or heavy metal," Betsy says. "They play nice music; just plain nice music. I leave it on all day. Apparently the previous owner didn't like the radio station either." Although more than two decades younger than Betsy, I find myself enjoying the easy listening as well, marveling at how it reduces my stress by a notch or two.

Dave pours me a second glass of wine. We sit in the lanai and enjoy the slight breeze. I see similar homes packed tightly together all around us.

"Nobody on the block even knew who they were," Dave continues. "Our neighbor Phil across the street—everybody knows Phil —he says they never even invited him inside."

"They didn't play golf," Betsy adds with finality.

"Clearly these people were unhappy for a long time," Dave says, packing his pipe with apple-spiced tobacco. "And much to our benefit. *Much* to our benefit."

I ask what happened to the couple. "Who knows," Dave says, puffing on his pipe. "Maybe they bought a house in a regular neighborhood where they can do anything they want."

Dave and Betsy take me out to dinner at one of the dozen or so country clubs to which all Villagers automatically belong. Dave offers to take me in the golf cart; Betsy will drive her Miata and meet us there.

Dave unplugs the golf cart and backs it out of the garage. He points out their new address shingle hanging from an old-fashioned driveway light pole. It gives their first names in a cheery script and the house number. I'm surprised when the light suddenly turns on. Dave tells me that all the driveway lights in the neighborhood turn on and off at the same time. I feel a slight chill as I look up and down the street and notice that all the driveway lights have switched on. I find it somehow creepy, and wonder if the couple who moved away felt similarly.

Dave puts the windshield down on the golf cart and flips on the headlights. He drives down the curving streets and then passes through a tunnel. We glide past golf carts traveling in the opposite lane. The sensation is oddly thrilling. Cruising along in a golf cart at twenty miles per hour is somehow more invigorating than traveling in a car at seventy. Occasionally a speedier souped-up golf cart flashes its turn signal and passes us on the left. Golf cart headlights and red taillights are all around us, traveling in a silent and orderly fashion, like a video game with the sound turned off. Dave has a smile plastered to his face, and so do I. We look at each other and chuckle with amusement.

At dinner, I notice that the entrées on the menu are surprisingly affordable, as if early bird prices are a permanent fixture, and it's always happy hour somewhere in The Villages. Many of the people I meet carefully adjust their weekly schedules around happy hours with free appetizers and two-for-one drinks.

After dinner, we stop on a balcony to admire the setting sun. "Quite a sunset," I remark.

"A lot of them are," Dave responds.

"There's no place I'd rather be," Betsy says. "This is home."

"Gosh, what a day," Dave continues. "A bad day here is better than a good day at most other places. Oh, well, I guess some of us are meant to suffer, and some of us aren't."

"That sunset is pretty as a picture," Betsy says.

"It's more like a postcard," Dave counters.

"I say picture. It's just like a painting you'd hang on a wall," Betsy says.

"No, it's definitely a postcard," Dave says. "But you'd need a wide-angle lens to capture it."

I look out over the championship golf course with its undulating carpet of green, punctuated by palms that stir in the mild breeze. Across the way is yet another golf course, this one designed by Arnold Palmer. In the distance I see a cluster of homes big enough to be classified as McMansions, but designed for very few occupants—a retired couple, perhaps, or a widow.

Dave is in as good a mood as I've ever seen him, as if a huge burden had suddenly been lifted from him. He is positively light on his feet as we leave the country club. To my astonishment, he grabs an antique light pole near the door and swings—yes, swings—around it. He even attempts to kick up his heels like Fred Astaire.

Back home, Dave generously gives me keys to the house and a guest pass, which allows me to use many of the amenities, such as family swimming pools. To obtain a guest pass, Dave had to register me with The Villages, and my birth date and other information rest in their computer system. Non–family members, like minors, are permitted to visit for only up to one month a year.

Since each visitor is registered and handed a bar-coded pass, it would be difficult to overstay one's welcome, as access to all amenities would be denied. In effect, my guest pass is a visa that entitles me to experience The Villages' lifestyle, but like most visas, it also expires. This is one way The Villages keeps tabs on minors. But it's the residents themselves who generally keep a close eye on occasional scofflaws: a youngster wearing a school backpack has little chance of escaping the attention of one's neighbors.

Dave also hands me his and Betsy's "calling card." Villagers have revived a quaint tradition that seemingly died out not long after the time of Edith Wharton and Henry James. Instead of business cards, many Villagers carry cards that list their name and village. The Andersons' also displays a 1950s-era image of a man and a woman swinging golf clubs.

As Dave and Betsy wind down for the night, I head out in search of nightlife. As I drive off, smoke sputters out of the exhaust, and the loose muffler roars. There's oil splattered on the street, but thankfully, none on Dave's driveway.

Spanish Springs is buzzing with people of all ages strolling along the sidewalks. A group of giggling retirees walk past me wearing giant sombreros and carrying oversize cocktails in their hands. They tell me they are on a scavenger hunt. A friend shouts greetings to them from a restaurant patio across the street.

A crowd has gathered around the center gazebo for the nightly bread and circus of free entertainment and inexpensive drinks. The band's front man is wearing faded jeans and a blue blazer. A partially unbuttoned shirt reveals a forest of glistening blond chest hair. He hops around the gazebo with his cordless microphone, pointing this way and that as he sings the chorus, "God is with me, yeah!" He then breaks into a rendition of Chuck Berry's classic "Johnny B.

Goode," descends from the podium, and starts mingling with his audience of boogying grandparents and shrieking grandkids, several of whom jump up and down in their motion-sensitive sneakers with blinking red lights.

I chat with a man named Joel who moved to The Villages shortly after turning fifty-five. "I love it here," he tells me. "The neighborhoods are neat and clean. We've got covenants here and they're enforced, which is good, because they keep out the riffraff." Joel, however, ran afoul of one of The Villages' deed restrictions: lawn ornaments are prohibited in many neighborhoods. "It was just a boy and a girl holding hands," he explains sheepishly. It wasn't even two feet tall. I got a knock on the door the very next day. It's my own fault—I should have known better."

The band finishes its final set and the audience clears out. Empty drink cups litter the ground. The nightly cleaning crew silently picks them up and collects the 100 or so folding chairs. One of the crew, a stocky man with a thick southern drawl peculiar to rural Florida, approaches me. "Shit, these old folks do more drinking than them college kids. And that's a lot. They got nothing else to do. You watch."

I head across the street to the last place open in Spanish Springs: Katie Belle's. There's nobody at the door to check my resident ID, so I just sneak in. A country and western band is onstage playing one of Shania Twain's hits. The dance floor is packed with older couples, dressed casually in shorts or jeans, swaying back and forth. Some are wearing sandals with athletic socks. Although my outfit is somewhat par for the course around town, I nevertheless resolve to leave my sweater vest, loafers, and argyle socks at home next time. I belly up to the crowded bar and order a draft. It arrives in a mug that looks heavy, but out of consideration for the older clientele is made out of plastic and is light as a feather. To my surprise, a bartender announces last call moments later. I look at my watch: it's nine forty-five.

An older man taps me on the shoulder and asks if he can borrow my pen. He holds it carefully in his arthritic hand to take down the phone number of a woman wearing bright red lipstick. He returns a few minutes later to borrow the pen once again, to jot down another woman's phone number.

I introduce myself to two guys farther down the bar who look to be in their mid-twenties. They're brothers, they tell me, visiting from Iowa, where their mother used to live before she packed up and moved to The Villages. Carl, the younger brother, gulps down several shots of tequila lined up in front of him. He sports a goatee and a baseball hat with the brim squeezed into a tight semicircle. He spots my notebook and pen.

"You writing a book?" he asks. I nod. "It's a good thing, because this place is *fucked up!*" His brother, Ben, nods in agreement. I ask them if their mother is happy here. "She misses some things," Carl says.

"Like what?" I ask.

"Home."

They invite me to the equivalent of after-hours in The Villages—a late-night karaoke bar inside a bowling alley. It's just outside Spanish Springs in a strip mall that is also owned by The Villages. The facade is designed to look like the Alamo, and it's called, not surprisingly, the Alamo Bowl. It is one of two thirty-six-lane bowling complexes built for residents so far: one smoking, the other nonsmoking.

The three of us squeeze onto the front bench of their mother's golf cart. Ben unrolls the cart's plastic siding to protect us from a nippy wind, while Carl whips out a six-pack from a cooler behind the seat. We each pop open a beer. Carl flips on the battery, and the cart shoots forward. "Golf carts are definitely the way to go," he says. "You can drink and nobody screws with you."

Outside the Alamo Bowl, the parking lot is filled with golf carts, four to a space. "Bowling alley bars suck dick," Carl offers, then pops open another beer. We step inside the karaoke bar, a popular Mexican-theme place called Crazy Gringos. It's full, and we struggle to find seats. An older woman with a bright red sweater and skinny legs is singing "Tainted Love."

We pull chairs up to a crowded table and I'm introduced to Jan and Darryl. They were neighbors when Carl and Ben were growing up in Iowa and remain good friends with their mother. Now they live in The Villages, too. Several pitchers of beer arrive. Carl leaves to sign his name on the karaoke list. Jan turns to me, asks if I'm looking for a "sugar mama," and winks. With her short hair and bouncy energy, she passes for younger than her seventy years.

As is often the case when a Villager greets a stranger, the conversation veers to life in The Villages. "You can be anyone you want to be here," Jan says. "If you ever, in your younger years, wanted to play softball, be a pool shark, or twirl a baton—maybe you weren't any good at it, or didn't have the time to do it—well, you can do it now. After living here, Darryl and me, we're not going back to Iowa. The kids are there and all, but we're not going back. It's too friggin' cold.

"This place is so unique. You can't really compare it with anywhere else. Anything you need or want; it's just a golf cart away. It's unreal. And you don't have to be fifty-five to enjoy it—well, you do if you want to live here—but it's fun for everyone. My kids love visiting. Heck, my daughter would move in tomorrow if she were old enough. We were in a rut back in Iowa. But we're here now, and it's a party place. It's been like a vacation from day one."

Darryl looks at me with rheumy eyes. "I don't say a lot," he says, slurring his words. "But I like it, too. I just want to spend my days here; the ones I have left."

Onstage, Carl is singing a rap song about big butts and getting "some booty." I'm surprised to see several younger men on the dance floor make like they're having sex from behind with their young dates. Then it's back to the golden oldies with Elvis's "Can't

Help Falling in Love," and the dance floor fills up again with inebriated seniors. "They play anything from the 1950s or 1960s and the floor is packed," Jan shouts over the music. "That's the age group you got here."

Several drinks later, I stagger to the toilet, passing alongside the closed bowling lanes. Once there, I bump into a man wearing a Veteran of Foreign Wars baseball cap. "I was a marine at Guadalcanal," he says, and then lets out an impressively long belch. "I was wounded there and now I have diabetes. But after all these years, at least I can still party at The Villages."

3

The Golden Years

RETIREMENT IS A RELATIVELY NEW PHENOMENON. FOR THOUSANDS OF years, with a few exceptions, humans would simply work until they couldn't. People lived in extended families because they needed to do so: survival generally required a collective effort. Parents worked hard to raise their children, and as they aged and their health faded, the roles were reversed, with elders relying on their children to care for them.

Beginning about a century ago in America, our growing prosperity made other living arrangements possible. The middle class gained enough of an economic foothold for the elderly and their adult children to consider establishing separate households: why live crowded under one roof when a family could afford to spread out in several homes? Then came the Great Depression, which—among other things—wiped out the pensions and savings accounts of many of the nation's older citizens. With unemployment at all-time highs, young families, who could hardly support themselves, were once again forced to care for their elders.

Social Security was in part designed to humanely pull older workers out of the workforce so that unemployed younger workers could fill their jobs. But it also shifted much of the economic burden of caring for elders away from individual family members and onto society as a whole; seniors now had a safety net.

The covenant implied in Social Security is deceptively simple: you pitch in now for today's senior citizens, and subsequent generations will pitch in to keep you from abject poverty. As my yearly Social Security statement explains: "Social Security is a compact between generations."

The first checks from the Social Security Act of 1935 were cut in 1940. The original payouts were rather small, more of a contribution than a real replacement for income. Because the age requirement was sixty-five years and the average life expectancy was then only sixty-two, few Americans at that time lived to see their check from the government.

But in time, rapid medical advances and the economic stability afforded by generous company pensions as well as monthly Social Security checks led to the creation of a whole new class of people—retirees.

What was retirement supposed to look like? What were these retirees supposed to do with the few remaining years during which they were viewed as too old to work, but too young to die? Mass retirement was a new phenomenon with few guidelines to follow. To many, the word "retirement" itself had a negative connotation, implying that seniors were being taken out of circulation, like old horses that were no longer useful.

As the extended family continued to disintegrate and the nation became infatuated with a youth-centered culture, seniors were left to chart their own way. Few knew what to expect from these years besides loneliness, declining health, and possible abandonment in "God's waiting room"—a gloomy nursing home. To some, retirement might as well have been a death sentence.

Out of this anomie, a new idea began to take shape—the creation of communities where active seniors could live together, free from the confines of dreary old-age homes. Although religious and fraternal organizations flirted with the concept of retirement communities as early as the 1920s, the nation's first age-segregated community was not built until the 1950s. It was called Youngtown, and it was little more than a modest housing development with a clubhouse in the middle of the Arizona desert. But its elderly inhabitants were grateful for it.

According to Youngtown's founder, Benjamin "Big Ben" Schleifer, its inspiration was an old Jewish prayer: "Do not forsake me, God, when I get old." Schleifer says he first heard the prayer as a youngster living in a shtetl outside Minsk, where his father worked as a timber surveyor. In 1914, the Schleifer family fled czarist repression and Cossack raids, and immigrated to America.

In New York, the thirteen-year-old Schleifer skipped school and went to work as an errand boy. An avid reader, he says he educated himself with discarded newspapers that he found on the subway. He eventually held a succession of jobs: farmhand, textile mill worker, flour miller, and grain broker. In the late 1940s, a bout of asthma forced him to relocate to Arizona, where he began to dabble in real estate, often unsuccessfully. He formed Big Ben Realty and worked out of an office not much larger than a phone booth.

Homesick for the east coast, Schleifer returned several times in the hope that Arizona had cured his asthma. He had no such luck, but one trip back east proved to be fortunate. He visited a friend in a nursing home in Rochester, New York, and was struck by the man's frustration with the regimented and confined lifestyle. Schleifer thought he could do better. He committed himself to building an entire community devoted to retirees and resolved to call it Youngtown, so that it "would be associated with youth and ambition." He wanted "to make elderly people not feel old."

In 1954, Schleifer bought a 320-acre desert ranch about twenty miles from downtown Phoenix, which was then a small city. At the time, an older widow and her 175 head of dairy and beef cattle were all that populated the land. To save money, several of the original ranch buildings were incorporated into Schleifer's new community. The milking station became the hobby shop, and housing for the ranch hands became the town hall. "My idea was to keep the costs down," Schleifer said at the time. "I didn't build a community for millionaires. Millionaires can go to Bermuda."

By most accounts Youngtown was a success: Schleifer had created a place where the blunt indignities of old age were softened, at least for a time. People came from all over the snowbelt for the warm weather and fellowship. And, more important, they didn't come to die; they came to live.

There were games of canasta, potluck picnics, garden clubs, and Saturday night dances. Residents staged musicals, pitched horseshoes and learned to tap-dance. Crime was practically nonexistent, and taxes were impossibly low. It was like one big family, albeit a family without children to disturb the peace and quiet of the blissful desert idyll.

Within a year, 125 homes had been built and eighty-five of them had been sold. Soon, enough homes were built that businesses opened up to serve the new residents. In contrast to friends they left back home—many of whom were slowly atrophying in nursing homes—Youngtown's pioneers considered themselves fortunate. In 1960, optimistically, Youngtown incorporated. A nascent American Association of Retired Persons selected the community as the site of its first chapter. Membership cost twenty-five cents.

The philosophical underpinnings of Schleifer's preference for age segregation were more practical than purposefully discriminatory: children cost money. A community without kids is a community without schools and with no high taxes to pay for schools. One of Schleifer's main objectives was to ensure that Youngtown's residents could afford to live with dignity, even if their sole income was Social Security.

"Nature divides the generations," he said. "So let's not blame the older people for not wanting children in the community. We didn't build Youngtown for social advancement. We built it for the economic security of the elderly."

Although Schleifer's biggest contribution to American history was his decision to exclude children from the development, the father of age-segregated housing married a much younger woman with two small sons, just one year after founding Youngtown.

According to his surviving stepson, the exclusion of children was secondary. "The intention was to create a community of elder retirees, and a natural consequence of that was not to have any children around except visiting grandkids," Paul Metchik told me. "At the time it seemed like a good thing, a place for older people to go. I don't think his foremost intention was to be exclusionary. He liked kids. He was a wonderful father."

Schleifer later admitted some embarrassment when the residents of his community helped shoot down a local school district's bond issue. "Our first obligation when I was a boy was to give young people an education, no matter what sacrifices it took," he said. "He who has the Torah has bread."

But asked at the time if he would have done anything differently, Schleifer said only that he would have tried to save residents even more money by modeling Youngtown on the Israeli kibbutzim, where members pool their labor and finances for a common goal— the overall health of the community. After completing Youngtown (which had no religious affiliation), Schleifer pursued his American kibbutz for retirees. Located twenty miles farther into the desert, Circle City was designed to attract lower-middle-class Jewish retirees. It was called Circle City for two reasons: it had circles and spokes radiating from a central civic area; and it was affiliated with the Workingmen's Circle, a Jewish society with socialist leanings. But it was a failure and left Schleifer bankrupt.

"He was a bighearted visionary, but sometimes his vision took him too far from the mainstream," Metchik told me. "A socialist Jewish community in the middle of the Arizona desert is a hard sell." Schleifer retired quietly on Social Security and spent the rest of his days playing pinochle with friends at a neighborhood park in Phoenix. "I'm rich with the good health Arizona has given me," he would say.

As the first of its kind, Youngtown made big news. It also made a big impression on a wealthy Arizonan entrepreneur, Del Webb. The legendary, charismatic Webb owned one of the nation's largest construction companies (as well as the New York Yankees) and had a history of building large-scale projects: military bases, missile silos, casinos, and the Flamingo Hotel for the mobster Benjamin "Bugsy" Siegel. Webb had also built internment camps for more than 25,000 Japanese detainees; which gave him experience in designing and implementing planned communities. Webb, who never had children of his own, was intrigued by the idea of a large-scale age-segregated retirement community, and had his company meticulously explore its financial feasibility.

Early feedback was not encouraging. Experts on aging claimed that it would be nearly impossible to tear senior citizens away from their extended families; and if this attempt did succeed, the elderly would feel displaced and isolated. Although the multigenerational household was fast becoming little more than a fond memory, many social scientists were nonetheless convinced that retirees remained dependent on their children and grandchildren for emotional sustenance.

But as Webb's lieutenants conducted their own research, they came to a different conclusion. Sure, older folks cared about their families, but this didn't mean that after decades of devotion, old people wanted to dedicate the rest of their lives to the family. Webb's market research suggested that retirees would welcome the opportunity to distance themselves from their offspring and limit contact to visits. Higher up on their priorities were good weather and something to do. They had worked hard, and now it was time to pursue hobbies, play golf, and socialize with their peers.

Given this information, Webb began to depict old age in a decidedly more favorable and promising light. Old age wasn't so bad, he declared. In fact, it could represent the best years of one's life, something to look forward to rather than dread. To help spread his message, Webb called late life the "golden years." Using this marketing pitch, Webb set out to create and sell his vision of carefree retirement—a metropolis of leisure named Sun City. "Together we can realize a way of life unprecedented in America," he declared.

The Webb Company had hoped to attract 10,000 potential home buyers to the opening of Sun City on New Year's Day 1960. There was some fretting about the numbers; perhaps they were too optimistic. Research or no research, building Sun City still required a tremendous leap of faith—the firm belief that America was on the cusp of a sociological revolution.

Apparently it was: 100,000 seniors visited Sun City that weekend, creating a mile-long traffic jam in the desert. Several hundred homes were purchased on the spot, and Webb's bewildered staff ran out of blank contracts. Despite the obvious hurdles to marketing thirty-year mortgages to aging retirees, the money rolled in; Webb sold 2,000 homes by the year's end.

Sun City had what seniors wanted: moderately priced ranch homes in a sunbelt community anchored by a golf course and a recreation center. Webb called his utopian creation "resort-retirement living." It was a new version of the American dream, designed exclusively for the nation's fastest-growing leisure class.

"In the average community there is no way of controlling the age bracket of our neighbors or the number of their children," Webb said at the time. "This we can control in Sun City, thus avoiding the problem of mixing conflicting living patterns and forcing social contacts that constitute an invasion of privacy, with resulting inconveniences for senior citizens."

Time magazine put Webb on its cover, with the caption "The Retirement City: A New Way of Life for the Old." His creation was heralded as a triumph, and Webb was feted as the man who put "active" into retirement. Few questioned the community's long-term sustainability, its segregationist premise, or the potentially negative impact of that premise on American society.

Sun City, with its emerging cultural cachet, would soon eclipse Youngtown. In time, Youngtown would be seen as a home for poorer and less sophisticated seniors, and its housing stock would fall into varying degrees of disrepair.

Schleifer had considered amenities expensive and generally unnecessary, but Webb had bigger dreams: he eventually built seven Olympic-size swimming pools; thirty miles of golf fairways; a substantial lake with docks, pedestrian bridges, and faux waterfalls; and a large outdoor performance facility. Schleifer kept the population of Youngtown purposely small to ensure a sense of affinity. At 40,000, Sun City would be Arizona's seventh-largest community by 1977. Webb soon built housing for another 30,000 people farther down the road and called the new development Sun City West.

Webb's once diversified company eventually committed all its energies to building retirement communities. It was a bold move. The building of these projects was considered by many in the industry to be nothing more than an interesting specialty for a niche market. Few could have predicted that it would one day become so central to the real estate business.

Decades after the creation of Youngtown and Sun City in the Arizona desert, retirement in America is undergoing numerous changes.

For many people, it remains an unattainable aspiration, but for tens of millions of Americans, retirement represents a chance to start afresh and put together a whole new life—one that is often centered on leisure. Today's retirees are the healthiest and most affluent generation in history.

Average life expectancy has risen sharply in the past century, from forty-seven in 1900 to seventy-seven in 2000. Quality of life is also rising, and age sixty-five is often described as "the new forty-five." Many of today's retirees want to remain fully active, especially given that many, such as civil servants and teachers, retire as early as fifty-five. It's expected that these early retirees will spend a full third of their lives in retirement; consequently, some experts recommend a more realistic retirement age of eighty-five in coming decades, as well as the creation of fifty-year and seventy-five-year mortgages. Some see the beginnings of an entirely new life stage (much like the "invention" of adolescence a century ago), in which people are neither middle-aged nor old, but rather "pre-elderly."

We are once again entering uncharted territory, and the painful alienation that seniors experienced more than half a century ago has not lessened. If anything, it has been exacerbated by the rise in wealth and life expectancy, and by the increasing transience of our country's population, which puts additional stress on the family unit. Average Americans move about a dozen times during their life.

With few guideposts to follow, older Americans continue to search for terra firma. To a significant number of retirees, such as the Andersons and their neighbors in The Villages, living with their peers in updated versions of Webb's cloistered playground is an attractive solution. And given the generational bulge of 78 million baby boomers just now entering this "pre-elderly" stage, the nation will soon be flooded with healthy "active adults" with similar needs. In 2001, the first boomers turned fifty-five, the point of eligibility for most age-restricted communities. By 2014, the number of Americans aged fifty-five and older is expected to reach 85 million.

Not surprisingly, the marketing campaign for the "active adult lifestyle" is well funded, highly polished, and revved up. Still a leader in its field, Del Webb's company, for one, provides its prospective clients with a free online "lifestyle adviser" service that begins with a questionnaire. Visitors are asked to respond to a number of statements on a sliding scale, from "strongly disagree" to "strongly agree."

To learn more, I took the questionnaire—albeit with my daughter sleeping in my lap—and was prompted with, among others things, the following statements: "It's too easy for my kids to ask us to baby-sit." "I want a community with twenty-four-hour security." And my favorite—"I want to leave our past behind and have a new future." When I failed to score a marketing bull's-eye, Jennifer, my new lifestyle adviser, mailed me a few questions to consider: "What is it that really keeps you connected to where you currently reside?" "Can you truly relax there?"

I was soon congratulated for considering a move "that will improve my life," and was invited to celebratory events at Del Webb age-segregated communities around the country: a costume contest for pets in southern California; a faux harvest festival in North Carolina; and an evening of Greek food and belly dancing in New Jersey. I was also sent handsome newsletters from existing communities with photos of joyful gray-haired potential neighbors. Another company mailed me a DVD in which a celebrity tennis player invited me to buy into a particular age-segregated community so that I could "play like a champion and live like a winner."

Although I may be far from retirement, other members of my family are currently navigating their way through it. They were young professionals when Sun City first opened, and their living choices today continue to be influenced by Webb's vision. An aunt and uncle live in an upscale gated, age-targeted community in central New Jersey, where children aren't forbidden so much as discouraged. They enjoy the community's demographics as well as its country club–like amenities. As my aunt says, "We've earned it!"

At this stage of their lives, community to them isn't so much a particular geographic location as easy access to new friends and senior-oriented activities. My uncle doesn't share a long history with his neighbors, but as a member of the community barbershop quartet and the bell choir, he shares hobbies with a good number of them.

And in many ways, that's about the best he could have hoped for: the communities in which he and people like him grew up and raised their families don't really exist anymore. Their communities may exist in a physical sense, but the people they knew have all moved away. "One sister is in California; two are in Minnesota; my son is in south Jersey; and my daughter lives in Westchester, New York," my aunt says, of her family from a previous marriage. Adds my uncle, "My son is in Kansas, my daughter is in California, and my brother is in Chicago."

My immediate family and friends are scattered as well. Most of them have moved repeatedly and live at least one time zone away. The remnants of our community exist mainly in the form of e-mail, cell phone calls, and the deep recesses of memory. Given our transient population, one wonders just where retirees are *supposed* to live. How does one adjust when social bonds are stretched thin by geography, when there's no longer a direction home? As our society fragments, the message many seniors are receiving is that they had better band together and take care of themselves, because nobody else will take care of them.

To adjust to this growing reality, my aunt and uncle picked a location that gave them access to cultural activities as well as the best chance of living near family. They live within driving distance of their grandchildren. "It's a long drive, but seeing them every week means a lot to us," my aunt explains. But just in case their children move, like so many others, they have also surrounded themselves with peers who stay put—so many that their community doesn't celebrate Halloween. No pumpkins. No kids. No candy.

"I miss the pumpkins," my uncle says wistfully.

4

Free Golf!

THE VILLAGES STARTED OUT AS NOTHING MORE THAN A SMALL TRAILER park for retirees in the boondocks of central Florida. The exact story has been clouded by the distinct lack of enthusiasm of the developer, Harold "Gary" Morse, for speaking with the press, especially about his family.

Morse clearly prefers to *make* news in the physical sense—his privately owned development company runs its own print and broadcast media outlets. Reporters working for the mainstream media tell me that obtaining information from official channels is akin to squeezing information out of the Kremlin. One told me, "You can ask if the sky's blue and they still won't comment."

When I call the public relations department seeking an interview with Morse, my request is instantly rejected. Gary Lester, the vice president for community relations, seems only moderately interested in meeting with me himself, even after I explain to him that I am writing a book about The Villages.

"We feel pretty secure," Lester tells me, when we finally meet for a cup of coffee. A former Protestant minister, Lester is a tall thin man with a sharp nose, piercing eyes, and a blow-dried mop of hair. "We don't feel the need to spin you. The residents are the real story, and they love it here. Just go up to anyone and ask. They'll all tell you the same thing: The Villages provides a lifestyle that can't be beat. We have businessmen visiting from South Africa, Central America, China, Japan—they all want to learn how we do things so they can copy us. They even try to incorporate the word 'villages' into the names of their developments."

When asked, he once again informs me that an interview with his boss, Gary Morse, is out of the question because, "Mr. Morse is a very shy man." I ask him why such a shy man named The Villages' major thoroughfare after himself: Morse Boulevard is the development's main artery. Lester declines to comment.

As Lester says, The Villages is very secure. Not only are most residents bursting at the seams to heap praise on the development, but within hours of touring the community, many visitors decide to buy a home. Northerners are flocking to The Villages, as are hurricane-wary Floridians in search of safer weather and affordable home insurance. Growth and revenues are through the roof.

According to industry experts, The Villages was the top-selling planned community in America in 2005, for the third straight year. In that year alone, The Villages sold 4,263 new homes, or nearly one every two hours, and pulled in gross revenues of more than $1 billion. The Villages has sold more homes each year than the last for ten straight years. One industry consultant told me, "Even the military doesn't build houses that fast. This is a retirement community on steroids."

There are nearly 75,000 people living in The Villages in about 38,000 homes, and that number is expected to grow rapidly as the development finishes its build-out—an industry term for the point when a project is complete—in the very near future. The Villages will then encompass over 20,000 acres in an area of roughly thirty-three square miles, and house 110,000 residents. Manhattan, by comparison, is twenty-four square miles in area.

Gary Morse's father, Harold Schwartz, is considered the founding father of the community. Schwartz died in 2003 at age ninety-three, and his ashes are kept in Spanish Springs, inside a statue built to honor him while he was still alive. As Schwartz's colorful persona slowly attains the status of legend, it also becomes harder to piece together the true story of the man and his business. To do so, one needs to cross a six-lane highway spanned by a steep golf cart bridge. On the far side, less than half a mile from the center of Spanish Springs, lies another, humbler "village." It's called Orange Blossom Gardens, and it's here that The Villages' history begins.

By most accounts, Harold S. Schwartz, who was born in Chicago, was lively and peripatetic. The grandson of Hungarian Jewish immigrants, Harold came from decidedly modest means. The family was so impoverished that Harold's father and two uncles were placed in an orphanage. Harold's father later married outside the faith, set up shop as a tailor, and moved his family into a crowded tenement on Chicago's South Side. Although something of a violin prodigy as a youth, Harold had to put aside his artistic pursuits and instead work as a traveling salesman for his father's business. Harold later branched out into the mail-order business, selling vitamins, cuckoo clocks, and leather billfolds with zippers. He wrote his own advertising copy, placed it in comic books and other publications, and shipped the products from his office.

Harold's first wife, Mary Louise—Gary's mother—grew up in the same tenement building as Harold and attended the same high school. Once married, the young couple moved in with Harold's extended family. They divorced about ten years later, and both remarried. Mary Louise left Chicago with Gary and his sister, and eventually resettled in a small town in northern Michigan called Central Lake, a vacation area not far from Sleeping Bear Dunes National Lakeshore.

Mary Louise shared her ex-husband's entrepreneurial streak. When sugar was rationed during World War II, she and her second husband, Clifford Morse, raised bees and produced honey. She and

Gary sold the honey door-to-door, as well as at a makeshift road-side stand. In time, the roadside stand, which was enlarged and renamed the Brownwood Honey House, carried vegetables and flowers grown by the family, and local crafts such as moccasins and pottery. Not surprisingly, Mary Louise turned to mail order as well: first Christmas greens, then gift boxes with honey and home-made jam. To further promote the growing business, Gary's mother relocated an old one-room schoolhouse to the Brownwood site and opened a small country store.

Mary Louise's next marketing idea brought her regional fame for its bravado: one winter she moved an abandoned stagecoach inn across a frozen lake to her growing tourism complex. Halfway across the lake, the ice began to shudder and crack, and the workmen jumped to safety as the inn slowly sank. Fortunately, it sank atop a sandbar and the frigid water reached only the first floor windows. Residents far and wide gathered to catch a glimpse of the half-sunken country inn, many opting to figure-skate around it once the ice refroze. Mary Louise refused to admit defeat and was said to have been furious when several local men offered to set the inn afire. Two weeks later laborers were able to cut a path in the ice and float the inn to shore. The Brownwood complex eventually added an ice cream parlor, history museum, and tearoom. The family's farm-house was soon transformed into a small steak house.

Gary seems to have inherited his family's drive to make money and its uncanny ability to promote its business ventures. As a teen-ager, he took his stepfather's name—Morse. After high school he left town for college, but soon dropped out and moved back in with his mother.

Gary put all his energy into making the Brownwood complex grow, paying particularly close attention to the steak house. He began offering free nightly entertainment, and the restaurant soon became the place to hang out for locals and the legions of tourists visiting during the summer months. At one point, Gary had to erect

41

a giant circus tent to accommodate all his customers. He eventually built a dedicated concert space, and continued expanding the restaurant until it sprawled across the Brownwood property.

Many locals fondly refer to that time in Central Lake's history as the "Brownwood era." This was a time when scores of attractive coeds worked for the restaurant and partied intensely after work. In contrast to the Brownwood's lively reputation, Gary is often described as somber, aloof, and a "hard guy to get to know."

Meanwhile, Gary's father, Harold, remained in Chicago, but traveled extensively, buying radio stations, gas stations, office buildings, and other real estate across the country. At one point he owned the maximum number of broadcasting stations permitted for one person and circumvented the federal law by setting up two "border blasters"—extremely high-power radio stations that broadcast to the United States from across the Mexican border. It was at one of these stations that the legendary disc jockey Wolfman Jack launched his career.

Harold also turned to land speculation. He and a business partner bought land cheaply in Florida, New Mexico and elsewhere, subdivided it, and sold it sight unseen by mail order to American and British retirees dreaming of owning a home in the sun. At the time, Harold owned a hotel in Miami and took occasional trips around the state scouting out additional real estate to flip or develop. That's how he came across the several hundred acres of remote pastures and watermelon fields in central Florida that would become Orange Blossom Gardens. Harold paid $150 an acre and sold it by mail in quarter-acre parcels for $295 each.

When the Florida legislature banned mail-order land sales in the late 1960s, Harold and his business partner were left holding the watermelon fields. Harold left his business associate in charge of the land. The partner decided to manage a trailer park on it, but after ten years and only 400 homes sold, he wanted out. Harold wasn't sure if he wanted to keep the investment either.

But then, like "Big Ben" Schliefer, Schwartz paid a visit to Arizona—in his case, to his sister, who had recently moved to Sun City. He was impressed by what he saw. In contrast to his dinky mobile home park in the boondocks, Sun City was selling the dream of retirement on a grand scale, with recreation centers, numerous golf courses, and an active lifestyle for "those lucky enough to retire." Schwartz marveled that Sun City was in the middle of nowhere and yet managed to attract legions of retirees with promises of the good life. Webb's vision soon became Harold's road map.

In 1983, Harold bought out his business partner and set about selling more than homes; he started selling a lifestyle. "I got rid of everything I owned," Harold later said. "At an age my friends were retiring, I put every cent I had into a high-risk venture. I was seventy-three."

In need of a new business partner, Harold urged his son, Gary, to join him. The invitation couldn't have come at a better time. Because of Central Lake's tourist economy, local businessmen had to make three-quarters of their revenue in just the summer months; the rest of the time, the businesses catered to a local population of about 500. But Gary had saddled himself with a sprawling restaurant and entertainment complex designed to seat hundreds. By most accounts he had overexpanded his steakhouse and was now deep in debt.

Gary flew to Florida and walked around the Orange Blossom Gardens property with his father. He agreed that it had potential and promptly moved to central Florida with his wife and children. Although Gary's steakhouse soon went belly-up, he proved his business acumen at his father's trailer park in Florida.

When Morse arrived, the community consisted of small homes connected by narrow roads, and only one small recreation center, called the Paradise. Father and son quickly set about building a community like Sun City on a modest budget.

Gary brought more than just his family with him to Florida; he also brought tradesmen. If someone had a small lumberyard or a one-truck cement business, Gary invited him to relocate his business to central Florida. Many of these men, previously the owners of small businesses, now run multimillion-dollar companies that service The Villages' empire.

Although not a golfer himself, Gary decided that the little dimpled golf ball was the crucial factor in making Orange Blossom Gardens a success. He transformed a field of watermelons into a decidedly modest nine-hole golf course and began advertising "Free golf!"

"Free golf" is still one of The Villages' major selling points, but it's more a slogan than a reality. Golf is "free" only on the nine-hole executive courses, and Villagers must still pay a trail fee if they want to use their golf carts. The cost of building and maintaining these "free" golf courses is included in the monthly amenity fees. In effect, all Villagers are subsidizing these executive courses for the minority who actually use them. Championship eighteen-hole courses can cost upwards of fifty dollars a game.

Regardless, the little mobile home park swelled with retirees practically overnight. By 1987, the development had $40 million in annual sales. In short order, Gary built more and more amenities: eighteen more holes of golf, an unpretentious country club, more pools, and another recreation center with its own restaurant.

As the community expanded, father and son tried to attract businesses that would cater to the residents' needs. They knew that conveniently located retail stores and doctors' offices were important to the creation of a truly self-contained community. But they couldn't find any takers. The area was still in the middle of nowhere, and retirees were often assumed to be poor, thrifty, and generally bad business. So the family members themselves opened and operated several businesses, including a gas station and mini-mart, a restaurant, a liquor store, and a Laundromat.

Flushed with success, they began building more homes on the other side of what was then a small county road but today is a six-lane highway. Within ten years, the family had built its own down-town (Spanish Springs); and soon a Winn-Dixie supermarket, a few banks, and other businesses flocked to the development.

Each phase of housing was more upmarket than the previous one, but the neighborhoods were configured similarly with adjoin-ing recreation facilities and golf courses, just like Sun City. Faced with an increasing number of new neighborhoods, Harold hit on an idea: he would call each one a "village." Orange Blossom Gardens, with its little trailer homes and modest recreation center, was re-named "The Village of Orange Blossom Gardens."

Golf carts quickly became a way of life. At first residents used them primarily to travel on actual golf courses, and then between golf courses, but pretty soon they used the carts to get around every-where. Carts were inexpensive and easy to use, especially for people in failing health. And as The Villages grew, there were more and more places to take them.

Because these neighborhoods were surrounded by intense rural poverty, and in an area with limited services, father and son sus-pected that residents would want to keep their world of leisure as self-contained as possible, so they provided just about everything the residents might need—and all of this was accessible by golf cart. It didn't take long before golf carts were ubiquitous and residents lost interest in driving anywhere outside the compound.

Harold acknowledged the peculiar primacy of the golf cart when, with the help of a local politician, he built a golf cart bridge across the highway between the older Village of Orange Blossom Gardens and the ever-expanding newer areas. The bridge is still there, rising steeply on both sides of the busy highway, with seniors zipping across it daily.

Harold soon became a local celebrity. Unlike his son, he en-joyed socializing with residents, and some say he was a heck of a la-dies' man. He built a modest home in the middle of Orange Blossom Gardens and took long walks around the neighborhood. In time, the family learned to capitalize on Harold's popularity, and embraced his emerging reputation as The Villages' kindhearted "founding father."

Harold's iconic smile was soon everywhere, even on The Villages' own scrip—promotional paper money given to prospective residents and redeemable at businesses owned by The Villages. When the family wanted to promote its efforts to build an emergency medical facility near Spanish Springs, an enormous photo of Harold appeared on a billboard. He was shown, dressed in a loud sports jacket and porkpie hat, pointing at an empty parcel of land: "I'll live to see The Villages Regional Hospital right here!" He did.

It's hard to tell if the decidedly less fancy Village of Orange Blossom Gardens is a place filled with fond nostalgia for Gary Morse, or an embarrassment of sorts, much as Jay Gatsby's humble beginnings were for him in the novel by F. Scott Fitzgerald. At heart, Gary is a businessman, and since the Village of Orange Blossom Gardens was built out long ago, it probably holds little interest for him, at least financially. Curiously, few residents have any recollection of Gary from the early days; others have no idea who he is. But they remember Harold fondly, making Orange Blossom Gardens the center of Schwartz' personality cult.

A walk through the original development is a trip down memory lane. Unlike the sea of upscale homes, fancy boulevards, and state-of-the-art recreation centers in the fantasyland across the highway, Orange Blossom Gardens feels as if it belongs to an earlier era, as in fact it does. Younger Villagers call it the community's "prehistoric" area, or the "Old Burial Ground."

One day I made the foolish decision to walk across the bridge connecting Orange Blossom Gardens with Spanish Springs. I was forced more than once to hug the walls as retirees zoomed past in golf carts. Once safely across, I strolled through the neighborhood. Many of the houses were gussied-up trailers with postage-stamp yards; some of them were already being torn down to make way for

larger homes on double lots. The deed restriction against lawn ornaments had evidently been dreamed up after the development crossed
the highway; I saw ornaments everywhere: a family of plaster deer
lying down in a circle of red mulch; the obligatory lawn gnome; and
a cutout of a little boy peeing while his toddler girlfriend shields her
eyes in red-faced embarrassment. I also saw old women in curlers
and hairnets —something that one rarely, if ever, sees across the
highway, although there is no rule against wearing them.

I knocked on the door of Elton Mayer, one of the fledgling
community's first residents. He is sometimes referred to as Orange
Blossom Garden's "first Mayer." Unlike many of the residents on the
other side of the bridge, Elton was actually old. Given the relative
youth and vigor of the residents across the way, I was surprised to see
someone walking with a cane. At eighty-six, Elton was in good health,
but he was clearly not about to hop over the net after a game of tennis.

Elton's house, like the homes of many of his immediate neighbors, was small but tidy. He greeted me hesitantly at first, but was
soon happy enough to talk about the old days. His time was limited, however: his second wife, whom he met at a square dance in
Orange Blossom Gardens, was in the hospital.

Elton told me he had first learned of the new trailer park while
reading an ad in *Elks* magazine at his home in central Michigan. At
the time, the ads for Orange Blossom Gardens had a dated yet poetic
style, perhaps reflecting Harold's years of experience in mail-order
advertising: "For the residents of Orange Blossom Gardens, theirs
is a quality of life that is so softly civilized, richly varied, infinitely
better, and in one of the most desirable areas of Florida." Although
Orange Blossom Gardens is an hour and a half from Orlando, the
literature nevertheless described the community as the "Gateway to
Disney World."

Contemplating an early retirement because of his first wife's ill
health, Mayer found himself intrigued by the ad. It was a lifestyle
he could afford: a cozy single-wide trailer home on a lot beside a

small lake cost just $9,995. The couple took a visit in 1973 and liked what they saw. "I bought this lot the first day I saw it," Elton said. "It was a piece of paradise—a house on the water in Florida, with orange trees in the front yard."

There were just thirteen trailers, three model homes, and the beginnings of a small recreation center. There were no age restrictions at the time, although a few years later Harold restricted occupancy to people over thirty. Local shopping was sparse, and nearby towns were run-down and sparsely populated. Elton described a time when he used to walk down the road—now a highway lined with strip malls—and buy pecans "from a native." Then came the free golf.

"There were just a few hundred homes at the time," Elton said. "But when they started with the golf, the population tripled in no time, and the homes got bigger. They started out as single-wides like mine, and then they went to double-wides, and then to those modular homes. They put them up in a big hurry because they were selling so fast. They even built their own modular home factory. I had no idea the place would grow so big, but Schwartz was a good businessman. He knew exactly what he was doing from the start. And he did everything first-class."

Old-timers like Elton rarely venture farther than Spanish Springs, if they even go that far. One wonders if they fully comprehend just how big The Villages has become. "There's no reason to go over there, across the bridge," Elton said. "We've got everything we need on this side."

Farther down the street, I met a man named Sam who retired here in 1984 in a house next to his parents, after a life of laboring in midwestern steel mills. He offered to drive me around in his golf cart for a short tour. "Now mind you, back then there weren't any golf carts," Sam told me. "If we wanted to go somewhere, we had to walk." I'm caught by surprise when he floors the accelerator and my back slams against the seat.

The development's oldest streets have charming Hawaiian-theme names like "Aloha Way," which happened to be where Harold lived. Sam pointed out Harold's old house, a simple ranch on a waterfront lot. A little dock led to a small gazebo on stilts. Beyond the oldest streets, the roads were named for members of Harold's family. Four streets were named for Gary's wife and children: Sharon, Jennifer, Tracy, and Mark. There was a Schwartz Boulevard, and a boulevard named after one of Harold's former business partners.

Sam stopped briefly to chat with a friend in his friend's driveway. The garage door was open, and I spotted an elaborate train set with bridges, tunnels, and its own make-believe village.

Sam took me farther into the development, where the golf courses are located and the bigger homes are modular. The streets had ambitious names such as Pebble Beach Lane, Saint Andrew's Boulevard, and Palm Aire. There was a hilltop country club (not all of Florida is flat), which housed the Villagers' perennially favorite pool: a whimsical creation reminiscent of the Flintstones, with a waterfall masking a hidden cave and a Jacuzzi. There was a tiki bar on one side, and on the other, a small karaoke tent with an older DJ wearing a big grin and blasting music loud enough to make me cringe. Inside, the locker rooms betrayed the club's age. They were really just shabby bathrooms with an extra stall for a shower, and a few lockers.

Sam floored the accelerator again and headed home. "I remember when this was all watermelon fields," Sam said, motioning to the homes below. "You could reach back and pick one to eat."

Near the bottom of the hill, Sam nearly ran over a pedestrian. "Mind pulling to the side?" the man asked gruffly.

"This is a *street*, asshole," Sam shouted back, without slowing down. "What a moron."

I asked Sam what he thinks the major difference is between the two sides of the highway. He didn't hesitate. "Money."

5

How Bananas
Got Their Curve

To get a better handle on The Villages' sprawling expansion, one morning I resolve to take a trolley tour. The tours are run out of the sales office, which is housed in a tall mission-style building that takes up a whole city block in Spanish Springs.

I start the day by pressing the snooze button on the clock radio until the Andersons' automatic sprinklers shut off and my bedroom is filled with glorious Florida sunshine. The fresh air coming through the open window smells of wet grass and budding flowers. The New England winter gloom feels far, far away. "It's another beautiful day here in The Villages," the announcer on WVLG says before I switch off the radio for good. It's hard to disagree.

I turn on the television. "The weather's great here in The Villages where golf's free and it never snows," a smiling blond anchorwoman chirps. "Now here's a Villager showing his stuff at the Alamo Bowl yesterday. Just two pins standing; Yup! He gets the job done. Nice job, Bob!" The camera then turns to a group of women on a putting green. One older woman connects with a golf ball, and it rolls toward the hole. "Oops, a little too much," the announcer says. "Let's see if she gets it on the second try. Wait, wait, and yes! It's in, for a par four. Nice job, ladies! We'll be back with more sports and recreation updates on the 'twos.'"

It's The Villages' own morning news show, which is broadcast on Gary Morse's television station, the Villages News Network, VNN. The anchors look surprisingly like real anchors even though they work for the developer and generally report only happenings inside the gates. They even have that little box above the left shoulder showing graphics and video. There are two companion stations as well; one that lists the plethora of daily activities and another that gives current weather conditions from The Villages' own National Oceanic and Atmospheric Administration weather station.

The next news story is about a resident teaching her grandchildren how to make unusually large soap bubbles using a length of string attached to a wand. "You can make long bubbles and they go really far," one granddaughter tells an on-site interviewer. The newscaster then cuts back in: "Here's a tip—the more humid the weather, the better the bubbles."

The following segment is about a ribbon cutting for The Villages' fifth fire station. The last news segment is a surprisingly brief piece about a resident who drove a car into the side of his neighbor's house: "No drugs or alcohol involved, but officials say the driver's blood sugar was low." Then it's time again for an update on sports and recreation. The blond woman cuts to more footage of residents playing golf. "These residents are enjoying golf without snow!" she says. Next, there's a feature about an amateur dog show called Bark in the Park.

I shower, dress, and take another peek at VNN before leaving the house. The stories are beginning to feel repetitive. There's a story about blowing big bubbles and an amateur dog show in the park, and footage of Bob knocking down two bowling pins. The morning show cuts to a commercial break with the tagline: "Covering your hometown like nobody else can." Apparently, that means over and over again.

After a relaxing breakfast of fresh grapefruit with Dave and Betsy on the lanai, I hop into my car and switch on the radio: "It's such a pretty day and a pretty world in The Villages," the announcer says. Once in town, I pick up Gary Morse's local newspaper, an unusually handsome broadsheet called the *Daily Sun*. The newspaper dispenser has a sentimental drawing of a newsboy hawking papers, which is ironic, for obvious reasons. The two lead stories are about blowing bubbles and Bark in the Park. As I pass through the lobby of the sales office, I pick up the developer's glossy monthly magazine, which is filled with comforting articles on life in The Villages.

I am in the lobby for mere moments when a resident named Marvel walks up and introduces herself. She is one of several greeters, all of whom happen to be residents of The Villages. A lot of residents choose to work for The Villages, mostly as part-timers looking for a little extra cash and something to do.

Marvel jumps right into a friendly sales pitch. "Oh, goodness, there are so many things to do here—more than a thousand activities each week," she tells me. "It's such a wonderful place for parents. You know what they say: people live longer when they stay involved and active!"

I sip a complimentary cup of coffee and ask her what it's like to live in a community that restricts visits by younger family members. "It's true that children can't stay longer than thirty days in any given year," she responds. "But gosh, we're so busy; they're so busy. We're living our lives; they're living theirs. We visit them; they visit us. It works out just fine. Oh, look, I think the trolley's back. Let's go see!"

Waiting outside is a bus masquerading as a San Francisco cable car with the aid of a colorful vinyl veneer. Buddy, a paunchy midwesterner with a big smile, is the driver. He is wearing a festive miniature top hat—a child's party favor—held in place with an elastic band that might ordinarily fit under one's chin. It is too small, so Buddy wears the elastic around the back of his head. Mindy, also a heavyset midwesterner with a contagious smile, is the tour guide. She wears a festive miniature plastic tiara. "Looks like Mindy is the Trolley Queen today!" Marvel remarks.

I board the intensely air-conditioned bus. Mindy sits in the front on a raised seat facing me. I take out my pen and paper and look around. I am the only passenger. Nevertheless, Mindy puts on her headset and turns up the volume. "The Villages is the place to be," she says, in her sing-song Scandinavian cadence of the upper Midwest. "It's unbelievable! Buddy and I are both proud to call it our home. If you're bored here, it's your own fault!" Buddy turns his head and nods emphatically from the driver's seat, and then puts the bus into gear. Mindy tells me that above all The Villages stands for GLC: golf, lifestyle, and convenience. "You can buy a home anywhere; we're selling a lifestyle that you can't find anywhere else in the world. Now keep in mind, everywhere we go today is accessible by golf cart."

We drive around the town square, which Mindy compares to New York City's Times Square "because there is live entertainment every night." We drive past several churches: "No community is complete without houses of worship!" Then Mindy points out the hospital. "Take a good look at it now because we're about to add three more floors and an intensive care unit." Mindy doesn't mention that despite the expansion of the medical facility and its self-proclaimed status as a regional hospital, there is no maternity ward.

Buddy makes his way around another large traffic circle and then pulls up to a guard booth. "These are our lovely gates," Mindy announces. "We're going to drive to some more established neighborhoods so you can get an idea of what your house will, uh, look like in a few years." Mindy looks at me awkwardly. "Um. OK. We're in the neighborhoods now; that's why we came through a controlled-access gate."

Every quarter mile or so, we pass additional gates on either side of us. These are the so-called residential "villages." The preponderance of gates, guard booths, walls, and security cameras is a touch peculiar, given that The Villages bills itself as Florida's Friendliest Hometown. But it is representative of how an increasing number of Americans live. More than 10 million Americans live in communities protected by some form of fortification. Forty percent of new home construction in America's sunbelt is gated; in some communities, it's difficult to find middle- and upper-income housing that *isn't* gated. In an age of globalization, building moats at home has become something of a national pastime.

This trend has been seen for many years in South America, where members of the wealthy elite barricade themselves from the multitudes of the poor; and in the Middle East, where western workers take cover from an increasingly angry local population. In America, the main reason for turning one's community into a fortress is ostensibly to reduce crime. Yet studies have found that long-term crime rates are only slightly altered. Regardless, Americans want their slice of paradise gated, with a uniformed Saint Peter.

Gates create a gated mentality, which is quite contagious. The debate over illegal immigration was heating up when I was visiting The Villages. I can't say I was particularly surprised by one resident's solution to the problem, published in the *Daily Sun:* build a bigger wall.

Even after my arrival, I continue to find the nomenclature of "the village" and "The Villages" frustratingly vague and confusing. That's because there is no real taxonomic definition for what The Villages itself considers a "village" to be. From what I can tell, a "village" is little more than a monotonous grouping of similarly priced ranch homes built on spec by the Morse family. There are about fifty villages in The Villages, although the development is expected to continue growing at a breathless pace. Most have distinguished-sounding yet meaningless names such as "Village of Lynnhaven" or "Village of Winifred."

A village can range in size from several dozen of these spec homes to hundreds of them, with the underlying principle being financial segregation and preservation of assets. As one realtor in The Villages explains to me, "You wouldn't want a basic ranch home next to your 'premier' home. We can guarantee that your home will be surrounded by a product line just like yours."

Except for the occasional recreation area and clubhouse, each village looks basically like any other suburban subdivision, with its mostly dead-end residential streets that curve aimlessly. Besides the front door, the visual centerpiece of each home is the driveway and garage; there are no sidewalks and few if any front porches.

There is nothing about these housing clusters that even slightly resembles a "village" in the traditional sense. There are no cafés, no corner stores, no newsstands. No commercial enterprise of any sort is allowed to take place within a village. Planned developments like The Villages generally spurn the one thing that make traditional cities and towns so varied and entertaining: mixed use. Commerce is shunted to a "commercial zone," i.e., strip malls, which one must drive to in either a golf cart or a conventional automobile.

Developers and home buyers believe that such measures will protect and even enhance property values. According to this reasoning, the opening of a corner café, let alone the construction of a home worth ten percent less than yours, could put your investment at risk.

This thirst for standardization and stability is also why deed restrictions are so popular with home buyers, who pay a premium to live under them. Tens of millions of Americans have voluntarily given up certain liberties to live under private covenants enforced by fellow residents because they no longer trust their neighbors (who are increasingly transient) to do the right thing. For many communities, deed restrictions are a source of pride, and signs are posted at entrance gates proudly declaring their enforcement.

Deed restrictions were developed in fourteenth-century England and were particularly popular in America in the pre–civil rights era, when they were used to keep out Negroes, "Mongolians," and

Jews, among others. Early homeowners formed associations to enforce these "gentleman's agreements."

Today's deed-restricted communities like The Villages are similarly although less offensively, "utopian." Most restrictions are designed merely to keep life's usual surprises at bay, addressing such mundane issues as home renovations, paint colors, and what kind of flowers one may plant. But some deed restrictions—and their rigorous enforcement by powerful homeowners' associations—can be severe to the point of being comical. For instance, one woman in California was repeatedly forced to weigh in her overweight poodle because it hovered around the community's thirty-pound weight limit for dogs. The Villages' covenants require the removal of weeds and the edging of lawns, which must be at least fifty-one percent sod. Hedges over four feet high are prohibited, as are clotheslines, individual mailboxes (mail is collected at central kiosks), the keeping of more than two pets, window air-conditioning units (all homes must have central air-conditioning), door-to-door solicitation, and Halloween trick-or-treaters. In newer neighborhoods, lawn ornaments are forbidden except for seasonal displays "not exceeding a thirty-day duration"—the same time limit put on visiting children.

Many people feel that careful planning and mandatory conformity is a small price to pay to ensure that your neighbor doesn't threaten your investment by changing his oil in his driveway, or building a swing set in his backyard. This is part of what makes The Villages' villages so predictable and manicured.

Gary Lester, The Villages' spokesman, made this abundantly clear to me during our interview. "I bet you're wishing right now that your neighborhood was better planned," he said. "I bet you wish that there were rules about when and how people could put their trash out and how they can park a boat or an RV. I bet you're thinking that you don't want that RV parked on the road or in the driveway for a month or more, that you'd like the trash to be carefully bagged and placed outside the day of pickup."

"You have a point," I responded. "But where does it all end, and at what cost? Do you, as a former minister, think that age restrictions have a positive effect on our nation's social covenant?"

Lester paused, considered the question, and then, to my surprise, declined to answer it.

Back on the bus, Mindy enlightens me about the community's three dozen or so pools. There are four pool classifications: family pools, adult-only pools, member-only exercise pools, and premium-membership social pools. "Any resident can use any pool," she says. "There are no class distinctions at The Villages. The amenities are for everyone."

Buddy calls her over and whispers in her ear, and Mindy hastily corrects herself. "Actually, the social pools are for priority members only, but the golf courses and country clubs are open to all residents."

The bus crosses a four-lane thoroughfare as we head to an even newer area of the development. I see golf carts descend out of sight like burrowing animals as they approach the highway, only to re-emerge effortlessly moments later on the other side. "Those are our golf-cart tunnels. Aren't they neat?" Mindy asks.

With so much territory to cover, the tour begins to quicken its pace. I scribble furiously to keep up in my note taking. "Now put that pen down and look up for a moment, Andrew," Mindy says. "I don't want you to miss this—our very own boardwalk and lighthouse!" We are entering Sumter Landing, The Villages' second manufactured downtown. The Morse family hired a design firm with experience working for Universal Studios to invent this make-believe town, including its history, customs, and traditions. After all, if you don't have a history, why not invent one? Unlike the real thing, an imaginary history is nonthreatening and noncontroversial, so why not choose one to your liking and invite people to stay awhile?

A recent promotional DVD for Walt Disney World cheerfully lists all its theme resorts, each with a make-believe history. "Had it up to here with the twenty-first century?" the narrator asks. "All that hustle and bustle? Then this is the place for you." The narrator goes on to describe a fake seaside resort from the 1880s "just like all those seaside resorts that popped up along the eastern seaboard." If the 1880s aren't to your liking, there are plenty of other possibilities. As the narrator says, "Choose your experience!"

In a sense, injecting fantasy and entertainment into more permanent communities is the logical next step. At The Villages, you even have a choice of themes, depending on which downtown you visit.

Built less then two years before my visit for an estimated $120 million, Sumter Landing rests beside a small man-made lake dotted with partially sunk boats. There is a rustic boardwalk of sorts, as well as a functioning lighthouse whose purpose and effectiveness are not quite clear given the size of the lake and all the shipwrecks. Unlike Spanish Springs with its adobe construction, Sumter Landing has facades covered in clapboard and decorative second-story porches for the traditional feel of the Florida Keys. Mindy points out the attractive central square, with its bandstand, fountains, and shops lining three sides. Embedded trolley tracks run alongside the main street—presumably, in the imaginary history, these were abandoned after decades of use in favor of golf carts.

Mindy turns our attention to a tract of land farther down the lake beside what appear to be rowboats for rent but are also just props. Nearby construction will soon begin on a Barnes and Noble superstore and a large hotel. "Sumter Landing has all the grace and charm one could ask for," Mindy announces. "You can just feel that it's a real hometown!"

From a planning perspective, The Villages' saving grace is in fact its downtowns. Although few residents live within walking distance, the downtowns provide an environment where people can stroll and mingle effortlessly. Most planned communities lack this pleasant design feature.

But there's no hiding the fact that these aren't real downtowns —they are "themed" by entertainment specialists and are owned almost exclusively by a single family that leases out space for businesses. Calling them downtowns is just as disingenuous as the using the term "Villages" or "hometown."

An authentic community is more than a collection of buildings designed to look old, like makeup applied to a young actor's face. Real towns are defined by a complex and multilayered web of interactions between businesses, residents, and civic institutions—little of which Spanish Springs or Sumter Landing possesses. Instead, Villagers have settled for a Hollywood facsimile that could one day be sold en masse to another investor.

Much like Disney World's "Downtown Disney," The Villages' so-called downtowns are really glorified shopping malls with souvenir stores and theme restaurants. That is why they look like ghost towns at night when the "mall" closes—no one lives there, or even actually shops there for necessities. Want to buy a quart of milk or a stick of gum? You'll need to jump back into your car or golf cart and drive to the development's periphery, which is crowded with big box stores and acres of asphalt parking lots.

Historically, downtowns have provided senior citizens with a convenient place to live near basic services. Planners call them naturally occurring retirement communities (NORCs). My grandmother lived in downtown Philadelphia for just that reason—ease of access. If she wanted a quart of milk, she'd walk a block to buy one.

When it comes to NORCs, the gauge of convenience isn't the number of drive-throughs, but rather the number of things that can be reached on foot or by public transportation. Much of Europe is chockablock with NORCs because its living patterns were well established before the advent of the automobile.

I suspect that The Villages' downtowns could be easily retrofitted to encourage genuine downtown living, but such a future seems remote. Although many of the buildings in Spanish Springs and Sumter Landing have second and even third floors (often with elevators), no one is permitted to live there. The spaces are either used for offices or for storage, or left empty.

Downtowns often reflect the character of the people who live in them. The Villages' downtowns don't have residents, but they do reflect the character of the development—a society in which leisure is the guiding principle. Because there is no real shared history, the pursuit of leisure becomes the glue that bonds the residents to the development and to one another.

This is not a surprising outcome, given that America has had a decades-long love affair with convenience and leisure. We invented and popularized fast food, drive-throughs, and the La-Z-Boy recliner, among other La-Z inventions, such as homes designed to look historical but without the hassles of a genuine restoration.

Even vacations have been made "easier," as can be seen in our obsession with all-inclusive resorts and cruise ships where you never really have to *do* anything. About ten percent of American leisure travelers now choose all-inclusive resorts as their destination. And the number of people opting for cruises grew from 1.5 million in 1980 to 10 million twenty-five years later. What could be more a convenient form of leisure than a cruise, especially when many cruises now offer "sanctuary decks" guaranteed to be free of children? Convenience and leisure, we've been told, make life easier. So why not build an entire community predicated on convenience—even if it's an illusion?

The bus leaves Sumter Landing and continues along gently curving boulevards past one gated village after another. The monotony is partially broken up by landscaped retention ponds and undulating golf courses. Several of the more expensive houses —some of which cost well over $1 million—have what appear to be zoo-size aviaries attached to them. These are actually screened-in porches big enough to accommodate pools with waterfalls and outdoor auxiliary kitchens. "That's where we party!" Buddy says. Many of these homes are ringed with additional security cameras.

We pass by a Veterans Administration clinic, an animal hospital, and a few of The Villages' larger regional recreation centers, which have tennis and basketball courts; Olympic-size pools; and large indoor rooms where Villagers work out, play billiards and hold club meetings. An annual amenity fee gives every Villager access to these and other smaller recreation facilities, as well as archery ranges and workshops for cabinetry and metalworking.

"Take a look, Andrew," Mindy says, pointing out the window at an expanse of athletic fields bordered by grandstands. "This is polo!" she says excitedly. Mindy nods her head, as if to forestall my disbelief, and repeats the word, this time in a hushed reverential tone: "*Polo.*" Villagers don't actually play polo. Rather, they watch a polo team consisting mostly of Gary Morse's friends. Popular with Florida's moneyed class, polo is undoubtedly a status booster for the developer as well as his residents.

Mindy tells me that one of the fields on the edge of the complex serves as a popular site for golf cart tailgates and drive-in movies, which, Mindy adds, serve as "a fond reminder of the old days."

Next door is the Savannah Center, a performing arts facility which was built to resemble Scarlett O'Hara's beloved Tara, and which attracts touring Broadway productions. "I just can't imagine what we don't have here," Mindy remarks. "It seems like we have everything we could possibly need. And it's so beautiful—like living in a Thomas Kinkade painting, but in real life."

The tour ends back in Spanish Springs, at a small reflecting pool with a bronze statue of Harold Schwartz in a sports coat, one arm outstretched in a gesture of welcome, much like the statue of Walt Disney at the Disney theme parks.

"Mr. Schwartz is dead now," Mindy explains, "but he founded The Villages—and I thank him for that." Mindy falls silent as Buddy the bus driver turns around to face me, still wearing his miniature top hat. "Me too," he says. "Mr. Schwartz always said, 'You shouldn't have to be a millionaire to live like one at The Villages.' And by gosh, that's still the way it is."

After lunch I set out to find The Villages' only playground. It's shown on the map of the development, but finding it is another matter. I finally locate it in an area isolated from normal pedestrian traffic at the far end of a vast parking lot, hidden behind a bunch of bushes. It's small, with a cute little imitation ship for children to run around on, but there are no swings, seesaws, or other playground basics. A mother with two children arrives and sets her kids loose on the fake boat. A short while later, they run up to their mother and profess boredom. She gathers them up and heads back to their car.

Two county sheriff's cars are parked outside the playground. The cars are idling, air-conditioning running full blast, windows wide open. The deputies are clearly taking advantage of the area's remoteness. One is sound asleep, his arms slack in front of him, head tilted back. He snores lightly. The other deputy is quietly reading a magazine. I approach and ask him if there is another playground.

"Nope. If you're looking for a real playground, you'll need to drive to the town of Lady Lake," he tells me. "It's about fifteen minutes away, depending on traffic. There are usually other kids there, so your little ones might find someone to play with. There's also a Burger King with a playground if you're really in a pinch."

I ask him if there's much crime in The Villages. "I'd say ninety-five percent of our calls are medical. We call the folks here 'frogs' because they come down here to croak. We're basically here as a 'presence.' I think that's the way the developer wants it to be." The other deputy lets out a snort and readjusts himself without waking up.

Back in town, I sign up for a boat tour of the lagoon that provides Lake Sumter with its modest shoreline. The sightseeing skiffs leave from a set of docks at one end of the boardwalk. I pay two dollars and step in with eight other visitors. A man wearing stripes on his shoulders and bifocals on his nose introduces himself as Captain Marvin. He directs our attention to Dickie, his potbellied first mate, who proceeds to show us where the life jackets are located. Dickie warns us that if conditions get rough we should "move away from the edge of the boat." I look out onto the shallow, motionless body of water designed by the developer's architects. It doesn't appear likely that we'll need life jackets.

As the canopied boat put-puts away from the dock, Dickie points to the lighthouse up ahead, and claims that it was built by a "Yank" named Willie B. Wagner more than 150 years ago. "He was a character among characters, but the locals liked him and called him the Commodore," Dickie tells us. "It took him ten years to complete the lighthouse, starting in 1835. The Historical Society came in and restored it some years ago." The other passengers nod their heads hesitantly, unsure whether or not to believe this tale.

We quickly run out of lake and the boat turns to port. Dickie recites for us a tale about a Seminole chief named Billy Bowlegs "a friend to whites who lived on this shore." Bowlegs eventually moved to Tampa to open a banana plantation. Dickie adds, "It used to be that bananas were straight until Billy Bowlegs put the curve in them."

Billy Bowlegs actually did exist, but he didn't live on "these shores" and his biography was more tragic. There is no evidence that he was actually bowlegged, yet his nickname persists in the pages of history, most likely derived from an earlier Seminole chief. Billy Bowlegs's real name was Holata Micco, or Alligator Chief, and he led a band of guerrilla warriors during the Second Seminole War. When he finally tired of fighting, he moved his tribe farther south. The whites followed and harassed him, thus starting the Third Seminole War. Bowlegs eventually surrendered, and joined his defeated brethren on the Trail of Tears to the Indian Territories of Oklahoma. Later, in the hope of receiving favorable treatment from the federal government, he fought bravely alongside Union soldiers during the Civil War, but he died soon afterward of smallpox.

We pass along the far side of the lake. We're told that this stretch of waterfront is rumored to be the secret meeting place of the now defunct "Fraternal Order of Exalted Alligators." It's an attractive spot with undulating banks quilted with fairways and sand traps. Some golfers cheerfully wave to us as they drive by in their cart. A passenger on the boat interrupts Dickie's presentation with a question: "Are those two par threes in a row?" Captain Marvin spins the wheel and put-puts back to the docks.

Safely back at port, I walk off in search of a can of soda, but I have difficulty finding a simple corner store—because there isn't one. I step into a shop advertising "Sassy Sizzlin' Styles" and ask the saleswoman where I can find a soft drink. "Hmm. You could get a soda at Johnny Rockets," she says. "But you'd probably have to sit down and drink it there. Well, gosh, I can't think of anywhere you can buy a can of soda around here."

As I continue strolling around the square, I'm overcome by a peculiar sensation. I can't quite put my finger on it until I walk past a bantering rock and then a chatty lamppost. It's the afternoon's headlines from WVLG streaming out of hidden speakers. Curious, I move closer to the lamppost to catch the day's news, and then a commentary by Paul Harvey, a nationally syndicated conservative radio host. After the news, a DJ spins Neal Diamond's "Sweet Caroline." "Hey, it's OK to turn up the radio real loud on this one," he announces gleefully. "Your kids still live up north!"

Retailers have long known that music affects customers' purchasing habits and employees' morale. Music is frequently piped into elevators, stores, offices, restaurants, and factories. Now it's being used as a mood enhancer for an entire town. It's so well integrated that gauging its effect is difficult, but the people strolling around the central square appear blissfully calm and cheery, much like the music.

I walk over to Johnny Rockets for a quick bite. Although it was founded in 1986 on Melrose Avenue in Los Angeles, Johnny Rockets bills itself as "the home of the original hamburger." Inside, one is greeted by smiling teens in snappy costumes reminiscent of the 1950s. These teens don't shout, push, smoke, or curse; they just smile and hop to it, and then leave The Villages' fenced perimeter each evening.

I ask an eager young waiter wearing a sharply creased paper hat how a restaurant chain founded two decades ago could have invented the hamburger. "Gosh, I don't know," he answers while scooping ice cream for a malted milk shake. "I never thought about it. Maybe they mean *their* original hamburger."

The company's philosophy, displayed on the cheery menu, looks as if Harold Schwartz himself could have written it. "Johnny Rockets was founded on the belief that everyone deserves a place where they can escape today's complicated world and experience the food, fun, and friendliness of feel-good Americana."

I step outside again and witness an unusual sight. Across the street in the town square I spot a black kid on a BMX bike. He's wearing a white stocking cap and headphones. A moment later, he is gone.

6

The Chaz Incident

ALTHOUGH THEY KNEW IT WAS HARDLY A CHARITABLE THING to say, early residents of Youngtown, Arizona, were quick to point out that the success of their community was predicated on the exclusion of children, and they must have felt vindicated when Del Webb copied the idea next door. But as time progressed and the desert scrub around them turned into strip malls and suburban housing developments, the residents of Youngtown saw their bubble repeatedly threatened by droves of young families moving into the area. Lured by its cheap real estate, some of these families even tried to sneak into Youngtown.

Ever vigilant, Youngtown residents strove valiantly to keep these clandestine families out of their community. In 1990 alone, the town fathers boasted of evicting thirty-two underage families from housing in Youngtown. Three hundred more were evicted over the next four years. The evictees protested against Youngtown's age segregation but never successfully challenged it. Youngtown continued to hold the line and evict nonconforming residents with impunity.

Then came what old-timers refer to as the "Chaz incident." Depending on whom you ask, Chaz Cope was either a sensitive teenager, or a "young thug" and a "terrorist who held the town hostage."

Chaz, a skinny sixteen-year-old, moved in with his grand-parents in 1996 to escape a physically abusive stepfather. Accord-ing to Youngtown's rules, children under eighteen were allowed to visit for only up to ninety days a year. Rather than try to hide him, Chaz's grandparents went to the town officials and asked for an extension because of the extenuating circumstances. They were charged a $300 filing fee and had to plead their case in front of the town council. A three-month extension was granted, and the town officials put a placard on the grandparents' front lawn informing neighbors that the family was housing a juvenile.

It was the grandparents' hope that Chaz could live with them until he finished high school the following year. But when they went before the council a second time, their plea for another extension was unanimously denied. The council further voted to fine Chaz's grandparents $100 a day for illegally housing a child. Chaz was rele-gated to the status of human contraband.

Chaz's grandparents appealed their case to the state attorney general, who decided to give the history of Youngtown's ordinance a good hard look. The standoff made international headlines and put Youngtown's age-segregation policies in the spotlight. Mean-while, Chaz and his grandparents suffered frequent harassment. Their car was vandalized; neighbors tried to prevent Chaz from play-ing basketball in his driveway before school, claiming that he was violating antinoise ordinances; and a town councilman circulated a fabricated juvenile court record alleging that Chaz had been charged with possession of marijuana. "My goal was to let people know that this boy wasn't the kind of angel that he was portrayed to be by the press," the councilman later said.

The residents of Youngtown could survive the black eye they were getting in the press because they had already dropped out of society to a certain extent, but the attorney general's much-anticipated ruling proved to be a crushing body blow. According to the state's findings, Youngtown wasn't an age-segregated community, and legally it never had been. Therefore, the town's attempts to enforce the policy were entirely unlawful.

For all his bravado in marketing, Big Ben Schleifer never actually wrote any language into Youngtown's original deed restrictions to ensure the community's future as an oasis for the aging. It probably never occurred to him to do so: who else would want to live in a retirement community in the middle of nowhere with no schools and no access to any other family-oriented amenities? Schleifer was so far ahead of his time that it would take the legal system—and the spread of Phoenix—decades to catch up, but in 1998, they eventually did.

When Congress passed the Federal Fair Housing Act in 1968, many types of discrimination in the sale, rental, and financing of housing were outlawed. But age discrimination wasn't addressed; the act was designed to eliminate only discrimination based on race, color, religion, and national origin. It was later amended to prohibit discrimination based on sex, in 1974, but it did not address age at all until 1988, when it was further amended to prohibit discrimination based on handicap and something referred to as "familial status"—households with children under the age of eighteen.

The congressional debates over the protections given to familial status were particularly contentious, with the result that these households were not granted the same blanket protection as the other categories. Family advocates pointed to well-documented reports of discrimination against families with children in the housing market, but landlords' groups and advocates for senior citizens argued that some housing should be reserved exclusively for older citizens because they often have special needs, as well as a preference for an age-homogeneous environment. The early developers of housing for baby boomers were also among the many industry opponents to the legislation. At the time, child-free, amenity-rich suburban condo complexes for singles in their twenties and thirties were rapidly growing in popularity.

Although Congress acknowledged that discrimination against families with children was prevalent, it sided with the powerful landlords' and seniors' lobbies, thus making prohibitions against children the only type of housing discrimination specifically protected by federal law.

"We recognize that some older Americans have chosen to live together with fellow senior citizens in retirement type communities," a House report stated. "We appreciate the interest and expectations these individuals have in living in environments tailored to their specific needs." The amendment of 1988 exempted "housing for older persons" from the Fair Housing Act, thus, under certain circumstances, permitting an absolute ban on children age eighteen or younger.

The amendment permitted the banning of children under the following circumstances: the housing was specifically designed for senior citizens under the aegis of a government program; the housing was occupied exclusively by persons age sixty-two and older; or at least eighty percent of the housing was occupied by households with at least one person fifty-five or older. (If the percentage of homes owned by residents of the qualifying age drops below eighty, a community loses its age-segregated status and the gates are suddenly opened to one and all.)

Commercially, this "fifty-five and older" exemption was the most malleable and therefore became the darling of developers. Limiting housing to people who are sixty-two or older severely limits the demographics of potential buyers. Imagine having to turn away an interested couple because one spouse is only sixty-one. Such restrictions greatly reduce the marketability of a development. Nursing homes usually apply this restriction, since they are unlikely to attract younger residents anyway.

Lowering the age limit to fifty-five opens the market to a much larger demographic of potential buyers, especially if only one member of a household has to qualify. A sugar daddy can still live with a twenty-five-year-old wife or even a college-age child. And if the real estate market sags, a developer has the option of abandoning the eighty-twenty mix and opening up the properties to all ages.

To help justify the need for age restrictions, the amendments of 1988 to the Fair Housing Act required such communities to provide "significant services and facilities specifically designed to meet the physical or social needs of older persons." The wording was somewhat vague, but the intent was not: retirement communities may exist because they cater to the special needs of their elderly residents. The Department of Housing and Urban Development came up with a long list of what serves these special needs, such as communal cafeterias, wheelchair accessibility, and specially designed athletic classes, but developers complained that these requirements were unduly onerous, especially for no-frills lower-income mobile home retirement communities. Congress scrapped this provision altogether in 1995 with passage of the Housing for Older Persons Act, and retirement communities no longer had to justify their existence.

Despite the amendment's obvious drawbacks, the civil rights community nevertheless saw progress through the haze of compromise. Not only did the legislation require the federal government to strictly enforce the entire Fair Housing Act and pave the way for physically and mentally handicapped renters and homeowners; it finally addressed the plight of a previously ignored demographic— families with children. Even the choice of the relatively young entry age of fifty-five was seen as a small victory because the barrier age for many retirement communities, such as Sun City, was then just fifty.

The civil rights community had a particular interest in the legislation because it saw discrimination against children as a proxy for discrimination against poorer minorities in general, who often have large families. Minorities were routinely turned away from potential rentals on the pretext that children were not permitted. A study conducted at the time by the Department of Housing and Urban Development found that neighborhoods with a white majority were twice as likely as predominantly nonwhite neighborhoods to have anti-child housing restrictions.

Before the legislation, landlords, developers, and neighborhood covenants could arbitrarily discriminate against families with children. There was no federal law addressing this situation, and only a few states attempted to forbid such discrimination. It was not unusual for housing complexes to routinely charge higher rents for families with children, or forbid them altogether without cause. Moreover, couples could be evicted if the woman was pregnant.

The first language addressing age segregation in Youngtown didn't appear in deed restrictions until 1975—much later than had been presumed. With an increasing number of young renters moving into the community, Youngtown city officials sensed trouble on the horizon. To neutralize the threat, the city council voted to officially incorporate age restrictions into the town's bylaws. Nearly two decades after its founding, children were finally verboten, or so the town elders thought. They aggressively enforced the new law and evicted more than 100 families until their legal charade collapsed in the face of the attorney general's finding in 1998.

The ruling hit the seniors of Youngtown hard. With the law no longer on their side, their humble paradise was inevitably going to be invaded by hordes of children. To add insult to injury, the state ordered Youngtown to pay Chaz's family $30,000 in restitution. Although this was a meager amount under the circumstances, it was nonetheless seen as a princely sum for a troublesome brat. When news of the settlement was announced at a packed town meeting, it was greeted with an audible gasp, then silence. Sensing that things could soon turn ugly, the town attorney warned residents,

"Retaliation . . . is a violation of state and federal law and will be prosecuted accordingly."

Chaz and his grandparents moved out anyway. Chaz had been briefly celebrated in the media as the Rosa Parks for his generation, but he soon fled the spotlight. I was eager to speak with him on one of my trips to Arizona, but locating him proved to be quite a challenge. It was as if Chaz had simply vanished.

Even after I eventually located him, by means of an unlisted cell-phone number, it took numerous awkward calls to persuade him to meet with me. "That was a long time ago," he complained. "I'm living a different life now." When I told him that I came bearing greetings from Dan Connelly, Youngtown's current police chief, who was an officer during the incident, Chaz began to relent. "The chief said he hoped your life was going well since the events at Youngtown, particularly because they should never have happened in the first place," I told him.

Now in his mid-twenties and married, Chaz is the picture of earnestness. Still skinny as a beanpole, he is casually but neatly dressed when I catch up with him at a coffee shop in Phoenix. He wears his hair combed straight back, has a thin mustache, and wears eyeglasses.

"I don't begrudge older folks who want to live alone together," Chaz says, much to my surprise. "There's a lot of crime and violence in today's society. There's no respect for old people anymore. They have wisdom and stuff to hand down to people. But kids today are unruly. The way kids are dressing, talking, and acting, it makes *me* feel like an old man. But people in general don't care about each other any more. The world is a wicked, violent place. And it's not going to get better until people start living the word of God. That's the only real solution."

Chaz informs me that he is now a Jehovah's Witness, and spends much of his time knocking on doors bearing witness to the glory of God. He hands me a religious booklet titled "What Does the Bible

Really Teach?" One illustration depicts an intercontinental missile circling the Earth and a crazed criminal holding a gun to victim's head. The caption reads: "The casting of Satan and his demons out of heaven brought woe to the earth. Such troubles will soon end."

As far as Chaz is concerned, Youngtown did two things wrong: it broke the law, and it didn't show any sympathy for his family's special circumstances. "I didn't move to Youngtown because I wanted to; I moved there because I *had* to," he tells me. "Things were really bad back home. It was an abusive situation. My grandparents pleaded with the town council. All they were asking for was nine more months. But the council wouldn't budge. They didn't show any compassion or mercy.

"What they were doing was illegal anyway. Youngtown wasn't age-restricted; they were just faking it. If it had been legal, I would have left. I wasn't about to chain myself to my grandparents' house. I'd have gone back to live with my mom if I had to.

"It got real nasty. You'd think, being old people, they'd be more mature. I wasn't a pristine kid in those days, but I was a still a nice kid. One neighbor said I was a real sweet boy. I didn't go around vandalizing and creating havoc. I don't see how I was such a hardship. I didn't even hang out in Youngtown. I met my friends in Peoria. But I don't think those old folks really cared whether I was a criminal or not. They didn't want young people there, period. They didn't want to get to know me."

Given its close proximity, I asked Chaz if he ever visits Youngtown. "I go back sometimes," he answers. "It brings back a lot of sad memories. I'd hate to see it happen to somebody else, another young person. I think there's always room for compassion, for empathy for what someone else is going through. When I drive by Youngtown and see all the families, I can't help thinking, 'Is that because of me?' And you know what? I won't lie—I do like the fact that Youngtown is filled with young people."

* * *

Youngtown's transition into a multigenerational community was awkward, to say the least. The town had no schools or playgrounds, and the library, well stocked with large-print books, had no children's section. "We don't have the land or resources to build these things," the mayor at the time said. "Youngtown is an island. It was never designed for children." The police chief was equally perplexed —what would happen to the seven PM curfew for visiting children? "We used to pull over a carload of kids because they didn't belong here," he said. "Now they might be residents."

In many ways, Youngtown before Chaz was already a dying town on the wrong side of the tracks from Sun City. Many of Youngtown's residents were doing their best just to hold on. The geriatric community reinvested little to nothing in its public structures and common areas, let alone its private residences. Its businesses left, residents of Sun City avoided it, and the nation forgot its historical significance.

Ask anyone to name America's first retirement community and the answer will probably be Sun City. It was Del Webb on the cover of *Time,* not Ben Schleifer. And it was Sun City that grew and grew, while Youngtown stagnated. Schleifer said his biggest regret was that Sun City wasn't at least ten miles away so that his community wouldn't have to be compared with it.

But after years of stasis and benign neglect, the housing market was opened up to everyone. Young families flocked to Youngtown for many of the same reasons its older residents had come: crime was negligible, homes were unusually affordable, and taxes were incredibly low—Youngtown doesn't tax its residents, but relies instead on state revenue sharing and a local sales tax. Once Youngtown was thrust into the greater real estate market, its artificially low property values shot up more than thirty percent practically overnight, and well over 200 percent in ten years. Many seniors chose to sell their homes at a handsome profit.

As Youngtown's aging retirees died or fled across the street to Sun City, the town filled up with young families. The retirees and their treasured traditions were fast disappearing, swallowed up by youth culture, much as everywhere else. Boom boxes blasting rock and rap replaced tabletop radios playing golden oldies; children's shrieks and teenagers' shouts replaced gentle greetings; and complaints about kids playing in the street fell on deaf ears. The Saturday dances, barbecue picnics, and quiet strolls were a thing of the past, replaced by a lingering fear that crime would soon threaten whatever remained. A deep well of resentment grew between the generations, who interpreted the name "Youngtown" to mean different things.

Desegregation has never proved to be an easy undertaking, and integrating Youngtown had its own particular challenges, many of which were lost on the newcomers. To the seniors the issue was simple: they didn't want younger people around. But to the newcomers, discrimination based on age was probably a difficult concept to understand. After all, a white person can't have been born black, but everyone was once young.

The seniors suffered yet another perceived indignity when the young invaders flexed their political muscle and elected one of their own as mayor. A youngster born after 1960 would now govern the veterans of World War II and Korea. The new mayor arrived at his first council meeting riding a Harley-Davidson, and gunning the engine for effect. He immediately set about carrying out his campaign pledge to spend more money on the town's children by building playgrounds, athletic fields, and a skateboard park.

Meanwhile, a group of seniors worked to discredit the mayor, much as they had done before with Chaz. They dug up and circulated damning court documents, but this time the documents were real and the mayor was guilty as charged. To Youngtown's older residents, the crime could hardly have been more emblematic of their predicament: the mayor had once been arrested for parking in a space reserved for the handicapped—albeit thirteen years earlier and halfway across the country. Worse yet, unlike the town's penny-pinching elders, the young mayor proved to be a profligate spender, and many people blamed him for draining the municipality's reserve funds.

Given Youngtown's tumultuous recent history, it's somewhat surprising how little its historic center has changed when I visit. Compared with old photographs I had seen, it looks much the same as it did decades ago, with a bandstand in the middle of a modest green, and a one-story town hall that originally served as housing for ranch hands. Across the way is the town library, where there are now children's books as well as computer terminals popular with Youngtown's teenagers.

Farther down the street is a small playground and just beyond that is Maricopa Lake, which resembles a retention pond. But any amount of water in the desert is a luxury, and this tiny body of water is no exception. At the far end is a picnic gazebo and a few scattered pieces of old playground equipment. Lake or no lake, the heat and dust never let you forget where you are.

Many of Youngtown's streets sweep around in the lazy curves that characterize so many subdivisions today. The homes that are well maintained are charming in the suburban style of the 1950s: ranch houses with small footprints, little carports, and carefully manicured gardens. But there are also plenty of run-down homes with ratty yards, peeling paint, and tinfoil hanging from windows to keep out the searing desert sun.

The commercial area is still recovering from the exodus of businesses in the 1970s and 1980s. The town's big grocery store left in 1978; and a cooperative failed, owing to a lack of volunteers. I see two massage parlors and a tattoo business. Across the street, Sun City and its palm-studded boulevards beckon.

The most radical new addition to Youngtown is also the one that is most difficult to access. One either has to drive halfway around the edge of the community or across a steep and creepy (at least at night) storm wash to reach a subdivision called Agua Fria Ranch. The development represents the community's first substantial residential construction since the early 1960s, and it is a source of great pride. The subdivision looks much like any other—uninspired homes with large garages facing one another—but there are plenty of basketball hoops and children playing in the streets.

Much of the subdivision's infrastructure—such as flood control —was paid for with a $3 million special assessment for which only those living in the new development are responsible. The assessment's purpose is to make sure that the residents of "old Youngtown" don't have to pay for improvements exclusively designed for residents of "new Youngtown."

On my way out, I spy one homeowner participating in an activity feared and despised by most deed-restricted communities, including old Youngtown. His car is hoisted up on a jack in his driveway, and he is buried somewhere under the chassis, presumably changing the oil. In many of the communities that I have visited, such activity is quickly reported and the perpetrator is warned to refrain from it in the future or face expulsion. Most members of a homeowners' association will tell you that taking a hard line is necessary to keep a community from spiraling downward.

Nonetheless, Agua Fria is considered a complete success, because it quickly doubled the town's population, from 3,000 to 6,000. It also balanced out the community's lopsided demographics. There is now the same number of younger people as older people, although time is ultimately on the side of the town's younger residents.

Graffiti is not altogether rare, and according to Dan Connelly, Youngtown's sixty-five-year-old police chief, crime has indeed increased since desegregation. The department recently added a drug-sniffing dog to the force, to help deal with a growing problem: methamphetamine. But the crime is due to a number of factors, Connelly tells me.

When it was first built, Youngtown was more than thirteen miles from the city limits of Phoenix. The retirement community and its neighbor, Sun City, were islands of green in a vast expanse of desert. But as Phoenix rapidly grew from a small city to a sprawling metropolitan area—it is now the fifth-largest city in America—it expanded to within three miles of their boundaries. One look outside at the congested roads makes the region's inexorable growth abundantly clear.

"At this point, we're really just another bedroom community of Phoenix," the chief tells me when we meet. "In ten more years we'll be considered inner-city. We've got all the crime and the problems that other cities have."

But while Youngtown has its share of drive-through crime, he says that much of its criminal activity is now homegrown—just as the obstinate seniors angrily predicted it would be. "We used to get about two domestic violence calls a year," says Connelly. "Last year we had 337. Ages twenty-five to forty are the prime demographic for domestic violence. In general, we have the same number of calls for service today as we did in 1999. But they're no longer Mildred calling because she can't find her cat or can't figure out how to operate the air-conditioning now that her husband's dead."

Another measure of change is the so-called death patrol. "We used to collect thirty-five to forty dead bodies a year; now we find ten, if that many." As the town's demographics change, so does its sense of community. Requests for the death patrol now come from concerned relatives "back home" rather than from a neighbor. "It's usually some nephew from Canton, Ohio, asking us to check up on his uncle who turns out to be dead on the toilet," Connelly says.

And yet, the chief tells me emphatically that the increase in crime has been worth the sacrifice. "Look, where you have kids and young people, you're going to have problems. But on the flip side, we now have a vibrant, growing community. We even have a kids' soccer league. As far as I'm concerned, the banning of children was wrong. I don't see it as being any different from the overt prejudice against African-Americans in pre–civil rights America. When I was in the military, I was stationed in the South, and I remember that time well."

In his view, integration has actually led to better relations between the generations. To illustrate this point, the chief recalls an incident from the mid-1990s, just before age restrictions were lifted: an older woman ran over and killed a seven-year-old girl who had just gotten off her school bus. "The woman was *angry*. She told me that the child should never have been crossing the street, because schoolchildren aren't allowed to live in Sun City. That's how bad it was."

7

Mr. Midnight

It's a Tuesday night and after yet another long day of reporting from the front lines of "golf, leisure and convenience," I find myself feeling bored, and perhaps a touch mischievous. The perfect lawns, nostalgic architecture, and chatter about golf are beginning to get to me. Thankfully, there's always Katie Belle's in Spanish Springs, with its abundant cheap drinks and the elders' endless antics, to let loose in. And so tonight, as usual, I'm driven to drink. The bar is full of laughter and the people on the crowded dance floor are swaying energetically to golden oldies performed by a band whose bass player wears a hearing aid and whose keyboardist wears what appears to be a toupee.

You'd never know it was a weekday. With no Fridays to anticipate, or Mondays to dread, the days of the week just blend together, and eventually every night feels like Saturday night.

One woman appears to be having a particularly good time balancing a pencil between her breasts in response to a challenge. Although she is in her early seventies, she has bright orange hair and is wearing a short skirt and a low-cut blouse. Her bracelet and necklace are neon-colored and her belt jingles with golden medallions. Her name is Kat, and she's on a tear. She removes the pencil and then turns to the small group of friends gathered around her.

"Want to see my mouse tattoo?" she asks, angling away from the crowd and lifting up her skirt. She looks down at her bare thigh and turns her head in mock surprise. She then hooks a finger around her panties and gently tugs them toward her crotch, her expression gradually turning into one of growing concern and disbelief. "Where's my mouse?" she says. Just as she is about to reveal all, Kat drops her skirt and announces, "It looks like my pussy ate it!"

Somebody buys Kat another cocktail. "Aren't we silly?" Kat asks me, drawing me into her orbit. "I've been this way all my life. I didn't change when I came here."

When my own grandmother was Kat's age, she religiously watched Phil Donohue, chewed bonemeal tablets for her teeth, and occasionally treated herself to an early bird platter of broiled flounder (usually leaving the restaurant with a few secreted packets of Sweet'N Low). Her favorite activity was to take walks with her women friends. Once a week, they'd visit a beauty parlor to have their hair done. Whenever it was windy or threatened rain, the "girls" (as they called themselves) were sure to bundle their hair in crumpled plastic before stepping outside.

Kat tells me she works part-time in The Villages' regional hospital, where she sees an eye-popping number of seniors with sexually transmitted diseases. Seniors are now one of the fastest growing populations at risk of STDs because they are so promiscuous. Also, more than sixty percent of sexually active older singles have unprotected sex. After all, who's going to get pregnant at seventy?

Kat leaves for the dance floor, and I find myself sitting next to a man from New Hampshire named Tommy. At seventy-three, he is balding and wrinkled, with prominent liver spots on his hands. As I introduce myself, he leans over and tilts his head so he can hear me with his good ear.

"I love sex," Tommy tells me, unprompted. "I really do. I had a heart attack last year, so I've been out of the game for a while. That heart attack really knocked the stuffing out of me." But Tommy isn't easily deterred. "I'm back now and ready for some serious action. What better way to die than in the sack? Nelson Rockefeller died that way."

Tommy tells me that at The Villages he has slept with women as young as nineteen. He points out an apple-cheeked waitress with a cute blond bob, balancing a tray of cocktails on her shoulder. "I had her. I did her on the kitchen table. It was great. They're all great."

I'm a bit stunned, if not a little impressed, and it must show, because Tommy starts explaining his success. "They don't want to be stuck here earning a little here, a little there. They want to be set for life. They think I can offer them that. I've also been told I'm a good conversationalist."

Tommy's eyes stray. "Look at that one." He points to a busty brunette in her thirties who has sidled up to the bar. I've begun to recognize a few of these younger women as regulars. "Does that look like a senior citizen to you?" He takes another sip of the beer. "I like to sleep around. And I know how to love a woman. You don't rush into it. You take your time.

"You know, some guys around here don't object to sharing their wives. I got it on with this one guy's wife. But he didn't seem to mind. It was just another 'beautiful day in The Villages.'"

I ask Tommy if he's a member of the Village Swingers' Club, about which I've heard whispers.

"I've heard about one—some say it's masquerading as the Wine Club—but I'm not so sure. Some folks dig that sort of thing; some don't. There was this other woman. I really wanted to do her, but her husband was the jealous type. I thought I had her when he finally died of a heart attack. But then I had one, too."

"The Wine Club?" I ask, intrigued.

"Sure," Tommy says. "It's not like they'd advertise such a thing. And alcohol's a nice lubricant."

Tommy adjusts himself on his stool. I hear what sounds like a fart, and then smells like one. "It gets harder to keep 'em in when you get older," he says. "You'll see."

Some buddies stroll by and Tommy smacks them a high five. One friend, a Brit named Nigel with the looks of an aging movie star, pulls up a stool next to Tommy. Nigel tells me he first visited The Villages on a recommendation from a friend in his native Birmingham. "I bought a place within two days," he says. "That was back in 1998. This place is like a candy store for a single guy like me. It's like New Year's eve every night. I can honestly say I don't miss home a bit. And I'm far from alone: there are quite a number of us here."

Fresh from the dance floor, Kat walks up to me and gently rubs my shoulders. I can't tell if she wants to mother me, or if she's got a hankering for something more, but I'm not about to complain about a shoulder massage. She moves closer, until I feel the warmth of her bosom resting against my back. "You're so tense," she says. "I can just *feel* it."

The bartender announces last call, and I take this as my cue to exit gracefully.

The next morning I drive a few blocks to the Andersons' village recreation center, which consists of a pool, a few shuffleboard courts, and a wall of mailboxes. I've forgotten my guest pass and I'm not entirely sure I am allowed to swim in this pool—I've already been kicked out of two—but nobody's here, so what the heck, why not squeeze in a few quick laps? I enter the pool area and toss my towel and T-shirt onto a lounge chair.

I turn toward the pool, but stop abruptly and look back at the lounge chair. I wonder, Do seniors fold their pool towels? Would folding mine help keep me from looking like a young mischief maker? I fold my towel and carefully place it back on the chair. I turn again toward the pool, but the nagging persists. Maybe I should fold my T-shirt too. I fold the shirt and lay it across the towel at a pleasing angle, like an extra set of guest linens.

When I am not ten minutes into my swimming routine, a woman steps into the pool area and cautiously surveys the scene. I see her frown but continue swimming without breaking my pace in the hope that she won't catch a good enough glimpse of me to estimate my age.

The woman starts swimming laps at the far end of the pool, as far away as she can get from me. A few minutes later I pause to catch my breath and check the time. She stops in mid-stroke and calls from across the pool. "Do you belong here?" she asks. "Are you a member? I noticed that your license plates aren't from out of state."

I hesitate, pondering the significance of my license plates, but choose to ignore her diligent detective work. "I'm staying with friends," I manage to say. "I thought it would be OK, especially since nobody was. . . ."

She cuts me off. "What street do your friends live on?" She's got me. I can't remember. In a development that's building out to 55,000 homes in countless culs-de-sac, the street names tend to blur together. Besides, I'm nervous about involving the Andersons in my reckless indiscretion.

"I think it's called Pine Hill or Pine Cone or Evergreen something," I offer truthfully. "It's the second—or is it the third left? Right up the street."

"I don't think you belong here," she says.

I can't help it. I have to ask. "What's the significance of my license plates?"

"If they were from out of state I'd know you were down here visiting," she explains. "But your plates are from Florida. Locals are always trying to sneak in here and use our amenities."

I look around at the otherwise empty little pool safely ensconced behind a gated guardhouse. I glance at my nicely folded and arranged T-shirt and towel. No matter. To her, I'm still just a local driving a crappy car. I'm the menace from the outside. I've been warned: pool-marm encounters are not uncommon. She watches me all the way to my car and then returns to her aquatic exercises.

On Kat's suggestion, I drop by her bungalow for a chat. Behind her zany exterior, I sense a bright woman with a big heart. Her place is just the way I had imagined it would be—a touch wild. The living room is decorated with comfortable lounge furniture upholstered in eye-popping colors with a scattering of zebra- and leopard-skin throw pillows. The 1970s flash competes with a nautical theme, which I find intriguing, given that Kat is from central Indiana. There are fishing nets hanging from the ceiling, lamps in the shape of whales, a mounted sea bass, and a fountain on her lanai in the shape of a dolphin.

She invites me to share a late-morning glass of wine with some pretzels. She plugs in the dolphin, and water calmly dribbles out of its blowhole. "There we go," Kat says. "A little ambience."

Kat wants me to know all about nightlife in The Villages. "It's why I moved here and why I'm never leaving," she says. "I'm having more fun here than I did in high school. I hope the carnival never stops." She pours me another large glass of wine, filling it to the brim.

"You should meet my friend Chet," she continues. "He's our big man on campus. All the ladies love him. They call him Mr. Midnight. That's what he calls his penis, and the name has kind of stuck. We all use it."

I nearly choke on a Triscuit. "His penis?" I ask.

Kat picks up a phone and dials Mr. Midnight's number. She gets the velvet-voice message on his answering machine, and leans over so I can hear it, too: "Hi, you're probably the one person in the world I'd really like to talk to today, but unfortunately I'm out. . . ."

"Hey, baby, it's Kat," she says when it's time to leave a message. "I've someone here you need to meet. Call me." Mr. Midnight rings back a half an hour later; he was outside working on his tan. He tells me to "c'mon over."

Try as I might to follow Mr. Midnight's directions, I find myself once again turning into and out of nearly identical culs-de-sac where most of the homes look alike. I know I've finally arrived at the right place when I see a sign hanging from a driveway light that flaunts a pair of Playboy bunny ears.

Mr. Midnight greets me at the door and gives me a hearty handshake. "It took me weeks of living here before I stopped getting lost," he says, putting me at ease. "Don't worry about it. It gets easier."

The house is surprisingly clean for that of a sixty-three-year-old bachelor, although the kitchen sink is full of dirty cereal bowls and the counter is crowded with empty take-out containers and a badly wilted head of iceberg lettuce. A refrigerator magnet reads, "If we are what we eat, then I'm cheap, fast, and easy." He offers me a seat in the living room on a plush recliner beside a large glass coffee table, and then casually sprawls across his white leather couch. A pastel print of exotic flowers hangs from a wall behind him. "I'm color-blind, so I had a friend pick out all the art," he tells me.

Mr. Midnight looks like an aging Adonis—six feet tall and broad-shouldered yet slender, with a full head of dark hair pleasingly salted with gray. Silver-rimmed glasses rest on his strong, aquiline nose. A former biology teacher from Illinois, he speaks with easy authority and charisma. Like most Villagers, Mr. Midnight dresses casually. Today he is wearing a Hawaiian shirt, khaki shorts, and flip-flops.

I ask him about his nickname. "A lot of ladies here are familiar with us," he explains, referring to himself as well as his legendary appendage. "Nobody calls me Chet anymore."

Mr. Midnight tells me it was the uncanny friendliness of the place that first attracted him to The Villages.

"I was with this woman—this is the gospel truth, mind you; I'm telling no lies—she was older, retired," he continues. "She takes me back to her place, lights up a joint, sticks it into my mouth and then takes off my clothes. I walked home that night thinking, 'I'm going to like this place.' That was my first night here. I was only renting. What you've got to understand is that there are at least ten women here to every guy. And they're all hot and horny. It's wonderful."

A typical day in what Mr. Midnight calls a "paradise of pleasure" looks something like this. He takes a short jog in the morning to keep fit, showers, and then sits at his computer chatting online for a few hours with licentious women from all over the state. Next it's lunch "in town" before he takes his daily afternoon nap. Then he heads to the pool to work on his tan. He's friendly with his pool monitor, who points out any new single women for him. At night he's on the prowl at Katie Belle's, which he fondly refers to as the "Pussy Factory," or just the "Factory." "I work the night shift," he says, with a mischievous grin.

"I'm a hunter," Mr. Midnight says. "That's what I am. But I believe in catch and release." Mr. Midnight walks me over to his computer and shows me how he enlarges the size of his already sizable pool of applicants. Up pop several photos of him on his favorite dating Web site. One photo shows Mr. Midnight resting against his Corvette. On his left hand he's wearing a ring, which is the cause of much confusion among his viewers. "I have a little arthritis on my right ring finger so I have to wear it on my left," he explains.

Another photo is a close-up of Mr. Midnight smiling into the camera. He's alone in the photo, but one can clearly see part of a female arm around his neck and her hand resting on his chest. He doesn't know how to use PhotoShop, but he liked the picture, so he simply sliced his companion out of it, or at least most of her.

His short bio describes him as "tall, dark, and handsome, or so I'm told. I've climbed all my mountains and now it's my turn to enjoy." He particularly likes what he calls "high-maintenance women" who spend considerable time fretting over their appearance, and he lists his preferred age group as forty-five to sixty-five. "I won't sleep with anyone younger than my kids," he says. "That's one of my rules. And I don't fall in love. That's another one."

There are stacks of e-mail lined up for him to read from prospective honeys with nicknames like Cute Coochie and Insatiable Sally. "That Sally; she's a wild woman," Mr. Midnight says. "She's passing through later this week."

I'm surprised by how bold many of the women are. Several list oral sex as among their favorite activities. This is just fine with Mr. Midnight. "I can pleasure some women for hours at a time. It's like they say, 'Show me a man who doesn't pleasure his wife, and I'll show you a woman that can be mine.'"

Mr. Midnight switches to a "gallery view" of his female queries, which exhibits the women like a deck of cards. "Hot, aren't they? I could sit here for hours. In fact, I do. There's no reason for anybody to be lonely anymore."

Mr. Midnight invites a lot of these women to "hang out" with him for a few days. Three days is his often-mentioned limit—another rule. They're all curious about The Villages anyway, he explains. "And you get a real bang for your buck here. I can take them out for a glass of chardonnay and a martini and it's about five bucks—tax included. Try finding those prices in Sarasota or Saint Pete."

The only downside to his frequent visitors is that he has to avoid his usual haunts for days at a time, lest he "muddy the waters." One inopportune encounter can set him back weeks with local women who have yet to succumb to his unbridled lust.

Mr. Midnight tells me he's on a short sabbatical from sex. "I'm not hunting this week. I'm too drained, literally." But this doesn't stop him from taking me on a field trip to the Factory. He changes into a clean Hawaiian shirt, freshens his breath, and combs his hair.

Minutes later, I'm in my car tailing Mr. Midnight's golf cart in what feels like slow motion. His shirt flaps in the breeze as he tops out at about twenty-two miles per hour.

At Katie Bell's, Mr. Midnight is in his element; he knows everybody and everybody knows him. I feel as if I'm entering a keg party with the quarterback of the high school football team. He's a social nexus for the "cool crowd," and he even refers to himself as the "party coordinator." He kisses the hostess and surveys the scene. The dance floor is a sea of mostly women line dancing to a lively country and western band.

One woman is wearing black slacks and a red blouse. Her hair is dyed a peculiar shade of blond. "Beautiful," Mr. Midnight pronounces. "Absolutely beautiful. I've had her a few times. She comes over, takes a shower, jumps in bed, and then gets dressed and leaves. She's simply the best."

There is a small coterie of younger women in their middle to late thirties at the bar. Mr. Midnight has slept with several of them (they're older than his children, albeit by just a year or two). "They like us older guys because we respect them," he explains. "We're not threatening like so many of the younger guys. It's just the opposite— we put them at ease. The only problem is that they're the ones who usually make us wear condoms."

I ask him whether he is worried about catching an STD. "Well, as you can see," he says flatly, "I've stopped having sex altogether."

A guy named Rico walks up to Mr. Midnight looking mildly dejected. "She gave me the engagement ring back," he says.

"Hey, how long were you engaged—two months?" Mr. Midnight asks. "That's not bad for The Villages. Have another beer."

An unusually buxom young blond waves hello from across the bar. She's wearing tights and a tight neon-colored getup that extends from just below her bust to her thighs. I've never seen anything quite like it and I can't help staring. It looks something like the low-cut unitards that Olympic weight lifters wear, and it accentuates her ample breasts. When she runs over to embrace Mr. Midnight, I feel as if I am in a 3-D movie and they're hurtling toward me.

"Hey, Jenny, you found love yet?" Mr. Midnight asks. Jenny shakes her head. "Getting any closer?" She shakes her head again, and her look of resignation is tinged with genuine sadness. Jenny, who is in her late thirties, divorced two years ago and now lives in The Villages. She rents a room from Martha, a woman in her eighties —the same woman who belted out karaoke on my first night at Gringos. "She loves to party," Jenny says, when I ask about her roommate. "She goes out more than I do."

"But why live in a retirement community?" I ask.

"I love it here," she says. "Everybody's just so friendly. They're all so welcoming. I have a great circle of friends. The Villages is just so peaceful. I could live here forever. As it is, I hardly ever leave."

An attractive southern belle catches Mr. Midnight's eye. She may be in her late sixties, but even I can see her obvious appeal. She's wearing a soft yellow blouse, a knee-length skirt, and diamond studs. She has a starlet quality about her that seems entirely out of place in the Villages. Mr. Midnight scopes her out, and then gives me the lowdown. "I had a friend who did her one night on one of those park benches around the corner. She visits from Palm Beach every so often."

"Was his name Tommy?" I ask.

"Yeah. How'd you know?"

The band plays the funk favorite "Brick House," and Mr. Midnight jumps onto the dance floor. He sways to the music in his shorts and flip-flops, a mug of low-carb beer in one hand, a pretty woman holding the other. The clock on the wall approaches ten PM, The Villages' witching hour, and the bartender shouts last call. I kid Mr. Midnight that "Mr. Nine-Thirty" might be a more accurate nom de guerre in The Villages.

A woman in a red leather jacket and a short black skirt who is carrying a designer handbag brushes past me. Like the aging starlet, she's dressed to the nines. Her high heels emphasize her unusually shapely calves. I try to fit in by scoping out chicks as well. "Nice legs," I say.

"That's Wendy Marie," Mr. Midnight says. "He's a she-he. And a lesbian." I reach for my plastic mug of beer and hastily empty it. "Good eye," he says, with a wink.

"I feel sorry for her," Mr. Midnight continues. "She could use a community where there are more people like her. And some butt pads. It's a little flat back there, like a skinny old man."

As usual, the party moves on to Crazy Gringos—the karaoke bar inside the Alamo Bowl. To my embarrassment, I'm starting to recognize many of the late-night revelers from my previous sprees after Katie Belle's. Mr. Midnight and I sit at the far corner of the bar and order a pitcher of beer. He takes a deep breath and looks me in the eye. I sense that he is preparing to pass on his wisdom. I listen attentively, sorely aware of my youthful shortcomings.

"How do I get one of these ladies from the bar to my bed?" he asks rhetorically. "I say 'Look, I'm not a teenager. I'm not going to put you in the back of my car and grope you. I'd like to take you home and make love to you.' But I don't want to appear anxious. When they're ready, I order us another drink. When we get to my place, I suggest they clean up. I always keep clean washcloths and towels around."

I ask Mr. Midnight how many women he's slept with. "I don't remember," he says. "I don't keep track." I throw out a number—100. "C'mon, were talking about my whole life, not just the last couple of years, right?" He orders another pitcher and we both scan the room. Jenny's roomate, Martha, is singing "Roxanne," by The Police.

"Do you really see spending the rest of your life here?" I ask. "Don't you miss the real world?"

"If a judge told me I could never leave The Villages again, I wouldn't care," Mr. Midnight responds. "I don't want the real world anymore. I just want to keep getting laid. Whatever happens now, you guys have to worry about it—it doesn't affect me. Hell, I didn't even vote in the last two elections."

"So that's it? You're just going to toss all your problems onto my generation's lap?" I ask.

"I paid my dues," he says, emphatically. "Isn't thirty years of teaching enough? Now it's your generation's turn. You work it out. I'll be here kissing the ladies."

"But you can't just hide from all the problems in the world, can you?" I counter.

"There will never be peace in the world, and I thank God that I'm old so I don't have to worry about that crap anymore," Mr. Midnight says.

"It just doesn't seem right," I say, deflated.

"Look," he says, "I know what it is like to be young. You don't know what it is like to be old."

A stout gray-haired man with another pitcher of beer approaches. It's Frank, a foulmouthed former plumber in his seventies.

"Hey, Frank, any luck last night?" Mr. Midnight asks.

"She was surrounded by her girlfriends," Frank responds. "It was hard to break in."

"Yeah, it's tough when they travel in herds."

Several beers later, Frank invites me outside for a smoke. Once we're in the parking lot, he lights up a fat, fragrant joint. "It's good shit," he says, exhaling an impressive plume. I accept the invitation; I've never gotten stoned with a senior citizen before.

And stoned we are. The breeze feels as though it's passing right through me, as if my body has hundreds of tiny pinholes. At my behest, we jump into Frank's souped-up golf cart with flaming decals, and drive high-speed lazy eights around the parking lot. Frank tells me about his latest female encounter. "She wasn't exactly a redneck; she was more of a country girl. But I wasn't sure if I wanted to spend the night with her. I don't sleep around. I'm not like my friend—he's a slut. To me, screwing represents a commitment."

I ask Frank what he does most days. "Get high and play Nintendo," he says, without hesitation. "I'm not much of a cook, so I just eat a lot of pepperoni."

"I like bacon," I say.

I stumble back into Crazy Gringos and order a plate of nachos. "He gave you the good stuff, huh?" Mr. Midnight says. "Frank's always got the best. The way he parties, you'd never know he's had two heart attacks and a stroke. If I were his doctor, I'd tell him not to bother winding his watch."

That night, I sleep fitfully and finally give up trying at around five AM. It's still dark when I drag myself out of bed and go for a drive. I pull into a nearby gas station to fill up and buy a cup of coffee. I'm not surprised to see that the parking lot is filled with day laborers, but I am surprised to see a group of retirees sitting to one side on benches and portable lawn chairs, chatting amiably over jumbo-size cups of coffee.

"Do you folks always meet this early?" I ask.

The group has little interest in me, but one man finally answers. "Yup."

"Why?"

"Habit."

I arrange to meet the transsexual Wendy Marie for a late dinner at R.J. Gator's, a reptilian-theme fish and burgers joint beside the docks in Sumter Landing. According to the menu, an alligator, who presumably craves fried food, owns the restaurant.

I arrive a few minutes early and pull on the restaurant's front door. It's locked. I peer through the glass and see a cleanup crew mopping the floors. I glance at my watch. It's eight fifty-five PM.

A sleek silver sports coupé pulls up to the curb. A stylish woman checks her hair in the rearview mirror and effortlessly glides out of the car. It's Wendy Marie, and she looks stunning in her low-cut blouse, white denim skirt, heels, and a pair of silver tear-drop earrings. There's a chill to the air, and she's wrapped snugly in her red leather jacket.

We find a restaurant that is still open and make ourselves comfortable in a booth. We are the only customers left. She removes a pair of bifocals from her purse, casually peruses the menu, and orders a small garden salad and a glass of chardonnay. I stare across the table, straining to find any trace of Wendy Marie's formally male persona. I'm stymied. If anything, she is the epitome of femininity.

Wendy Marie is The Villages' only transsexual and openly lesbian resident, and nobody is more aware of how her female neighbors dress. "I like women just as much as any guy, but the women here don't impress me," she says. Her voice is slightly raspy as a result of surgery to shave her Adam's apple. "They're overweight, dress like crap, and don't give a rat's ass what they look like. They're more interested in their golf game or canasta. Nobody wears heels, nylons, or even skirts. Women dress so casually that a lot of them look like their husbands. And their husbands are so fat they look like pregnant old ladies."

She rolls her eyes at the thought. "But the worst are the single guys at Katie Belle's. They're a bunch of dirty old men. You should see how they hit on me. It's never 'May I have your telephone number,' or 'May I take you out for dinner.' It's always 'Want to go to my place tonight?' One geezer invited me to a motel after ten minutes of conversation. And he was married. What are these guys thinking? Whatever happened to flowers and dinner—where did all that go?"

A retired major in the Air National Guard, Wendy Marie (then Donald) moved to The Villages in 1999 with his wife, Jennifer. Like most residents, they were attracted to the amenities. They bought a 1,100-square-foot ranch home with all the bells and whistles for $120,000. Donald and Jennifer quickly rose through the ranks of pickle-ball players. A paddle game played on miniature tennis courts, pickle-ball is particularly popular with retirees because it doesn't require as strong a serve as tennis or quite as much running. Invented by a family in the Seattle area in 1965, the game was named for the family's dog Pickles, who liked to chase after errant balls.

"We beat the shit out of everyone," Wendy Marie tells me. "It's a fierce game when played at a high level. We *slaughtered* our opponents. And we excelled at softball, too."

It didn't take long for Donald's deepest longings to surface. He was a she, and he knew it. The couple separated and Donald started undergoing electrolysis. "Ouch, that hurt," Wendy Marie says with a wince. The next step was facial feminization. Donald hired a top plastic surgeon in San Francisco to work on his face bones. "First he popped out my brow bones and sanded them down before putting them back in," Wendy Marie calmly explains. I glance down at my hamburger and then over at the waitstaff. They smile back, oblivious of our conversation.

"Next he raised my eyebrows, narrowed my nose, and raised my upper lip. And then he took out my chin and put a screw in and then shaved down my jaws. It was an eleven-hour surgery. The doctor even took a lunch break. I was hoping the surgery would be effective—after all, it cost me $37,000. The funny thing is, only one person said, 'You look different.' I just told them I lost weight."

In preparation for the surgery, Donald was careful to keep to himself—not an easy matter in a gregarious community like The Villages. "I just disengaged. I kept my car in the garage, so that no one saw me coming and going. And I no longer played pickle-ball and softball. Those people knew me when I was living as a male."

After the surgery, Donald renamed himself Wendy Marie. "I started leaving the house dressed as a woman. And I *looked* like a woman. One day I went to Wal-Mart and looked at everybody to see if they'd react. You know, yell out, 'Hey, you're a man!' But they didn't. It was then that I knew that I could live full-time as a woman and not be ridiculed or discovered. Now I love going out. I love being called 'm'am' and 'hon,' and being asked, 'What would you ladies like?' when I'm at lunch with a friend."

Next came breasts and then permanent makeup. "I didn't want to have to pencil my eyebrows and put on eyeliner and lipstick every time I wanted to leave the house. Don't forget, I was born male. You have no idea how high-maintenance women are: the clothes, the manicures, and the shoes—*definitely* the shoes."

"I hate shopping for clothes, too," I say, jumping at an opportunity for common ground.

Wendy Marie is uncertain whether she will stay in The Villages. To me, it's amazing that she's even considering it. "I'm not sure I have a place here," she says. "There are a lot of boring people here, and there's not a lot of pizzazz. And there's certainly no gay scene. But there are people who know me and accept my decision. That says a lot about this place. Who knows? There's an outside chance it just might work."

For now, Wendy Marie is in what she calls a 'holding pattern'— betwixt the sexes. Her final "transition" surgery is scheduled for the fall, but it may have to be put off because of an ailment common among seniors—high blood pressure.

"Frankly, I don't have a burning desire to do it, but I can't keep walking around half male and half female." Her days are mainly spent indoors, protecting her privacy and tackling the boggling logistics of legally changing one's name and sexual identity. Unlike most Villagers, she doesn't belong to a single club.

"Sure, I'm lonely," Wendy Marie tells me. "A lot of people come here to live their second childhood. I just want to live my first. But I know there will be a rainbow at the end of it. Until then, I will just have to wait and see where I belong."

The next day I check the *Daily Sun*'s activity calendar for things to do. It feels like being at summer camp, where all I have to do is sign up for activities each morning. After a quick glance, I zero in on a listing for the so-called "Wine Club." If Tommy from Katie Belle's is right, then this is the front for the "Village Swingers." My curiosity gets the better of me. As much as I am repelled by the idea of walking in on two dozen naked seniors in the throes of sexual rapture, the material is simply too rich for a writer to ignore. I'd never forgive myself for not pursuing it, so I decide to drop in on a "tasting" uninvited. But I'm nervous; I have absolutely no idea what to expect. Will they kick me out? Will they invite me to watch or, God forbid, join?

I park outside a recreation center where the meeting is scheduled. I move quickly because the sky is filled with swollen clouds growing darker by the minute. At the club room I meet a man with a knee brace who greets me warmly. I give the room a curious glance; the participants look more like Elderhostel's travelers than the sort who sway lustily from indoor swing sets. Have I come to the right place?

I warily take a seat at one end of a long table. The first wine is poured, and I'm invited to participate. "Whoa!" the club leader says. "Anybody getting that *banana* flavor? Kind of *fruity*, don't you think?" The woman to my right pours me another taste. "Really gets the *juices* flowing, doesn't it?" she asks, and then winks at me.

Just then, a thunderous crack fills the room, followed by an intense flash of lightening. The skies open up and let loose sheets of water. The sound of thunder once again reverberates across the room, and the lights briefly flicker. "We just might have to *spend the night* here," the woman says. "Hope we have enough wine!" Everyone in the room laughs, except me. I manage a weak smile and contemplate my next move. Another wine is poured. "How about that last one?" someone at the far end of my table asks. "Nice *big* taste, don't you think? *Mmmm.*"

The wine keeps flowing, and everyone at the table insists I drink seconds. Before I know it, I'm tipsy. "This next one is a petit Syrah," the club leader says. "The grapes may be small, but not the flavor."

A couple from the Midwest, who are seated across from me, are real aficionados and explain the wines I'm drinking. He worked as a computer programmer and she was in middle management at a corporation. Now she is a part-time hostess at a golf club restaurant in The Villages, her husband cleans its bathrooms. They tell me this work keeps them busy and it affords them half-price golf. "I'm the 'head' pro," the husband jokes.

As the club members settle into warm revelry, the conversation is anything but kinky. It dawns on me that this night is unlikely to end with multi-partner sexual escapades. A guy down the table tells me about a new computer game that allegedly fights off senility with brainteasers. "Hope it helps!" he says with a hearty laugh.

"You have to have a sense of humor when you get older," a woman next to me says with a smile. "But we're all in the same boat."

"That must be comforting," I say.

"It *is* comforting. It's one of the reasons my husband and I love living here. The only thing I miss is seeing little babies. I just love babies. I tell my husband I want to have another one and he's like, 'Yeah, sure, the baby could be your eightieth-birthday present!'"

As we leave, half a dozen guys from Orange Blossom Gardens, who call themselves the Thursday Night Poker Club, take over the clubroom. Several of them wear terry cloth sports shirts and porkpie hats. A man with thick black glasses spins a toothpick around in his mouth and shoots me a glance. "What are you looking at?" he asks.

The next morning I search out Wendy Marie's potential companions, The Villages' lesbian community. But it's a deeply closeted group: among the hundreds of activity and affinity clubs in The Villages, lesbian-friendly listings are conspicuously absent.

I resolve to do what any other self-respecting writer with a relatively keen sense of gaydar would do—I drive over to the women's softball league practice. I am soon rewarded with what I conclude are numerous closeted lesbians. Unlike the coy nymphs who populate *The L-Word*, these women have generous figures and some sports crew cuts.

"C'mon, Barb, throw the ball already!" a batter barks out to the pitcher. Barb underarms it across the plate and the batter smacks it hard. It's a pop fly to center field. The fielder shuffles around uneasily, trying to get under the ball. "I can only see so far," she shouts, adjusting her eyeglasses. She catches the ball anyway. "Way to go, Tammy!" Barb hollers back to the fielder.

Soon practice is over and I cautiously approach Barb. Who am I to presume? She's sitting on a bench cleaning her cleats. A few other women sit nearby on lawn chairs, discussing the practice game.

"Hi, I'm writing a book about The Villages and I was looking to talk with all sorts of folks about living in a retirement community," I say to Barb. "I want to make sure I get a well-rounded view of things. I heard that there was a lesbian community here." I grimace and squint my eyes as if bracing for a car crash.

Barb is quiet, and doesn't take her eyes off her cleats. She doesn't introduce herself, nor ask my name. An awkward thirty seconds pass before I clumsily try again. "Do you know where I might find some, uh, lesbians?"

Another grimace, and then I really start tripping over myself. "Some of my best friends are lesbians. My brother's gay. I'm from Massachusetts." Several of the women walk away, not angry, but visibly uncomfortable.

Barb's silence isn't helping matters. She finally throws me a bone. "It's hard to tell who's a lesbian and who isn't," she offers. "It's not like they carry a banner that says, 'I'm a lesbian.' It's more like in the military: 'Don't ask; don't tell.'"

OK. This is a start.

"It's kind of like being an alcoholic," Barb continues. "It's part of who you are, but you wouldn't want to wear it as a label." I'm saddened by the analogy, which suggests self-hatred; Barb clearly belongs to an earlier generation.

"Do you live alone?" I ask.

"No," she says.

"Do you live with a housemate?"

"Yes."

"Are some of the softball players lesbians?"

"Yeah, most of the good players are."

"Do you consider yourself a 'good player'?" I ask.

"Yes and no," she says curtly. "Look nobody wants to break their anonymity. It's just not proper. Nobody knows what might happen to the information. It could make things hard on you in the neighborhood. It could be that your friends and neighbors wouldn't want to be guilty by association. It's not like people burn crosses around here, but still, it's never far from one's mind."

I tell her that where I come from, women who love each other walk hand in hand down the street. "That's not OK here," she says. "At least not in public."

"I had suspicions about one woman," she continues. "I caught her practicing her throwing at home with a man's sock—so she wouldn't throw like a girl. She said it was her husband's sock, but I don't think she was married. She said she had kids. Maybe she does. Half of us do. Maybe more. I thought that maybe I was wrong; maybe she's not like that. Then I saw her at a restaurant with another woman and they looked like they belonged together. You know what I mean?"

I ask if we could exchange names and phone numbers, just in case she might want to talk some more at a later date. She says no. I tell her that I'm not interested in outing anyone and suggest that she might give me a pseudonym. She ponders this for a while.

"Call me Ellen," she says brightly. "Like that comedian lady on TV. Yeah, call me Ellen."

"Ellen" walks away toward her car. A woman from across the way bellows out to her: "Hey, Barb! Barb! It's me, Fran! What time do you want dinner?" Barb keeps walking to her car, fighting the impulse, I imagine, to turn around and acknowledge her roommate in my presence.

An hour or so later, I run into Mr. Midnight standing in the sunshine outside Katie Belle's. "I've penetrated the lesbian community," I say. He laughs. But I can see that something's on his mind. After all his talk about sex and secession, he apparently doesn't want me to get the wrong idea about him.

"I want you to know that I speak to my maker at night," he says. "I ask for good health, peace in the world, and someone to love."

Listening to Mr. Midnight try to be pious is actually more painful than funny. There's an awkward pause, which I keep expecting him to break with a punch line. I yawn. Mr. Midnight fidgets and looks bored.

Is he really about to quit his hedonistic lifestyle, dedicate himself to making the world a better place, and even embrace monogamy?

I don't think so, but I probe a little deeper, just in case. "How was your visit with Insatiable Sally?" I ask.

Mr. Midnight hesitates, and then speaks his mind. "Excellent," he says. "But I had to let her go. She wants someone to love and cherish her. I don't love, and I don't cherish. So it's over. She knew the rules."

8

Government, Inc.

ONE PECULIARITY OF THE VILLAGES, PARTICULARLY GIVEN ITS GEO-graphic size and population, is that it doesn't have any municipal buildings. This is because The Villages, despite the fact that it spans three counties, is a privately held business situated on unincorporated land.

When asked, few residents can tell me how they are governed. Most queries are met with a blank stare and an abrupt change of topic, usually to golf or the weather. That's not particularly surprising, because few people understand how The Villages is governed even *after* it is explained to them.

It's an exceedingly Byzantine enterprise—and one that took me quite a while to comprehend as well—with an alphabet soup of legalisms. It's amorphous complexity obscures the fact that Gary Morse owns much of the community and exercises enormous political control over it.

By choosing to live under the Morse family's private regime, Villagers have voluntarily relinquished many of their civil liberties. In exchange for unlimited leisure and recreation, they've traded the ballot box for the suggestion box. The underlying assumption, it would seem, is that self-governance isn't really very important. Those who have run afoul of Morse's policies refer to the "Village vision"—a willful disregard by the vast majority of Villagers of anything that threatens their rosy outlook. I suspect that this laissez-faire attitude may well take a beating one day soon, as home values stop appreciating at a blissful twenty percent a year, and residents are eventually beset by problems that force them to confront a privately owned government. It's easy to lose oneself in The Villages' resort-like atmosphere, but reality has a way of intruding, and residents have little recourse when it does intrude.

To gain a better understanding of The Villages quasi-government, I sign up for a special class given weekly by The Villages: "Community Development District Orientation: Your Introduction to Your Special Purpose Units of Local Government." The two-hour class is taught in a building as nondescript and nearly invisible as the quasi-government it houses.

Several rows of folding chairs fill the meeting room. Sixteen people show up, including two reporters from the *Daily Sun*. A man named John Rohan steps up to the front of the room and introduces himself as the district administrator.

Rohan asks everyone where he or she is from, and then comments about the bane of most northerners' and midwesterners' existence: "Gosh, I hear there's a lot of *snow* back there! How deep is it? It sure is nice and warm here, isn't it?" When asked, one attendant responds that he's from the Florida Panhandle. "Gosh, that makes you a 'Gator fan, I bet!" Rohan says.

"OK. Cool. Let's get started. But this is complicated, so feel free to attend this course again as many times as you'd like. OK? Here we go. Sometimes folks think we're a municipality because of our size, but we're basically one big master-planned development. It started out as a mobile home community surrounded by farmland on a lonely county road. There were contractual-based fees for utilities, public safety, and golf, so the developer, in his wisdom, created districts and numbered them. Each one is a unit of 'special purpose local government,' which is a general-purpose government for a region. But it can't issue building permits, comprehensive plans, annex, or do law enforcement. But with the exception of those four things, it operates just like a regional government; only it doesn't lie within incorporated boundaries. OK?

"You see, growth pays for growth in Florida: somebody's going to pay. This is a mechanism to fund and finance infrastructure and support services. At some point in time the last nail will be nailed and the last slab poured, and the developer will be finished with his dream, but he knew that someone would have to manage those golf courses. The developer knew that this lifestyle would have to continue after he's done. To provide for this, he builds recreation centers and sells them back to the community. OK? Everyone still with me?"

Rohan takes out an easel filled with large complicated charts. The audience members begin to have a glazed-over look. He moves quickly, and the many numbers rapidly blend into one another. Every so often, there's something recognizable that I try to hold on to, such as "bond debt," "impact fee," and "amenities fees." But mostly it's a slew of puzzling terms like "adjusted taxable revenue" and "ad valorem." He proceeds to explain an algebraic equation where "assessments equal total costs times the number of acres in the unit divided by the number of assessable acres in the district." Women look to their husbands, but several of the men are already asleep. "I bet you all are ready to get out of here and go golfing, aren't you?" Rohan asks cheerfully.

To break up the monotony, somebody asks Rohan a question: "Are you elected to your position?" "Uh, no," he responds. "I'm an employee." Rohan then takes out a seven-foot aerial photograph of The Villages with a clear plastic overlay identifying the development's ten districts, which together are big enough to encompass two zip codes. The color-coded districts are oddly shaped, much like gerrymandered municipal wards. In the middle of the photograph, which is devoid of color-coding, there is a large empty area as big as any district. It corresponds to the white space in the middle of the map I bought from the chamber of commerce. I ask Rohan why the area is left blank.

"Oh, that over here? Uh, that's private property."

"Whose private property?" I ask. It's a sizable chunk of real estate in the heart of the development, and yet it's outside any of the development's districts, which means that it's not governed by any of the rules or additional fees that every other resident must adhere to.

"Uh, uh, that's the developer's property," Rohan manages. "It's a private gated community."

"So that's where Morse lives?" I ask.

"Uh, yes." Rohan turns back to the flip charts. The next one is covered with so many calculations that it resembles a financial prospectus, or perhaps a classroom exercise for MBAs.

What Rohan is trying to explain is the rather unusual legal structure underlying Morse's mega-development, which grants him enormous powers. It's called Chapter 190, referring to the Florida statute's numerical designation. The legislation is nearly three decades old, and its origins date back even farther, about half a century ago, when Walt Disney brought his vision for a Magic Kingdom to sleepy Orange County, Florida. After a cross-country search for the right location—one that would give him maximum flexibility but still be near an interstate highway and a population center—Disney found himself circling in a small plane over a swampy, alligator-infested wasteland several miles outside Orlando, a small city that served as a hub for Florida's citrus industry. To ensure that he could buy the land dirt cheap, Disney kept his intentions secret for two years as he acquired more than 25,000 acres.

Disney lobbied the Florida state legislature for the creation of a wholly independent district, free of state, county, and local ordinances and land-use laws, and empowered with the ability to float its own tax-free bonds—and even to build its own airport and nuclear power plant if it so wished. When Disney described the $400 million investment he planned to make, and the thousands of jobs his new theme park would create, the legislature was happy to oblige. It was called the Reedy Creek Improvement District, and despite its inherently controversial and despotic nature—some people have likened it to an imperial land grant from the king of Spain—it is still in existence today.

In 1980, the Florida state legislature decided to help spur development by formalizing portions of Walt Disney World's special status, so that it could be imitated easily across the state. The ensuing legislation was called Chapter 190. There are now hundreds of communities in Florida governed by these special districts, and similar legislation now exists in more than thirty states.

From what I can tell, this peculiar form of government works as follows. A developer encounters a number of challenges regarding infrastructure when working with raw land. He needs to clear the land, grade it, and build—among other things—roads, sewers, and storm water retention ponds. This can cost a lot of money, particularly when the local government doesn't have the means to help with roads, electricity, and water treatment. A developer can finance this burden in a number of ways.

The most common method, which Del Webb used when he built Sun City, is to borrow money from a bank. Webb earned the money back when his homes were sold because the infrastructure improvements were included (front-loaded) into the price of the houses. Chapter 190 provides another way for developers to fund these infrastructural improvements without help from the county, by allowing the builder to create his own quasi-government with its own "community development districts" to help govern the development and pay for its infrastructure.

This financial structure affords a developer many advantages, such as the ability to obtain tax-free bonds, which are ordinarily available only to traditional governmental bodies, such as municipalities and school districts. This process makes it unnecessary for a developer to persuade a private bank to lend him a large sum of money, usually at higher interest rates. Rural counties generally give Chapter 190 projects their approval because the local government reaps all the eventual tax benefits from the new development (more people mean more gross tax revenues), without having to spend a penny.

The developer doesn't have to repay these bonds himself; he can pass them on to homeowners. Instead of paying for the infrastructure up front, Villagers theoretically pay a reduced rate when purchasing their homes; but upon closing, they must accept their portion of the bond's repayment. Because the costs are back-ended, the homes can appear to be less expensive than they are.

The Villages' ten mini-districts (or CDDs) are each governed by five supervisors, who for the first several years are appointed by the developer at will. These supervisors are often family members, friends, and business associates of the developer. It is during these first few years of existence as a governmental body that the CDDs borrow millions of dollars and set up conditions for repayment. By the time homeowners are allowed to elect their own representatives, most decisions of consequence have already been made. Residents are basically empowered to doll up roadside flower beds and repaint streetlights.

Morse began tapping into Chapter 190 financing when The Villages spilled across the county highway that borders Orange Blossom Gardens. This financing covered many infrastructure costs, but Morse was still left paying for his golf courses and recreation centers.

Morse created two special "central districts" (one for Spanish Springs and one for Sumter Landing), which govern the other mini-districts. The central districts encompass only the development's commercial areas, but they still govern the rest of the community. Not only did their creation help reimburse Morse for additional expenditures; they also ensured the family's control over the community for years to come.

Unlike the mini-districts, which eventually enfranchise their inhabitants when they revert to civilian control, the central districts are structured in such a way that no residents of The Villages live inside their boundaries. Hence, as the majority landowner in the central districts, the Morse family rules them unchallenged. Once again, the boards are filled with friends, business associates, and family members.

When Gary Morse wants to be reimbursed for his recreation centers and golf courses, he sells them to these central districts. It's important to remember the mantra of most developers: "Build; sell; leave." Maintaining pools and golf courses to the exacting specifications of demanding residents doesn't fit that model.

The central districts buy the properties—recreation centers, golf courses, swimming pools, etc.—as well as the amenities contracts connected to these properties. Consequently, a recreation center that the county tax appraiser values at $5 million could be sold to a central district for $50 million, because the central district is also buying future revenue. Villagers collectively owe several hundred million dollars for their community's infrastructure and amenities, and that number is likely to increase in coming years as the community continues to build out. Sixty percent of every monthly amenity fee goes toward debt service.

In the past, when evaluating the developer's asking price, the central districts have used a consultant who has also worked for Morse. The Villages refuses to acknowledge any conflict of interest. But even if such a conflict was acknowledged, it wouldn't much matter: Chapter 190 exempts these districts from Florida's laws governing conflicts of interest. And although the residents of The Villages pay the developer for these properties and contracts (and assume liability for them), they don't actually "own" them in the way they own their homes; the central districts (over which they have little control) own them. Residents are free to complain about these financial arrangements, but they have no leverage in the matter. And yet, to many residents, such details amount to splitting hairs. As far as they are concerned, the central districts, whose primary functions are to administer their recreational amenities for the benefit of the residents, are doing a fine job.

As Rohan's presentation winds down, a resident from Michigan asks if it's true that The Villages is planning a third downtown with a western motif. The Villages filed for permission with Sumter County years ago to build a third downtown, and for most people the information is common knowledge.

"A third downtown? Gee, I don't know," Rohan says. "But I would encourage you to keep yourself up-to-date the same way we do—by reading the *Daily Sun*."

I look over at the two reporters from the *Daily Sun*. One of them is staring out the window, and the other is impatiently jiggling her leg. Neither has asked a single question. At exactly noon a secretary comes in to remind Rohan that he has a lunch date. "Wow! It's noon already?" he says, then hastily hands out gold-stamped certificates of completion. Outside, I invite the two reporters—Mark and Kim—to lunch. They readily agree.

Perhaps the most insidious aspect of the *Daily Sun* is its ability to masquerade as a real newspaper. It's printed on state-of-the-art presses and carries local, regional, national, and international news, much of it from legitimate wire services. The hefty Sunday paper resembles that of any other mid-size city.

The *Daily Sun* is unabashedly conservative—not surprisingly, given Morse's political affiliations. Public records indicate that Morse, his family, and his associates have donated more than $1 million to the Republican Party, including at least $100,000 to President Bush's two campaigns, thus earning Morse the status of "pioneer." He was also a strong supporter of the former governor, Jeb Bush, who visited The Villages many times and even borrowed

Morse's private jet. More recently, Morse handed the Florida Republican Party its largest single donation ever—a check for $500,000.

The *Daily Sun* won't run "Doonesbury," but it does print a slew of conservative columnists, including Oliver North and Ann Coulter. Although most of the local news is unusually sunny, one gets the distinct impression that just enough bad news (drugs, crime, juveniles misbehaving) is sprinkled on top to make one feel relieved to live inside the gates.

My former neighbor Betsy Anderson tells me she is impressed with the *Daily Sun* because it concentrates more on cheerful profiles of fellow Villagers than on hard news. "It's nice to read about good news for a change," she says. "I like reading about all these peoples' accomplishments. It's the sort of thing most newspapers ignore. And the *Sun* only costs a quarter. The paper back home was twice as expensive."

The paper has a ninety percent penetration rate, something unheard of in the real world, and has thus cornered the advertising market, including the highly profitable classifieds. Morse's paper has another unique advantage: few residents appear to have an interest in other local newspapers or in the hard news they provide about surrounding communities. I spoke with a number of Villagers who even believed that deed restrictions prohibited home delivery of other papers. They were mistaken, but competing papers are hard to find. By comparison, the *Daily Sun*'s vending machines are everywhere, even though many residents opt for home delivery: the newspaper lands in thousands of driveways every morning.

Mark, a former bartender, is a rookie reporter, and Kim has about three years of experience. Mark tells me he didn't know where The Villages' government building was until now, and he's not sure why he was required to take today's course. "I can't see how it relates to what I'm doing," he says.

Because of their age, the two reporters necessarily live outside the community they cover. Both were hired after posting résumés on an Internet job site, and they suspect that their lack of training and experience helped them get a foot in the door. "I didn't even have any clips," Mark explains. "I'm not sure why they hired me."

"Me neither," Kim adds. "I was hired as a crime reporter, but there's no crime. I get the sense they don't really want me covering anything, so I spend a lot of time doing nothing. I see this being a better place to end a career."

"We're not allowed to cover anything even remotely controversial," Mark adds. "I wanted to write about the 1,000-person waiting list for new homes. I thought that was a good thing. But the editor told me I couldn't write about it. He wouldn't even let me call public relations for a quote."

"Look, every newspaper is owned by *somebody*, and that person usually exerts some editorial control," Kim says. "But this is extreme. The Morse family owns everything and controls everything. It's a true company town."

"All the businesses are linked," Mark says. "I've been told that I can't tend bar at any of the country clubs after work, because then The Villages would have to pay me overtime."

Like the owners of a theme park, the Morse family caters to the needs of a captive audience. From what I can tell, they own liquor stores and liquor distribution rights, a mortgage company, several banks, many of the restaurants, two giant furniture stores as well as a giant indoor furnishings arcade called the "Street of Dreams," a real estate company, golf cart dealerships, movie theaters, and the local media. You name it; they probably own it. They own so many different businesses that's it's nearly impossible to tell which are theirs and which aren't. And what they don't own outright, they often lease. The Morses own hundreds of thousands of square feet of retail space. In addition to rent, many businesses also pay the family roughly seven percent of their monthly gross.

Mark tells me about an orientation for new employees he recently attended. The other participants were restaurant workers, engineers, personal trainers, real estate agents, and liquor store cashiers. "They wanted to teach us the philosophy of the company, to let us know we don't work for the newspaper so much as for The Villages itself," Mark says. He shows me the back of his company identification card. It reads: "The Villages' Dream-Maker Passport. We're dedicated to building a retirement community where people's dreams come true."

"How does the *Daily Sun* cover bad news?" I ask.

"They don't," Kim responds.

I ask her if she could help me obtain some back issues. "I can't," she says. "We don't keep old newspapers on file. We don't even keep our notes. We are supposed to destroy them after a story is run. Taped interviews, too. And every few months somebody from the company goes through our computers and deletes all our files. I think legal counsel suggested it."

Mark has an epiphany. "I should change my résumé to say that I write public relations and marketing materials. I'm really just writing free advertising."

"This place isn't normal," Kim says. "I keep waiting for everything to just unravel."

The Villages is not entirely without homegrown opposition. Relations between homeowners and management first soured years ago, when residents accused Gary and his father Harold of reneging on promised free cable television and trash pickup.

Residents banded together, took the owners to court, and won. In anger, father and son refused to acknowledge the scrappy group, which named itself the Property Owners Association (POA). Gary and Harold then sponsored the formation of a competing organization. To this day, there remain two resident groups: the Village Homeowners Association (VHA) backed by the developers, and the feisty POA.

I meet with Joe Gorman, the current president of the POA, over a cup of coffee in downtown Spanish Springs. Joe, a mergers and acquisitions analyst for a Fortune 100 company, opted for early retirement, and for The Villages as the place to spend it. "I liked it immediately, and I still do," he tells me. "This place is ninety percent great. Not merely good—but great."

Joe says he "woke up to the issues" about five years earlier, when the *Orlando Sentinel* ran an investigative series about Chapter 190. It explained how Morse sold common property assessed at $8.8 million to the central district for $84 million. "When I saw that, I thought it was a typo at first," he tells me. "I later learned that the business valuations weren't completely off base, but what concerned me was that there appeared to be very little arm's-length negotiating. I've been in business long enough to know that you never give someone exactly what they ask for. We had to make repairs to the Savannah Center not long after purchasing it."

When Joe talks about Morse's ability to levy fees on residents with near impunity, he uses language borrowed from the American Revolution. "It's taxation without representation," he says. "If the central districts are going to tax us, then residents should be able to serve on the board. If there were just one thing I could ask for, it would be to open up these districts to fair representation." The POA's ten demands, incorporated into its "Residents' Bill of Rights," are actually quite modest. The document is filled with basic requests that most of us take for granted, such as "a local government that is free of conflicts of interest."

But few requests are too rudimentary in dealing with Morse's autocracy. Although the First Amendment ensures that "Congress shall make no law . . . abridging the freedom of speech . . . or the right of people peaceably to assemble, and to petition the Government for a redress of grievances," Morse and his central districts recently tried to do away with that protection.

They instituted an "Activity Policy," which outlawed the gathering of two or more residents for the purpose of protesting against The Villages' policies without first filling out a lengthy application to gain permission from the central districts, and obtaining a $1 million liability policy. Even then, there was a ten-day waiting period, and protesters were still forbidden to demonstrate near areas with high traffic. When the POA called the American Civil Liberties Union and the local independent press, The Villages quickly backtracked.

Joe says the Activity Policy originally slipped by without anyone's even noticing it. "There's hardly any discussion at central district meetings. The board recites the Pledge of Allegiance and then votes on whatever is presented to them by staff. There's never a dissenting vote. The whole thing lasts maybe twenty minutes."

Technically—and company officials are quick to remind you of this—the mini-districts and central districts don't "belong" to the developer; employees of these districts don't work for the developer directly; and the company is a separate entity that must petition the districts just like anyone else. But it's difficult to ignore the obvious: the family owns the company that controls the government.

The family members themselves rarely speak with residents. Gary Morse's son Mark, who now runs the company's day-to-day operations, gives an annual "state of The Villages" address sponsored by the VHA. Several Villagers describe it to me this way: the younger Morse jumps onto the stage and delivers a quick speech. He doesn't take questions from the audience, insisting instead that all queries be submitted in advance. This past year, they say, he didn't even respond to submitted questions.

I ask Joe how much support he thinks the POA has in the community. "It's kind of like during the American Revolution," he tells me. "About one-third support the king, one-third support the rebels, and one-third are generally more concerned about the annual Christmas parade."

Later that night, I attend a campaign rally for U.S. Senator Bill Nelson of Florida, a Democrat, in one of the recreation centers decorated to give a feeling of the old South. After delivering a basic stump speech to a crowd of 200, Nelson takes questions from the audience.

A man wearing sandals, shorts, and a hearing aid is passed the microphone. "Senator, are you aware that the developer of The Villages is abusing Chapter 190?" The man is clearly nervous: his voice trembles, his eyes water, and his hands shake, but he soldiers on. "The developer controls everything. If he wants to sell residents an outhouse for $50 million, his people on the central districts say 'Sure!' He has sold property to us at ten times assessed value." The audience erupts into applause, but Nelson shows little interest in the issue.

"As a member of Congress, I get all sorts of calls like, 'Can you help me get my cat down from my tree?'" the Senator responds. "Now what can I do about that? I have no jurisdiction over that Chapter 190, or whatever it's called. One thing you can do is demand accountability from your local elected officials."

Several audience members shout out, nearly in unison: "We don't have any!"

After the rally, I meet one of the few residents elected to a minidistrict, Rich Lambrecht. He is trim and clean-cut, and looks almost too young to be living in The Villages. Like Joe Gorman, he has a financial background.

"Once we finally got a majority of residents sitting on our five-member CDD board, the developer's two appointees simply stopped showing up," Rich tells me. "They weren't used to the sort of issues we brought up, like competitive bidding."

Sinkholes—and the resulting liability—have become an issue in Rich's mini-district. These impromptu ponds dot the landscape all over this region of Florida. Until recently, it wasn't an issue; a sinkhole in a cow pasture isn't exactly big news.

In the middle of Rich's district is the Nancy Lopez championship golf course, which Morse decided to retain rather than sell to the central districts. The golf course has a complex drainage system that includes retention ponds. Not long ago, one of these disappeared down a sinkhole. Given the fact that the retention pond is on Morse's property—you can't reach it without first walking across the golf course—you might assume that Morse would be footing the bill to repair the damage. You'd be wrong.

When Morse first built the golf course and the surrounding residential area, he had the mini-district approve the building of a storm management system, and then assume debt and liability for it, even though portions of the infrastructure are located on his private property.

Although the retention pond serves Morse in many ways, he left Rich's mini-district with the bill for repairing the sinkhole, which ran well over $150,000. When Rich dug a little deeper, he also found that Morse made residents of the district financially responsible for landscaping a nearby strip mall owned by The Villages, costing residents of the mini-district another $50,000 a year.

"Somehow I keep expecting Mr. Morse to pull me aside to see if we can find some common ground," Rich says. "But he won't even show us his face."

A few days later, I attend a meeting of the developer-friendly VOA—the Village Homeowners Association. The meeting is advertised as a question-and-answer session with representatives of The Villages. Gary Lester, Morse's spokesperson, sits at a table facing the audience. Several colleagues join him, including Pete Wahl, who manages The Villages' entire quasi-governmental system. All questions have been submitted ahead of time.

I sit beside a veteran member of the VHA, and he volunteers to fill me in. "Pete Wahl's the old-timer. He knows what the hell's going on. You'll see him and Gary Lester clash a bit because Lester works for the developer, but Pete doesn't; he sort of works for us. He won't speak for the developer because he wants the developer to speak for himself. Pete doesn't want there to be any conflict of interest. He's basically paid by the developer, so it's a real delicate line he walks." I nod in agreement.

The questions are all innocuous. "Why are folks driving so fast in their golf carts? It should be illegal!" "Will the developer widen the golf cart paths near Spanish Springs?" "When's the new golf course going to open?"

"People shouldn't be driving so fast; I guess that's just human nature," Lester philosophizes. "But it's not right. And it's not safe." When he is asked about any construction plans in The Villages' near future, Lester pleads ignorance. "I don't really know. We're just so busy doing what we're doing. That's about all I can tell you."

Wahl addresses the next question, about the nine-hole golf courses, which are owned by the central district. He then passes the microphone to Lester to speak about eighteen-hole championship golf courses, which are still owned by the developer. My seatmate nudges me. "See how Pete didn't answer for the developer? See the difference? Pete's a very knowledgeable guy, but a lot of people still don't like him. They say he should be elected, and that if there were an election, he'd never get voted in."

The next question is about the possibility of making the church in downtown Spanish Springs off-limits to visitors without passes. I've heard other Villagers express outrage that their downtowns are inundated with local families. Another church congregation also considered limiting its parishioners to those age fifty-five and over; children under nineteen would be able to attend the church only as guests. The question makes Lester a touch uncomfortable. He pauses, then says he doesn't think placing age restrictions on the church downtown is such a good idea.

Lester then ends the meeting with an impassioned sermon about "truth and cow doo." The Villages uses millions of gallons of water a day, and the regional water district has recently expressed concern that the water table is dropping. Lester is clearly pissed off because several local newspapers had the temerity to report these preliminary findings as news.

Much of Florida sits atop a giant aquifer, but it's not big enough to meet the needs of endless growth. After years of bruising water wars, every county and municipality in Florida has adopted stringent standards that regulate water use. Regional water districts use these standards to establish minimum water levels in order to ensure that the state's aquifers don't dry up.

The Villages is challenging the way the water district collects its data and then applies the data to establish minimum water levels for the surrounding area. By negating the water district's methods and findings, The Villages is potentially unraveling Florida's water policy.

Water, or the lack of it, is The Villages' Achilles' heel. Restrictions on water use are one of the few things that could prevent Morse from building thousands more homes. The Villages makes a good faith effort to irrigate with reclaimed water, but this still covers only a small fraction of total water use. The possible overuse of water has some very real consequences: dropping water levels could lead to an epidemic of sinkholes, and put the regional ecosystem and economies under enormous strain.

During his speech, Lester belittles a local environmental activist who lives outside The Villages, and insinuates that she doesn't understand the issues well enough to be criticizing The Villages' complex water system. In reality, the woman is a highly educated young retiree who quit a lucrative career developing power plants to home-school her three children.

"I don't have any financial incentive to stand up and take the heat to do what's right," she explains to me when I speak with her later. "This is my community. My children live here. I'm not in it for personal profit and gain. How much is the developer paying Gary Lester? Just how far is the developer going to chase the golden ring? Until our lakes are sucked dry?"

It's plain to see that the water table around The Villages has dropped, although it's hard to say exactly why. Lake Miona, which borders some of The Villages' more prestigious properties, has fallen by more than a foot. The docks are now so far above the water that it's uncomfortable to board a boat, and a metal fence pole sticking out of the water at a public beach clearly shows a foot or so of exposed rust. Many of the people I speak with say it's because of unsustainable water usage. Lester says it's because of a long statewide drought.

"If you read the local papers, you'd think the sky is falling, that we're running out of water," Lester says. "I want you to know the facts. You should be very proud of the water program here in The Villages. Did you know that the water quality in Lake Miona has dramatically improved? You know why? Because it's no longer surrounded by pastures filled with cows that poop in the water! We've cleaned up Lake Miona by developing the land around it!"

Visibly moved, a member of the audience pleads with Lester to publish the truth in the *Daily Sun*. "We're working on it," Lester responds.

The man seated beside me looks satisfied with Lester's explanation. "No matter where you live, or what you do, there will be negative thinkers," he tells me. "I'm just glad that there aren't too many of those kind of folks here in The Villages."

A few days later, I see a headline in the *Daily Sun* that seems familiar: "Villages' Efforts to Protect Aquifer Working." A tiny sidebar is headed: "Villages Helps Recharge Aquifer." It's a short, awkward story quoting only one source: the developer's paid water consultant.

★　★　★

The next day, I meet with Pete Wahl, a stocky gray-haired bulldog of a man who used to work as the supervisor of Lake County until things soured, and he left to work for The Villages.

Wahl tells me that he left Lake County because he was pro-development and his board of supervisors wasn't. Like Lester, he expresses some disdain for the rural character of the three surrounding counties: Lake, Sumter, and Marion. "The worst kind of sprawl is low-density development," he tells me. "That kind of development can't even support sewer and water lines.

"Chapter 190 is perfect for Florida," Wahl continues, "because it helps developers build a fantasy in the middle of nowhere. Sumter County could never have provided us with the services we needed. The nearest municipality was poor and miles away. Chapter 190 let us do it ourselves. And the CDD form of government protects the development forever.

"A typical subdivision uses a homeowners association. But an HOA can go belly-up. We're a form of government and we can't cease to exist. Our assessments are collected with county taxes; and taxes must be paid. It's a guaranteed collection system."

Although much of Wahl's job is to represent the Villagers' interests, he is quick to express frustration with residents, such as the POA, who challenge Morse's policies. "Those people don't understand how the system works," he says. "They don't want to understand it, and they don't appreciate what they have—a lifestyle essentially unmatched in the continental United States, and probably the world. When it comes down to it, if they don't like it here, they can always move. Living here is voluntary."

Wahl clearly doesn't relish his role as the local punching bag. "All I ask for is fairness. There are two sides to every story." He tells me he has devised a system for dealing with errant reporters. "The first mistake, they get a phone call; the second mistake, they get an e-mail; and after the third mistake, we communicate on an e-mail basis only."

Although his soliloquies are aggressive, Wahl ends each one with the pained look of someone who's been terribly misunderstood. "I don't represent the developer," he insists. "I represent the district boards." I find this splitting of hairs tiresome and politely excuse myself for another interview. He walks me outside, and invites me to have a Swisher Sweet cigarillo with him.

Changing the subject, I ask Wahl if the rumors about Gary Morse's personal fortune crossing the billion-dollar mark are true.

"The Morse family isn't that kind of wealthy," Wahl responds. "And I can remember a time when things weren't so rosy. I can remember cash flow problems and all sorts of worries about making payroll." When I ask him what time period he is referring to, I am surprised to learn that it is the same year as Gary Morse's weekend-long surprise birthday party, during which hundreds of guests were flown in on chartered jets.

Wahl puffs on his cigarillo and exhales deeply. "Our commitment is to building a retirement community where dreams not only come true, but they exceed all expectations." he says. "I might be biased, but I think we're doing one hell of a job. This is my baby. I got it to adolescence, and soon adulthood. And it will continue forever without me."

"Any regrets?" I ask. "Could anything have been done better?" He takes another slow drag, glances out to the horizon, then turns to meet my gaze.

"I wish we had built the golf cart paths wider," he says. "And we should have had a lawn ornament restriction from day one. But you learn to live with your errors."

Many of the residents I speak with express little concern about their lack of representation. "Just as long as they keep this place looking so nice, and they keep on building more golf courses, then I'm happy," Betsy Anderson tells me. "I don't want to get involved in politics. I didn't come here for that. And frankly, I don't care how much the developer makes. He's done a great job."

Dave Anderson is more philosophical about what I perceive to be his voluntary disenfranchisement. "Forget the developer; he's already alienated himself. It's the people who now live here that define what the community is. We're the ones shaping things."

To me, The Villages' increasingly affluent residents just don't seem to feel the pain. Much as with American shareholders who are too often apathetic in the face of executives' obscene pay packages, the financial hit that Villagers are taking for the Morse family is spread across enough residents—tens of thousands of them—that it sparks little interest. New construction continues to be viewed as an expression of Morse's benevolence and business acumen. "Wow, they built us a new recreation center!" rarely translates into, "We are paying every penny of it, many times over."

As one might expect, Villagers are not alone in their lack of interest in something as basic as governance. And there's little correlation to age: a good number of younger families are also choosing to live in similar planned communities because they, too, want the reality of the outside world to go away. They don't want messy towns with messy town politics; they want orderly communities where decisions are often made for them, preferring to live in developments that *resemble* towns, as opposed to the real thing. When I think about my own town, with its century-old buildings, and our annual town meetings, where citizens vote on budget items and proposed laws, this sort of thing strikes me as a tragic parody. Sure, my town also suffers from voter apathy, but at least most people have an opinion—and we don't allow ourselves to be governed by a developer.

About an hour's drive from The Villages lies the town of Celebration, which is owned by Disney and markets itself as a "traditional" age-integrated community, although it too will soon have an age-segregated neighborhood. Surrounded by alligators, interstate highways, and theme parks, Celebration is nonetheless reasonably charming. The houses all have homey front porches within speaking distance of sidewalks so that neighbors can stroll and meet more easily. The schools and downtown civic and commercial buildings are all within easy walking or biking distance, and some people even *live* downtown, often in apartments above stores. The nostalgic nod to yesteryear is nearly movie-set perfect—the designers even provide fake fall leaves and winter snow for seasonal celebrations. Most residents I met spoke of their handsome community with great enthusiasm.

What's missing? A real government, for starters. Celebration was designed, owned, and run for many years by a global entertainment conglomerate in search of profit, rather than by elected officials. At this point, Celebration remains an unincorporated community with its residential areas partially "governed" by a homeowners association, but much of the commercial area remains in private hands. Disney recently sold the town center to a private real estate investment firm based in New York City.

There's a stately building in the center of downtown Celebration labeled "Town Hall," but it's really just a meeting place for the homeowners association as well as the board of directors appointed by the developer. The governance of Celebration is anything but simple. Thrown into the mix are the following: the developer, the Celebration Company, which is a subsidiary of the Walt Disney Company; the Residential Owners' Association, the Non-Residential Owners' Association (consisting of commercial landowners and appointed by the Celebration Company); the Celebration Community Development District (now consisting of residents); something called an Enterprise Community Development District (governed by the developers' appointees); and a "managing agent," Capital Consultants Management Corporation, which has headquarters in Phoenix and Dallas, and bills itself as a "full-service community management firm."

Andrew D. Blechman

When I ask a woman at the front desk (I had assumed she was the town clerk) for an explanation of the community's complicated organizational structure, she tells me to contact a local realtor. A notice in the public restroom asking visitors to turn off the lights adds to my curiosity. It's signed: "The Management."

On one of my trips to Phoenix, I visited a new planned community with the blandly patriotic name Anthem. Built by Pulte Homes and its subsidary Del Webb, it has both "traditional" and age-segregated neighborhoods. Located thirty miles north of Phoenix, Anthem is a true exurb in the middle of nowhere, at least for now.

As with The Villages, segregation is a theme that seemingly runs throughout the community's design, with similarly priced housing clustered in "neighborhoods." Adults over fifty-five have the choice of living in a separate gated neighborhood where they can exercise and socialize in their own child-free recreation center.

I was naturally drawn to a large park and sports complex in the center of Anthem, where I introduced myself to a young supermarket executive taking a walk with his daughter. He spoke enthusiastically about the planned community's amenities—the park has a toy train that children can ride, and the recreation center has a water park and an indoor climbing wall.

To be sure, it is leagues ahead of the usual housing development, many of which lack even a rudimentary community green. A typically dreary American subdivision isn't even in the same ballpark. I suspect that most Americans, myself included, if given a choice only between the two, would be tempted to live in a faux wonderland like Anthem.

"We *love* it here," the young man told me. "Crime is low. We can let our children run around, and they have plenty of other kids to play with. There's so much to do! And it's easy to make friends. Anthem's like it must have been in the old days: one big community."

But although Anthem may be a community—with a recreation center, ball fields, schools, and even some strip malls for shopping—is it actually a city? Or is it just an amalgamation of housing tracts like The Villages? "Just what *is* Anthem?" I asked.

"Gosh, I hadn't really thought about it," the young father responded. "I think we're part of Phoenix. Or maybe we're just part of Maricopa County. I don't know. I think we live in both."

"Who runs the place?" I asked. "Do you have a mayor?"

"A mayor? I think so. But don't quote me on that. Actually, wait a minute, I think Del Webb runs the government."

"Del Webb *runs* the government?"

"They're really good to us," he responded. "A bunch of us asked them for a skateboard park, and we got one. I thought that was awesome!"

9

Necropolis

Sun City, Sun City West, and the newer Sun City Grand all border a major thoroughfare called Grand Avenue, which connects the distant town of Wickenburg on one end with downtown Phoenix on the other. The Sun Cities sit just outside Phoenix, in an area called the West Valley.

Although Phoenix now dwarfs the little community of Wickenburg, this was not always the case. In 1863, a lone German miner, Henry Wickenburg, discovered gold in the far western valley. Several years later and some fifty miles to the southeast, another adventurer decided to revive a prehistoric canal system and cultivate produce for the rapidly growing population of Wickenburg. He transported the food using a wagon trail that connected the two settlements. At the time, it was called Vulture Road.

It is said that during the restoration of the ancient irrigation system, an Englishman looked at the parched ruins of the Hohokam tribe and said, "A city will rise phoenixlike, new and more beautiful, from these ashes of the past." He was right about Phoenix, but as far as Del Webb was concerned, the Englishman might as well have been talking about Sun City.

By the time Sun City came onto the scene in the early 1960s, the surrounding area with its bountiful aquifer was mainly used for growing long-fiber cotton named after the Pima tribe. But when the price of cotton plummeted after World War II, landowners began courting developers, like Webb, who bought up thousands of acres. Webb cut swooping curves into the starkly angular fields, and steered the West Valley's flagging economy from cotton balls to golf balls.

Although Sun City's first residents complained of cricket infestations, tumbleweed, and valley fever (a lung infection caused by windblown spores), the community's early years were nevertheless brimming with promise. Webb developed the community in phases, but the homes sold so briskly that it was as if the construction never stopped. Every year or two residents saw the completion of yet another recreation center, golf course, or shopping area, in addition to hundreds and hundreds of homes. It was an optimistic era fueled by Webb's seemingly continuous investment.

Sun City's very first recreation center, called the Oakmont, has undergone some minor renovations over the years, but for the most part it looks much as it did when it opened in 1960. It's decidedly small by today's standards. There's one large room that can be used for small theatrical presentations, dances, and other gatherings. Down the hall is a workout room with equipment that looks about twenty years old. On the day I visit, a few men in trousers and collared shirts walk on treadmills or slowly pedal stationary bicycles, as "Start Me Up" by the Rolling Stones fills the room.

In the other direction is a room for the jewelry club, which costs just four dollars a year to join. One door down is the pottery club. I find several women giggling as they trade gossip and paint molded ceramic kittens, puppies, and other tchotchkes. One woman lightheartedly pokes fun at my book project: "I'm sorry to disappoint you, but I left my cane at home!" The others all share in the laugh.

Outside there is a nine-hole golf course, and a swimming pool with seniors tanning on lounge chairs. There is no kiddie pool, nor is there a playground; Sun City does not have a dedicated area for children to play. A sign on the pool lists the hours during which children ages four to sixteen may use the pool: eleven AM to one PM.

Next door to the Oakmont are Sun City's first five model ranch homes, each measuring a mere 860 square feet, which 100,000 people visited that first weekend in 1960. The recreation center, golf course, and nearby shopping center were built before these homes were completed, to counter the image of other, less scrupulous developers who promise future amenities, but don't deliver. This clustered configuration—neighborhood, recreation, retail—is the basic pattern one still finds in many of today's larger age-segregated and planned communities.

One of the five homes—the first to be sold—has been converted into a museum housing the Sun City historical society. With its wavy gingerbread touches, Formica countertops, vinyl flooring, and pink tiled bathroom, the home is a perfect period piece. The director of the society is an intellectually active but physically frail woman, Jane Freeman. Curious about The Villages' future, I decided to take a peek into Sun City's past by visiting with her and spending some time in Arizona's West Valley—the birthplace of age segregation.

Freeman moved to Sun City from New York in 1970 with her husband, now deceased. "I raised my children and I didn't want to raise anyone else's," Jane tells me. "A lot of grandparents become dumping grounds for kids. So I came here. My brother used to ask me why I don't move back to be with the family. I'd ask him why he doesn't move out to Sun City."

Like many Sun Citians, Jane takes Webb's retirement revolution very seriously. She sees it as her duty to chronicle and preserve this significant piece of America's history. "People say that because we weren't born here and didn't go to school here, we don't have roots here," she says. "They say we don't have any history, that our history is back home. But we *do* have a history here."

To prove her point, Jane hands me a tattered red paperback. It's a surviving copy of Sun City's first narrative history, which she wrote decades ago in celebration of the community's twenty-fifth anniversary. The dedication reads: "To Delbert Eugene Webb, a man of genius, who, together with men of competence, courage, and foresight, explored and conquered untried frontiers that opened new vistas for thousands of retired Americans. And to those Sun City Pioneers who dared to leave old ties to establish new homes, new friends, and a whole new life of active retirement."

In many ways, the early settlers in Sun City were pioneers: they left behind all they knew for an untested and uncertain but hopeful future. Webb may have created a city out of dirt, but it was these pioneers who created a community from scratch.

Although he personally had little to do with the day-to-day planning and development of the retirement community, a reverence for Del Webb, the man, permeates Sun City. There is an eight-foot bronze statue of him in the exterior courtyard of one of the main recreation centers. He is shown with one arm extended toward the future; his other arm holds blueprints.

The interior of the residence housing the historical society is filled with photographs from an optimistic and somewhat glamorous era (we're talking about a retirement community after all, not Camelot). The photos show residents dressed to the nines and posing in front of their new homes; listening to Rosemary Clooney and Lawrence Welk perform at the outdoor Sun Bowl; and gazing admiringly at a visiting Bob Hope on a golf course wearing a tam-o'-shanter and sharing a joke with Del Webb.

What the photos don't show is the mounting enmity and relentless quarreling between residents of the growing community, which often stemmed from Sun City's ambiguous governing structure. To seek clarification and redress, residents often found themselves organizing angry petition drives and filing incessant lawsuits to tackle such mundane matters of governance as garbage collection, regulations regarding dog walking, and restrictions on guests.

Webb was winging it when he built Sun City, and governance was something of an afterthought. His original vision didn't adequately address how residents would establish rules and resolve conflicts. He was more interested in providing amenities and selling homes. Webb made this clear when he called the second recreation center "Town Hall." As he stated in an early company memo: "We will build houses but we will not become involved with the population in any way, shape, or manner." But such a policy proved untenable as early attempts at self-governance continually devolved into acrimony. The company was forced to step back in and remain involved for a lengthy transition process, which has since become a proud company hallmark.

Webb soon set up a homeowners association and a nonprofit corporation to run the recreation centers in perpetuity. Neither of these organizations proved to be particularly popular, but the alternative—incorporation—was repeatedly dismissed by Sun Citians as too costly and unnecessary, even though the Webb Company recommended it. Sun City remains governed by these quasi-governmental entities with limited powers, as well as numerous very vocal special interest groups.

Age segregation became an issue early on. Webb's company attracted a handyman to the community, but to Webb's chagrin, residents evicted him because he had young children. Residents also tried to kick out the community's only doctor, an older man with a young son, but once they realized how difficult it was to recruit another doctor to the isolated desert community, they soon relented.

But what concerned residents most was the inescapable feeling that as the development reached completion, their progenitor and protector was slowly abandoning the community altogether. And they were right: Webb had made his money and he was now detaching himself and his company from Sun City. First to go were the shopping centers; then the restaurants, the office buildings, and the professional plazas; and finally any vacant land—all sold to other developers for a quick infusion of cash. The company's attention had already drifted to a dusty tract of land a few miles down the road named Lizard Acres, future home of Sun City West.

Sun Citians had to threaten and cajole Webb's company to build a final promised recreation center. The center was eventually built, but it has the cramped appearance of something designed on the cheap. A final shopping plaza was never built, because Webb couldn't attract any tenants. In Sun City West, plans for a centrally located shopping center were scrapped for similar reasons, and replaced with additional housing. Residents had little say in the matter.

Such are the vagaries of the marketplace when one developer owns an entire community: pieces of it can be sold off and projects abandoned at will. As with any developer, Webb's fortunes ebbed and flowed with fluctuations in interest rates and the natural cycles of construction booms and busts. Sometimes a community project simply lost its financial attractiveness, and cutting bait was considered a prudent business decision. Early incursions into Florida and California fared badly and were soon deemed nonperforming assets. They were sold off, leaving residents stuck with the highest bidder. To hedge risk and save on costs, projects were designed smaller and smaller.

As any honest developer will tell you, the building of these "communities" is a business and nothing more. Pursuit of profit is what guides decisions. Nearly three decades after Webb's death in 1974, Pulte Homes, Inc., one of the nation's largest home builders, bought Webb's debt-laden company. Corporations are even less sentimental than individual developers. Their purpose is to make money for shareholders, and if a development is not sufficiently profitable, or in line with expectations, it is usually in their best interests to sell and move on.

Five decades after its founding, Sun City is fraying around the edges. No longer a darling of the press, it feels anachronistic and dated. It's nearly forgotten as a cultural icon, except perhaps as the butt of an old joke. Many younger Americans have never even heard of the place. Like the once luxuriously green medians that have been left to yellow as a cost-saving measure, optimism has been replaced with financial retrenchment. Most of Sun City's residents are on fixed incomes, and because of that, they don't like to spend any more money than they have to. In communities with a traditional mixture of ages, these sorts of financial concerns are brought up in town meetings and elections—and then often ignored by younger voters who are usually more eager (and able) to reinvest in their community's schools and municipal infrastructure.

But Sun City is anything but a mixed community. According to recent census data, the median age in Sun City is seventy-five. Sun City is also about 98.5 percent white, and 0.5 percent black. What happens when you create a community consisting almost completely of senior citizens living on fixed incomes? A number of things, and few of them pleasant.

In order for a community to survive, let alone flourish, it must continually reinvest in its future, with current generations investing in future generations just as past generations invested in them—a generational giveback of sorts. My wife is German, and every time we travel to Germany, I am always impressed by how the Germans build public structures to last for generations. They don't skimp on materials; nearly everything is built with stone or a correspondingly high-quality and long-lasting material. Why build something that will stand for hundreds of years, well beyond our lifetime? A society that builds with stone clearly cares about its future generations.

By comparison, my town is repaving many of its sidewalks for the first time in decades. Because of mediocre building materials and a lack of craftsmanship, these sidewalks probably won't last fifty years before they rapidly deteriorate. Today's taxpayers are saving money by using cheaper materials and less craftsmanship, but tomorrow's taxpayers will eventually have to foot the bill.

Sun City is a place where seniors choose to live out their final years. They don't want to plan for ten or twenty years down the road. They might not be around then, and whose future would they be investing in, anyway—the next round of retirees?

For the most part, people who retire to age-segregated communities have already jettisoned their obligations to the community they left behind—the one that invested in *their* future many years earlier. The residents of Sun City have also made it abundantly clear that they don't much care about the new communities in their midst, either.

When it first opened, Sun City happened to be within the boundaries of the Peoria school district. This inconvenient fact led to the area's first generational war. Over the course of twelve years beginning in 1962, the residents of Sun City defeated *seventeen* school bond measures. School programs were cut and children were forced to attend school in staggered sessions. At wit's end, Peoria finally acceded to (some say embraced) Sun City's demands, and de-annexed the retirement community from the school district. After another prolonged battle, Sun City West was also de-annexed from its school district. With these communities no longer a part of any school district, the average retiree's tax rate is less than half of what surrounding families pay.

Some Sun Citians are ashamed of this history and the long shadow it cast on their community, but others point out that residents still contribute just like everyone else in the form of state taxes, which help fund school districts throughout Arizona. In reality, they don't have any choice.

A community that does not reinvest in itself is in real danger of petrifying into a geriatric ghetto, or—worse yet—a necropolis. Further complicating matters for communities like Sun City is that they are monocultures, the societal equivalent of an economy dependent on a single cash crop, such as coffee, bananas, or rice. The problem with such economies is that they have no diversification. If demand for the commodity suddenly drops, the local economy can crater.

Real economies—those not owned by a single corporation as in a banana republic—demand diversity. And so do communities. What happens if demand for Sun City's single crop—decades-old leisure housing for retirees—falls precipitously? Similarly, what happens in twenty or thirty years when the baby boomers begin to die off in significant numbers and there is a glut of age-segregated communities?

A meandering drive around Sun City gives one the feeling that such a fate has already arrived. Many of homes are petite and dated by today's standards. Today's retirees want more: an expansive kitchen, Jacuzzi tubs, home office with broadband access, and all the latest appliances. By contrast, when the first homes in Sun City were built, air-conditioning was optional.

And that's just the homes. Sun City's recreational centers—its historical selling point—are badly in need of updating. Whereas yesterday's retirees were content with a small dipping pool, a few bowling lanes, and a few shuffleboard courts, today's prospective residents are looking for lap pools, yoga rooms, full-service spas, and professional kitchens for cooking classes. Even a rock-climbing wall is not out of the question.

Local businesses have already had a taste of the future, as evidenced by the slowly withering strip malls at Sun City's commercial core. From the looks of it, the top tier of today's aggressive retailers has already concluded that this city's sun is setting. Not only do I see a number of vacant businesses and discount retailers in the community's badly aging retail core; it's what I *don't* see that is more troubling—businesses designed with baby boomers in mind, such as upscale coffee shops, organic groceries, and trendy restaurants. Investors are clearly more interested in chasing younger, more free-spending consumers housed in leapfrogging subdivisions just beyond Sun City's periphery.

To get a better idea of how Sun City is addressing these critical issues, I meet with Doug Kelsey, president of the Sun City Home Owners Association (HOA). Located in a small building beside a strip mall, the HOA has a staff of seven, four of whom are part-time.

Kelsey, who describes himself as the closest thing Sun City has to a mayor, greets me enthusiastically and invites me into his office. He was born in the Midwest, is the father of three grown children, and has six grandchildren. He wears a cardigan and white slacks; has a mustache; and has a thinning head of hair carefully combed flat. Framed copies of the Declaration of Independence and the Bill of Rights hang on the wall.

"Used to be we were the big dog out here," he tells me. "We could get our way on a lot of issues. But the towns have grown around us and they've surpassed us in sheer numbers. They've taken away our clout."

Adding to Sun City's woes, Kelsey tells me, is the community's declining volunteerism. Sun City calls itself the "city of volunteers," and since its inception, the community has relied heavily on its residents to perform many basic municipal functions. When I imagine a city of volunteers, I picture large numbers of citizens performing charitable work, perhaps for the needy. In Sun City, the motto has a slightly different meaning.

Although a good number of residents volunteer in local schools and hospitals, the majority volunteer inside their own community because the free labor saves residents tax dollars. The Sheriff's Posse, a neighborhood watch of sorts; and the much-celebrated PRIDES, who landscape medians and keep other public areas tidy, in effect serve as a police and public works department.

"Volunteerism is the backbone of our community," Kelsey says. "Without volunteers we have a big problem—and volunteerism is dropping. Boomers aren't as interested in it. They'd rather write a check."

Also keeping taxes artificially low is Sun City's dependence on Maricopa County for just about everything it needs—social services, planning and zoning, health inspections, and more. Some might argue that county government is not designed to handle the everyday issues of a de facto municipality with tens of thousands of residents. As Maricopa County continues to grow at a staggering rate (it is one of the fastest-growing metropolitan areas in the country), Sun City must compete for the county's attention. But Kelsey scoffs at talk of incorporation, calling it "just another layer of bureaucracy." He tells me that this lack of bureaucracy helps keep Sun City "vibrant."

Although Kelsey compares the HOA to a city council, it is by its very nature a reactive organization with very limited powers (let alone voluntary membership), and thus seemingly ill suited to charting the community's future. When I ask him what sort of long-range plans the HOA has for Sun City, he just shrugs his shoulders and says, "If something breaks, we fix it."

"What if volunteerism continues to decline?" I ask. "Then what?"

"Damned if I know," Kelsey responds.

According to Kelsey, the HOA's most important task is protecting residents from neighbors who violate neighborhood deed restrictions, such as by keeping messy yards and using nonconforming paint colors. The organization's four part-time employees spend their time investigating these complaints, the biggest of which is the discovery of underage children. And it is here that Kelsey chooses to focus much of his energy.

"It happens all the time," Kelsey says of contraband children. "And it's a public relations nightmare no matter how we handle it. Why? Because to a lot of people it just feels intrinsically wrong on a gut level to exclude children. But Sun City is not supposed to be a stopover place for kids in hard times. That's a violation of the rules. Everyone who moves here has read the rules and signed them. If their circumstances change—well, I'm sorry, but it's time to move on. Sun City is about lifestyle—and children are not included."

"Why live without kids?" I ask.

"Why not?" Kelsey responds. "Kids can be rude and noisy. What's so wrong with being in your sixties, having raised your kids, worked hard, and now wanting to live without children? It's a lifestyle choice. So what if we live in a bubble? It's our right. We pay our taxes. We vote." He points to the Bill of Rights on the wall. "There's nothing in the United States Constitution that says you have to have kids living next to you. I live like this because I can.

"Look, I understand diversity. But I don't want it shoved down my throat. Why can't someone be allowed to be comfortable when being comfortable to them means living in, say, an all-white community? Don't get me wrong; I'm a people person. I have friends of all persuasions. But I don't want to live in a community with children. I love my grandkids. I just don't want to be *forced* to live with them. People should be free to pick who they want for neighbors. Things weren't so great in this country when we were all forced to live together. And if there's something wrong with the way we live, then how come they're building Sun Cities all over the country?

"You know, people say we're selfish. Well, let me tell you something. Down the street there's a medical research facility. They have one of the largest brain tissue banks in the world. One day they'll discover a cure for Alzheimer's disease. Where do you think they get all that brain tissue? Sun City residents donated it. That's right— we volunteer our bodies and our brains. If you die, they can have your brain out within two hours. Ask *those* people what they think of us."

Over lunch, I meet a woman from Sun City Grand whose husband teaches in a neighboring school district. She says the children are wild, disrespectful, and impossible to discipline.

I ask her if she thinks the area's age segregation has anything to do with it. Surely the children sense Sun City's antipathy toward them. Could it be that, by their actions, Sun Citians are exacerbating the generational divide, encouraging exactly the sort of behavior they fear?

137

"I don't know," she tells me bluntly. "I hadn't thought of it that way. But I can tell you that things were different at my husband's last job. He taught on an Indian reservation. It was a traditional community, with elders. If a child misbehaved, my husband only needed to report the child to his elders and the trouble stopped.

"Come to think of it, my grandmother lived with me when I was growing up and she taught me a lot. But things were different back then. Everything revolved around family. People are so scattered now. Even cousins are like a foreign concept. The kids here don't really have elders, and their parents usually work long hours."

After lunch, I drive to the two-story doughnut-shape Lakeview Recreation Center, Sun City's most iconic and kitschy building, for an interview with another quasi-governmental group, the Recreation Centers of Sun City, Inc. (RCSC), whose elected board of residents governs Sun City's many amenities.

After completing the community, Webb handed these amenities to Sun City residents by creating this nonprofit organization, thereby freeing himself from a giant burden: 340,000 square feet of indoor recreation space, 122 holes of golf, and thirty miles of paved golf cart paths that all required maintenance. In the process, Webb created a laudable and fair-minded method for turning over recreational facilities and responsibilities to his residents.

Inside the RCSC offices, Norm Dickson, a retired schoolteacher who serves on the board, greets me. Although he is in his seventies, this athletic midwesterner represents the new progressive face of Sun City—people who are working hard to ensure that the community has a future.

The generational warfare that plagued Sun City's dealings with its youthful neighbors has turned inward, with older Sun Citians now at odds with younger Sun Citians. Aside from retirement, the two groups don't have much in common. And as the average life expectancy increases, the RCSC is finding the generation gap all the more difficult to bridge.

"We're basically a big country club and our job at the RCSC is to make everyone happy at the lowest fee possible," Norm tells me. "But that's like changing a wheel on a moving car. We have residents here in their mid-fifties and others that are over 100. There are folks who have lived here for thirty years and others who arrived yesterday. The older folks don't want their fees raised, because they hardly use the facilities anymore. But the new younger retirees want all the bells and whistles, and they're willing to pay for it."

Norm and his fellow board members are in the process of overhauling the community's recreation centers, in the hope that updated facilities will encourage the gentrification of Sun City. To pay for these projects, the RCSC charges new residents a onetime impact fee of a few thousand dollars when they purchase a home. Even though the snazzy renovations don't cost veteran residents a penny, the several-thousand-strong Sun City Taxpayers Association has filed several lawsuits against the RCSC and has circulated a petition to recall the board's president.

"Believe it or not, a lot of the older folks are upset because these projects increase the value of their properties," Norm says. "They aren't looking to sell their homes and, frankly, they don't care much about their heirs, either. What they care about is protesting anything that might lead to an increase in their taxes."

Because residents of Sun City don't pay municipal or school district taxes, the tax rate is actually quite low. Norm tells me that he was paying $5,000 a year in property taxes in Michigan before moving to Sun City a decade ago. He now pays about $750. "When I got my first tax bill," he says, "it was so low that I thought it was a monthly payment."

Given Sun City's aging demographics, the turnover of houses is relatively high. The consistent turnover is evidence that newer residents are still buying into the community. Norm intends to keep it that way, because the alternative is unthinkable.

"Communities either grow, stagnate, or decay. In order to remain a viable community, we must attract newcomers. When a community can't fill vacant houses, neighborhoods begin to deteriorate and things start to spiral downward until there are too few people to afford maintaining what's left.

"We need to be proactive. If we don't fix up our community, we won't attract new people and we won't fill vacancies—not with fifty-year-old facilities. There are simply too many competing communities out there. We need to give people a reason to continue choosing us. But convincing older residents of this hasn't been easy."

The results of these internecine battles—stagnation and decay —are already visible. Some of Sun City's apartment houses and condo complexes are run by miniature homeowner associations that don't have the money—or are unwilling to spend the money—to perform cosmetic repairs, let alone major renovations. "What happens when these units can no longer attract new occupants, and the association fees are spread across fewer and fewer residents?" Norm asks. "Then what?"

I ask Norm if these generational wars will ever end. "I don't know," he says with a sigh. "As far as I'm concerned we have a moral obligation to contribute to the future of those who come after us. But some of our older residents forget that they were once young."

After half a century of age segregation, Sun City's future remains anything but certain. One wonders if it will someday simply cease to exist, the unforgiving desert reclaiming it like the ancient Hohokam settlements before it.

By comparison, a decade of desegregation has breathed new life into Youngtown. Once the poor cousin across the street, the tiny municipality is seemingly filled with optimism and opportunity.

Mark Fooks, Youngtown's first and only town manager, promotes this hopeful image. The town has a total landmass of just one and a half square miles, so its worst drawback is its postage-stamp size. Municipalities in rapidly sprawling areas tend to compete with one another much as businesses do: the yardstick of growth measures success. For Youngtown to remain competitive, it will have to grow. Otherwise its revenue sources will be forever limited—a situation that in municipal (and business) terms, has a smell of death about it.

How will landlocked Youngtown grow? Youngtown is heavily dependent on its "sales team" to bring home the bacon. Aside from managing Youngtown's day-to-day affairs, Fooks's job includes attracting businesses to the town so he can continue to portray Youngtown as a "player" in the local municipal scene. He hopes to transform the resulting cachet into a mandate for annexing the aging behemoth next door. "The only real problem is what to call the new town," Fooks says, with evident satisfaction. "Do we call it Youngcity, Suntown, or what?"

Although the young mayor may be the face of the new Youngtown, Fooks is the architect. I met with him at his modest office in Youngtown's ramshackle town hall. A large man with a confident smile who is fast approaching retirement, Fooks gives the impression that planning for Youngtown's future is as easy as baking chocolate-chip cookies with store-bought dough.

Conversely, Fooks sees Sun City's days as numbered. "These folks have lived in a bubble for years, and they'll tell you, 'Please don't burst our bubble—that's why we came here.' It's only a matter of time before they're annexed. The only question is which neighboring municipality gets the honors.

"They *could* incorporate," he continues. "But why go through all the trouble of building a new town hall, establishing a police force, and creating a public works department when they can just join us? We'd turn into a city of 42,000 overnight. With state revenue sharing for municipalities at $230 a head, $8 million would float down to us without us lifting a finger. Increasing our size opens us up to all sorts of money. Just think of the additional $3 million in sales tax we would get from local businesses. And we'd qualify for federal monies as well. That's a heck of a budget to play golf with."

Because it is unincorporated—a city in name only—Sun City cannot charge a municipal sales tax; nor is it eligible for state and federal monies. Youngtown already receives these sorts of payments, but on a smaller scale.

Fooks tells me that even if volunteerism weren't waning, Sun City's problems are too big for volunteers to handle. "God bless volunteers, but you can't run a city with a bunch of amateurs. They don't have the training to administer a city with its buildings, streets, golf courses, parks, streetlights, water, and sewers. Do you have any idea what it takes to manage a golf course, let alone a sewage treatment plant? You don't turn a golf course over to somebody whose sole qualification is that they like to play golf. That's why most local governments are run by trained professionals."

Fooks predicts that the next wave of retirees (assuming there is one) in Sun City is likely to be wealthier, savvier, and more demanding of municipal services. "They'll want to incorporate once they realize they don't have a real voice in their own affairs," he says. "They're going to wonder why they don't have a real police force, and why they have to plead with the county just to get a road repaired. Having to knock on the county's door every time you want something is not what I would call local representation."

The police chief, Dan Connelly, drops by the office, and Fooks invites him in to join our discussion. Connelly has few illusions about the critical choices Sun City will soon face. As far he's concerned, it's only a matter of time before Sun City will have to face reality. "The driving force for Sun City's incorporation will be police protection," he says flatly. "Crime is getting worse and there's no way the Posse can even begin to handle it."

In Arizona, streets in gated communities are not eligible for road repair or police patrols; therefore, there is a strong financial incentive to remain un-gated. After years of de facto solitude, Sun City remains without gates, but it is now uncomfortably sandwiched between sprawling municipal neighbors. Residents of these other cities have necessarily turned many of Sun City's roads, such as Grand Avenue, into major arteries, and Sun City finds itself subjected to an ever-increasing amount of nonresident traffic, making it more vulnerable to crime.

"People want to feel safe, and the sheriff's department can't supply that with three deputies," Connelly continues. "Besides, how many of today's criminals are going to be scared off by an eighty-five-year-old member of the Posse wearing a hearing aid?"

10

Foreign Policy

ALTHOUGH THE VILLAGES EXTENDS INTO THREE COUNTIES, THE VAST majority of the development will soon roll across hapless Sumter County. Per capita income in Sumter County is about half the state's average, and sixty percent of its population is on some sort of state assistance. In addition to being poor, it's also far more rural than two adjacent counties—Lake and Marion—with less than one-fourth their population. When the build-out of The Villages is complete, Sumter will have 45,000 new homes, compared with 5,000 each for Lake and Marion counties. There will be roughly 90,000 Villagers living in Sumter County, outnumbering all other county residents by nearly 50,000.

Sumter County encompasses nearly 600 square miles of the quiet center of Florida. Even when fully built out, The Villages will remain a small rectangle on Sumter's northeast corner. I know this, but I'm still surprised when it takes me nearly an hour on back roads to reach Bushnell, the county seat. The number of run-down trailer parks that post signs advertising their age-restricted status also surprises me.

Along the way, I stop by the tiny Leesburg airport, just across the Lake County line, to sneak a peek at the "Morse air force," as Gary's planes are often referred to. I spot two gleaming Falcon jets in a hanger detailed to look like it holds thoroughbred horses. Morse successfully lobbied to have a U.S. customs officer assigned to the airport, thus giving it "international" status, and allowing him to fly directly into and out of the country with foreign clients. Morse has also lobbied for and received tentative approval for interchanges off Interstate 75 and the Florida Turnpike that will help make The Villages and its environs more accessible to motorists.

I arrive in tiny Bushnell early for a meeting with county officials, and park beside the county's handsome old courthouse. I ask a young, pregnant girl walking along the road where the center of town is. "This is it," she replies. "Unless you mean Wal-Mart. That's up the road."

The air is hot and seems to cling to my body, and the town of 2,300 is quiet except for chirping cicadas. I see a sign for Bushnell's one claim to fame: the nearby Dade Battlefield Historical Site, where in 1835 Seminole warriors (distantly related to Billy Bowlegs) ambushed and killed more than 100 American soldiers in a marshy meadow, thus starting the Second Seminole Indian War.

Inside the courthouse, which has served as the county seat for 100 years, I meet with County Supervisor Brad Arnold and Supervisor of Elections Karen Krause. She paints a picture of Sumter as one of central Florida's last sleepy counties, but rapidly changing under pressure from The Villages' development. "I guess it was just a matter of time," Krause says. "We've got The Villages in the north, and now the southern portion of the county near Orlando is filling up with that city's spillover. Those folks are tired of the mess down there—the crime, the traffic, the sprawl, the high cost of living—but now they're re-creating it here."

"Ten years ago, the number of registered voters in Sumter County was under 16,000," she tells me. "Five years ago it was about 28,000; now it's about 50,000. The majority of these registered voters are from The Villages. We knew it would happen; but we didn't think it would happen so fast. Used to be we had more cows than people in the county, and just three stoplights."

The trend shows no signs of abating, she says. "We are issuing 550 building permits a month for The Villages. We figure that each new house represents 1.9 voters. And unlike the rest of the county, Villagers are a conservative lot. Ten years ago, I was the very first Republican ever elected as a county commissioner. Now all the commissioners are Republicans."

Residents of The Villages, along with Morse, quickly flexed their new political muscle by changing the way county officials were elected, advocating a new system of power distribution in the county, ironically titled "One Sumter." County residents used to elect their five commissioners by district. Residents in district one, for example, would elect their own representative to the board, but not vote on a commissioner representing another district. But with just two district commissioners to vote for, Morse and the Villagers decided that they'd rather vote on the election of *all* the commissioners. Naturally, the rest of the county liked the protection the district system afforded them from the surge of new voters in The Villages.

The vote on "One Sumter" in 2004 was extremely close, but with a ninety percent turnout rate (twice the county average), The Villages won, and the era of big-stick diplomacy began. Villagers, with their overwhelming numbers, could now monopolize every county election. And yet many still felt stymied and underrepresented by the districting system. Although Villagers could now vote for all five commissioners, they could still run for only two seats.

To address this slight obstacle, Villagers pushed through a redistricting, which gave them a third seat on the county commission, and thus a lock on electing the county's government for the foreseeable future.

Although Villagers have already lobbied for—and received—their own Sumter County sheriff's substation and government annex, which is golf cart–accessible, they are no longer satisfied with the arrangement. There's now talk of moving *all* county functions out of the centrally located, century-old Bushnell courthouse and relocating them to The Villages.

At our meeting, County Supervisor Arnold tells me that Chapter 190 is "a wonderful thing. I haven't seen a downside. It helps grow an unincorporated part of the county in a rational manner." He adds that he recently said as much to a fact-finding group from Georgia, whose legislature is considering the adoption of a similar measure. "The Villages pays taxes and yet it's not a big user of county services," he says. "It's a win-win for us." Arnold says nothing of the fact that transplanted retirees have politically overwhelmed the local-born population. When I ask him if these retirees might have a different set of priorities from local families—regarding schools, perhaps—he says he doesn't think so.

He points with pride to the towns near The Villages, including the desolate municipality of Wildwood, which are preparing to benefit financially from the development. "Wildwood is annexing unincorporated land that will soon be commercial," Arnold says. "They will also provide homes for workers. It's a real boom for them. The Villages is a big economic engine. A lot of residents hope it'll give their children a reason to stick around after high school."

To gauge just how far The Villages has already expanded, I return from Bushnell along a sun-bleached, cracked two-lane county highway that passes through gorgeous rolling pastureland with broad vistas. I admire the shady stands of old live oaks in the meadows, and an occasional glistening lily pond. This is the Florida of piney woods, saw palmetto scrub, and sun-dappled hummock that Marjorie Kennan Rawlings describes vividly in many of her novels. Although an avid reader of Rawlings, I still had no idea that central Florida could actually be this stunning.

The Villages' executives often refer to this scenic idyll of delicately interwoven ecosystems as "inventory," and I soon see why, when up ahead the scenery abruptly changes. To my left I see a metallic water tower soaring above a treeless crest, surrounded by hulking piles of concrete sewer molds, partially finished streets, and mounds of sandy soil. Some of the landscape is carefully contoured and resembles the early stages of a new golf course.

To my right, mailboxes line the road beside old driveways scarred by tank treads. The homes are already demolished, and giant bulldozers have leveled what were once rolling hills. Pale sand and upturned oaks with their naked and gnarled roots litter the construction site for as far as the eye can see, which is pretty darn far. The development has leaped right across the road I am driving on, which will soon be converted into a multilane highway with strip malls. Concerns about the health of the area's aquifers have apparently had no effect on Morse's ambitions.

I head for what seems to be the eastern perimeter of The Villages' mammoth construction site. But it's hard to know for sure. The development is expanding so quickly that none of the local maps can keep up. I turn down a lonely lane that runs right along the Sumter and Lake county line, and I am soon rewarded with another vista of endless construction. The newest phase of nearly completed Village development sprawls to the horizon.

In the near distance, just across a brown rail fence, are scores of gently curving streets ending in culs-de-sac. Unlike the more rudimentary site I have just visited, here there are tidy curb cuts, sewer grates, utility boxes, stop signs, and even street signs. Only one thing is missing—houses—but they'll be there soon. A wave of homes is already cresting on a nearby hillside and is poised to roll across this neighborhood-to-be. Given The Villages' aggressive construction schedules, this neighborhood could be filled with homes built from scratch in a few months.

Across the street in Lake County, the land is still wooded and sparsely populated with older, somewhat ragged homes. I pull into the dirt driveway of one displaying a "For Sale" sign and walk a short way until the packed dirt ends and overgrown scrub grass begins. I meet a man who is leaning over a metal fence, with a yapping Chihuahua dancing about his heels. He's in his early seventies and wears leisure slacks, old loafers, and a stubbly beard. High-voltage electrical wires buzzing atop steel towers bisect his yard, which is dotted with small orange trees. I'm staggered when he tells me the asking price is $750,000.

His name is Alan, and he tells me he relocated to the area eighteen years ago to get away from "all the commotion" of his native Orlando. "When I moved in here, there were just two mobile homes and us," he says. "Now they're building 34,000 homes across the street. Kind of boggles the mind, doesn't it? And there's nothing any of us can do about it. So I'm moving."

"What do I think of The Villages and all this development?" Alan says. "I think it stinks. They're building without any regard to the land. I'm no tree hugger, but I hate to see the land raped the way they're doing it. They're shipping in all sorts of clay and sand just so they can make the land flat. They're cutting down trees, and putting in lakes where there weren't any. There's only one saving grace about this whole nonsense—it'll be gorgeous when it's done."

The Villages brushes off the complaints of locals like Alan. "Everybody complains about change," Gary Lester responds when asked about local opposition. "I'm still upset with the American League for adopting the designated hitter rule."

My curiosity once again gets the best of me when I drive past a sign for a county park and something called the Spark Level Baptist Church. I turn down a potholed road with run-down trailer homes lining one side and an empty pasture on the other. The road ends at the church and an overgrown park with a few scattered picnic tables at the edge of some piney scrub. According to local historians, this neighborhood was founded by escaped slaves and is one of the earliest settlements in the region. At the time, the area was a swampy forest located far away from prying eyes. A state map from 1837 labels it "Negro Town." Born in poverty, the small African-American settlement remains basically destitute. The trailers are badly rusted and the yards generally consist of packed dirt littered with discarded furniture, car parts, and empty gas cans.

I knock on the door of the trailer closest to the church. An older woman opens the door but doesn't invite me inside. I ask her about the sprawling development next door. "What we going to do 'bout it?" she says, in a breathy drawl. "I been here fifty-five years. They covered up our fishing lake. I heard one day they gonna come and offer us. But I ain't seen nobody. Guess they just going to put a big wall around us."

She recommends that I speak with a neighbor named L.T. and his wife, Ruby-Mae, so I walk a few hundred yards to their cinder block home, step onto the sagging porch, and knock on the door. An elderly man cautiously opens it a crack. I explain my visit, but he remains ill at ease. "I'm kind of busy right now," he says guardedly, his eyes not quite meeting mine. Try as I might to put him at ease, my visit is clearly making him uncomfortable. The Ku Klux Klan once held considerable sway over this area, occupying several local positions of power, including the sheriff's office. A few local white residents tell me they recall signs reading "No Niggers Allowed" displayed inside private businesses as recently as a few decades ago.

I walk back to the church to fetch my car, but notice a path leading off to the side. The path narrows until it is just wide enough for two sets of sandy tire tracks. I walk along it, listening to the clicking, chirping and buzzing of birds and insects in the long motionless grasses. Oak trees draped in gray Spanish moss line the way on either side of me. The sun is strong enough to heat the hair on my head, and given the clinging humidity, the shade provides little relief, and the mosquitoes and sand gnats are even worse beneath the high canopies. I come across a brick home that looks abandoned. Outside, a mutt sits in a shaded gully beside a plywood doghouse tilting to one side. He looks at me, rolls on his back in the dirt, and goes back to sleep. Across from the driveway in the scrub are the meager remains of a one-room schoolhouse.

I walk up a short rise and gaze at hundreds of partially finished homes. The air is punctuated with the pop-pop-pop of nail guns. In front of me is a metal cattle gate. I climb over it and continue down the rutted dirt path, now surrounded by homes on either side. The neck of land ends in a shady cul-de-sac dotted with a mixture of new and very old headstones. I am in the old "Negro Town" cemetery.

The Villages naturally has little interest in building homes overlooking a cemetery, let alone a cemetery for poor black people. It doesn't fit into the marketing plan. But the cemetery can't be bought, and even if it could, disturbing it would be illegal. What's the developer supposed to do when faced with such an obstacle? Surround it with a park and celebrate the site's historical value? Mythologize it as Billy Bowlegs's final resting place?

I climb over a fence and then a man-made earthen berm to see how Morse is addressing this awkward peninsula of land jutting into his housing inventory. I emerge in a parking lot beside a new recreation center. None of the homes are quite finished, but newspaper vending machines carrying today's *Daily Sun* stand at the ready beside a mail kiosk. A green-and-white sign welcomes visitors to The Village of Caroline. The cemetery, hidden on three sides by a dense row of bushes planted on steep mounds of earth, is nowhere to be seen. I know it's right in front of me, but I can't make it out.

With little or no connection to the land outside the gates, burial poses a problem for Villagers, many of whom have, in any case, little interest in being interred locally. Some military veterans opt for burial at a regional cemetery, but for the most part, the dead and dying are sent home by airplane. Few personal statements are more powerful than where one decides to be buried, and Villagers express a clear preference for the soil of the communities they left behind.

Gated planned communities often have about as much in common with the local area and population as a Club Med resort—it doesn't really matter where they're located as long as the weather is nice. For example, a consortium of Japanese investors is seeking to build an age-segregated community in New Mexico for Japanese citizens. They may not speak English, but such concerns pale in comparison with the benefits of warm winters and the yen's favorable exchange rate. As my former neighbor Dave Anderson tells me, he has always hated Florida—and still does. But as far as he is concerned The Villages isn't really in Florida: "It just happens to be located there."

Back in my car, I head toward the sleepy town of Lady Lake in the northwestern corner of Lake County to meet with the town manager. Lady Lake owes its existence to the railroad, which passed through the town beginning in 1884. The town was incorporated in 1925 but remained a rural farming community for much of its existence. During Prohibition, the swampier and nearly impenetrable portions of the county became popular with bootleggers. The Ma Barker gang hid out nearby until they were discovered by the FBI and killed in a dramatic shootout.

As late as the 1960s, Lady Lake was just a bump in the road with a population of 335. The town couldn't afford to buy its one policeman a car, so he enforced the speed limit on foot with a whistle, and when necessary, hitchhiked to chase down a speeder. Until The Villages came along, the town's only claim to fame was "Cathedral Arch"—a quiet street gracefully lined with giant oaks that once appeared on the cover of the *Saturday Evening Post*.

The area became popular in the 1970s with retirees of modest means searching for sun, good fishing, and low taxes. Land was cheap and zoning nonexistent. Much of Harold Schwartz's old Orange Blossom Gardens is inside Lady Lake's municipal boundaries. Three of the town's five council members are now Villagers, giving The Villages much the same stranglehold on the municipality as it has on Sumter County.

But although many Villagers tell me that they moved here to escape suburban sprawl, much of it has been re-created in the outskirts of Lady Lake, with all its attendant aggravations such as congestion and crime.

The urge to build on the surrounding pastureland is too strong for the Morse family, as well as other developers, to pass up. There's good money to be made erecting big box stores and housing developments—and that's what's happening. Driving into and out of the Lady Lake area of The Villages is becoming a real chore. Sadly, The Villages and local highway engineers are seemingly of one mind: they keep widening the roads, which then attract yet more cars.

I visit with the town manager, Bill Vance, a young, clean-cut professional, who is dressed in khaki slacks and a crisp white shirt. We meet at the Lady Lake town hall, a squat cement structure physically isolated from any other town landmark or neighborhood. When I ask him how he intends to manage the town's explosive growth, he hands me a snappy booklet titled "Commercial Design Guidelines," nods confidently, and invites me to peruse it during our interview.

After several years as a municipal reporter covering sprawling disasters across the country, I have a decent idea of what the booklet might contain: rules for managing sprawl, such as feeble landscaping requirements and gussied-up veneers for strip malls. One page displays a photo of a giant supermarket, considered a success story because it has "three or more roof planes per primary facade." I'd seen the same monotonous so-called "managed" development ruin towns from Connecticut to Iowa to southern California. It's one of the reasons I live in rural New England, where strip malls are not necessarily greeted with open arms.

"We want responsible growth," Vance tells me. "The Villages has raised the bar for all of us."

"What about designing for people, not cars?" I ask. "What about sidewalks?"

He points to plans he has for a sidewalk alongside the town's six-lane highway, where no sensible human would dare to tread.

Two days earlier, a young woman tried; she was killed—nearly sliced in two—by a speeding Lexus. The driver thought she had hit a dog.

"Would you walk on these sidewalks?" I ask.

Vance hesitates. "No. I guess not."

For years, Lady Lake sat on the sidelines and watched The Villages get bigger and bigger. Vance's basic strategy is to help this once sleepy town finally capitalize on The Villages' growth. "You've got tens of thousands of folks here with nothing but time on their hands and money in their pockets," he explains.

Living in a bubble takes a leap of imagination, but try as they might to insulate themselves from the real world, Villagers cannot survive without it. Every utopia has its soft underbelly; even the Biosphere 2 space-age terrarium project eventually needed oxygen pumped in. The Villages' weak spot is employees. Villagers need shops, restaurants, and supermarkets, and these businesses need to be staffed by human beings.

"We can provide both," Vance tells me. "But we'll need more schools. A lot of seniors don't want to pay for schools, but they want to go out for dinner and shop in local stores. Well, you need employees to staff those jobs, and schools for their kids. The same goes for the white-collar professionals. They're not going to relocate here if there aren't good schools for their children. It's all interrelated. If you want a nice community, you need nice schools. And that takes everyone chipping in."

On my way out, I ask Vance for something I can't seem to find: a map of the region. "There isn't one," he says. "Until recently, this wasn't a 'region.'"

On my way out of Lady Lake, I come across a group of pre-teens playing in the street with their younger siblings. They're dressed in jeans and shorts. The boys wear T-shirts, the girls wear tank tops, and most are barefoot. The oldest is named Tania, and she is nominally in charge. When I ask her what she thinks of The Villages next door, she pauses and looks at her debris-strewn dirt yard. "I wish I lived over there, too," she tells me. "It's so clean. And they have nice restaurants and stores. I bet the old folks are really happy there." Her friends giggle at the improbable sight of her being interviewed.

A dark-haired kid named Jimmy stops riding his knobby-tired dirt bike in circles when he hears us talking about The Villages. His hair is long and straight, and he pushes it out of his eyes when he speaks with me. His toddler brother, Billy, also approaches and starts playing with his belly button. Pretty soon, all the kids are gathered in a circle around me, bouncing rubber balls or carrying dolls.

"I don't like The Villages," Jimmy says. "It's a shame such a nice place is only for older people." The kids all watch him intently. "You have to act different there, or they yell at you." Several of the children nod their heads in agreement. Jimmy tells me that he was once dragged out of the movie theater for throwing popcorn at another boy who pissed him off. "My mom had to pick me up and she wasn't too happy."

I picture Jimmy's mom dropping off her cargo of youngsters at the town square. I can hardly imagine a more incongruous picture: retirees strolling about in their fantasyland suddenly invaded by a station wagon full of someone else's rambunctious children.

"I'm always getting in trouble for trying to skateboard there," Jimmy says. "The old people ask us to stop or they get the police to stop us. I haven't seen a sign that says 'No Skateboarding,' but they take your skateboard away anyway. I've had three of them confiscated. I'm getting a new skateboard, but I'm never going back there. The old people are always following us around like we were criminals."

Tania interrupts. "I don't want to live in a trailer anymore," she says. "It's too small for all of us, and I hate it. I want to live in a big house with fresh sod on the lawn—just like the old people."

A muscle car with rap music pulsating out of its sunroof pulls up with two men inside. It's Jimmy's dad and a friend. Jimmy's father is carrying a brown bag with what appears to be a liquor bottle inside. The children sense that he's not in a particularly good mood and quickly disperse.

Later that evening, I meet with Jim Roberts, a Sumter County commissioner whose views often differ dramatically from those of the county supervisor, Brad Arnold. Roberts, a high school civics teacher for more than two decades, is a tall gangly man with rubbery limbs and facial features. He meets with me at the county's satellite offices in The Villages.

He is in the middle of a reelection campaign, one made nearly impossible by The Villages' lock on elections. He has the overwhelming support of his district in the south end of the county, but he must now win the support of the entire county. Making matters worse, the Morse family is using its media machine to support his opponent.

We sit at a conference table. Roberts's sagging shoulders and the deep bags under his eyes betray his exhaustion. He pauses and then closes his eyes, contemplating where to begin. He starts with the gated roads that the county inexplicably agreed to maintain—by a vote of three to two, after the developer helped get a third commissioner who was friendly to The Villages elected to the board. Roberts shows me prior contracts plainly stating that The Villages would be responsible for maintaining its own roads.

Since the county is now stuck with maintaining the roads, they are technically open to the public, whether or not The Villages is gated. And therein lies one of bigger challenges to The Villages' marketing: how to promote a sense of gated security when, for the most part, it doesn't really exist. The Villages may look like a gated community, but most of the gates are actually little more than props. The guards (some of whom are semiretired Villagers) can ask questions, but they can't deny access.

Roberts finds the charade distasteful. "Why should any county resident have to push a button and pass through a security gate to drive down a county road?" Then again, who in Robert's district would even want to drive around in a closed subdivision? To further discourage such a possibility, many gates display an unsubtle "Welcome Home" sign.

But some locals have no choice. A carpenter who builds homes in The Villages told me about an incident when a Villager accidentally rammed his car. When he stopped to check the damage, she told him he didn't belong in The Villages and shouldn't be driving on "her" roads.

I find it increasingly difficult to take the role-playing that accompanies the community's simulated security seriously, particularly when I am returning to the Andersons' house after a rowdy evening at Katie Belle's. One night, when asked by intercom about my intentions, I said, "To pillage and plunder." The distracted guard gave me a cheerful "Okey-doke!" and opened the gates from a remote location.

Roberts tells me it's neither the development itself nor its residents that trouble him. As a pro-business Republican, he has always considered himself a strong supporter of The Villages. "It's a quality development which brings us lots of jobs," he says. "For a cash-strapped county, a retirement community makes for an awfully attractive industry. I knew the developer was getting rich, but I was OK with that because I thought we were getting a utopia with all the advantages and none of the expenses."

But Roberts grew wary when The Villages lobbied commissioners in Bushnell to approve, all at once, plans for 30,000 more homes. It concerned him that the massive expansion had too little of the sort of commercial development that keeps county coffers afloat through tax revenues. Retirees may use fewer county services than younger residents, but they still use some. Otherwise, Villagers wouldn't need their own sheriff's substation and county annex.

Roberts was also concerned about the environmental impact of the expansion. "Water levels are down, and what does the developer do? He challenges the same formula used in Tampa, Saint Petersburg, and Fort Myers."

When he argued that the county should move cautiously and approve only one-third of the expansion at a time, Roberts says, he earned the eternal wrath of the Morse family. "The developer was moving too fast. It's our job to protect residents of The Villages and the county as a whole from reckless planning. One day the developer will be gone and we'll all be left picking up the pieces."

Taking on the Morse family has consequences. The developer helps fund candidates for county office who are friends and business associates. And all candidates are dependent on his magnanimity. No candidate can win without securing a majority of votes inside The Villages. But because The Villages' deed restrictions forbid door-to-door solicitation (unless a resident is personally introducing a candidate to friends and neighbors), candidates must generally rely on Morse's own monopolistic media to deliver their message.

It comes as little surprise that The Villages' media empire takes a dim view of Roberts. The *Daily Sun* seemingly goes to great lengths to keep his picture out of its pages. A recent example was a ceremonial groundbreaking at which Roberts posed with his fellow commissioners.

"Just for fun, I sandwiched myself between my colleagues," Roberts said. "I wanted to see how the *Daily Sun* would cope with me in the center of the picture. Guess what? They cut the photo in half and displayed it in two pieces. You could just make out the knuckle of my little finger on one side, and my index finger on the other. The few times I'm actually in the paper, they print the same photo where I look like I'm snarling."

More often than not, the only mention of Roberts is as the butt of a political cartoon or the object of an angry editorial describing him as a "big-spending politico trying to kill the golden goose" with his "inexplicable" and "wasteful" voting.

Left unmentioned is Roberts's dogged refusal to accept any political donations. He runs a bare-bones campaign financed with a few thousand dollars of his own money. "I always teach my students that money is the corruptor of government," he explains. "If I take money from someone, they'll expect something in return."

Roberts worries most about what he fears are Morse's attempts to turn the entire county into the equivalent of one giant central district. Sumter County is run by what Florida calls a "constitutional" form of government—a boilerplate organizational structure generally favored by poor rural counties. In a constitutional government, all county officials are elected, including the sheriff, tax collector, property appraiser, and supervisor of elections.

Several commissioners backed by the developer have called for the creation of a "charter" government, in which county officials are appointed by majority vote of the board of county commissioners. If such a measure passes—as is possible—the board will soon appoint all other county officials.

"It's like the central districts all over again," Roberts says incredulously. "County government will just be a proxy for the developer—a developer who was never elected by the people. We're not talking about a typical situation where there are twenty competing developers. We only have one, and he wants to control everything."

The Morse family's clout in Sumter may one day end as the southern end of the county fills up with more young families commuting to Orlando. But as with the mini-districts, it may then be too late—many of the important decision may already have been made.

It's nearing midnight, and Roberts excuses himself. He has to be up early in the morning for school and he still has a long drive back to Bushnell. After teaching, he expects to spend the rest of the afternoon walking around his district asking for votes.

Morse is backing a different man in the primary, the county's former director of public works, who resigned a few years earlier after butting heads with Roberts. Not surprisingly, he is very well funded, having raised about $60,000, with many of the donations coming from companies doing business with The Villages.

The next day, I attend a meeting of the Sumter County Republicans. Given the community's conservative roots and active voters in a critical swing state, The Villages has become a favorite campaign stop for Republican candidates, both local and national. Jeb Bush was a frequent visitor, and his brother, the president, made a campaign swing through Sumter Landing in 2004. Tonight, Gary Lester is there, and he starts the meeting with a prayer asking God to bless, among other things, The Villages and the Republican Party. He then leads us in the Pledge of Allegiance.

He introduces Gary Breeden, the developer-friendly candidate for Jim Roberts's seat on the Board of Commissioners. Breeden speaks with an ingratiating folksy drawl, and describes Sumter County as a "diamond in the rough—now is its time to shine," and The Villages as "an absolutely wonderful development."

Someone asks him about a possible water shortage. Breeden dismisses the notion with a confident smile and a wave of his hand. "There's plenty of water," he says. "*Plenty* of water." Lester nods his head approvingly.

Afterward, I ask Lester whether he thinks his employer exerts considerable political influence over the county. He pauses for a moment to consider the question, and then looks me squarely in the eye. "He only has one vote, just like everyone else."

11

Cluck Old Hen

I REACHED THE NADIR OF MY EXPERIENCE OF THE VILLAGES' ABOUT halfway into my stay. It wasn't the result of any one incident in particular, but rather a growing discomfort with make-believe downtowns, talking lampposts, and the ho-hum predictability of living in a gated community with older, mainly heterosexual white people who love to play golf. I felt trapped in another generation's world and was becoming antsy. I wanted to hang out with people my own age. This was to be expected, but the long and somewhat creepy shadow of the developer was more surprising. It had never been my intention to write about him—in fact, I knew nothing about him when I started the project—but there was no avoiding it. Morse's influence was evident everywhere. His seeming omnipotence, however legal it may be, still didn't sit well with me.

And try as I might to keep an open mind, I grew increasingly disenchanted with those—my former neighbors included—who embraced the Villages' age-restricted lifestyle. It struck me as segregation, pure and simple, with children taking the place of previous "undesirables." I was homesick for a more authentic world, and began counting the days to my departure.

Back home, my family and friends lent me a sympathetic ear, but here in The Villages I felt alone in my brooding negativity. As I spoke with young families in Spanish Springs, a far different picture emerged. They didn't see life in The Villages as selfish. On the contrary, they were relieved that such a place existed for their older relatives. They no longer had to worry about Mom and Dad, who were now more likely to be found having fun at a recreation center than sitting at home monitoring a police scanner.

I met a man whose family was relocating to The Villages one generation at a time. "My grandparents have been here for twenty years," he told me. "My parents have been here for six years, and my wife's parents moved here four years ago. My aunt just bought a house here yesterday. It's nice to know that they're all in one place and can keep an eye out for each other. I can't wait to retire and move here myself, but I'm only forty!"

This man's little boy could barely contain his enthusiasm, either. "I love visiting The Villages," he said. "It's the happiest place on Earth—just like Disney World!"

How could this be? Sure, it's comforting to know that one's older relatives are in a safe, sociable environment where they can age gracefully, but is outlawing young families the only way to make such a thing possible? Didn't these people recognize that their relatives' land of make-believe is predicated on age discrimination?

One day, at the end of my rope, I found myself driving around aimlessly, and eventually I pulled into a parking lot for the local hospice. For better or worse, there's no sugarcoating death. Even a developer can't do that.

I've spent a lot of time in hospices as a journalist and a friend, and I've been greatly impressed not only by the level of care, but also by what these compassionate organizations represent. A community with hospices is generally a community that makes an effort to care for its own. And isn't that why so many seniors gravitate to The Villages in the first place?

The Villages' hospice is in a sunny, bright building with cathedral ceilings, lazy fans, and handsome furnishings. There's nothing depressing about it. If it were a hotel, I'd check in immediately. As with several of the local schools, Morse donated the land for the building and helped construct it. There are plans for several more.

On the day I visit, a spunky volunteer in her sixties, Doris, greets me at the front desk. She has a quick smile and enjoys talking about life in The Villages. "Back home, I'd be isolated by the weather and living in a neighborhood where everybody else works," Doris tells me. "But here I can feed my mind, body, and spirit. I've taken so many adult education classes that I can't even remember them all—twelve history courses alone."

Doris is a former teacher from Minnesota, and she tells me that she still finds time to tutor at the local elementary school. "I think it's important for the generations to approach one other. I want the younger ones to know that we care about them, just like there were adults who cared about us when we were young.

"A bunch of us volunteer, especially in the schools, but the majority of people here like to hide behind our gates and forget the world outside. They're the ones with the parades and the *Guinness Book of World Records* competitions. That's their involvement—stuff dedicated to good times. I think we reflect the community at large; apathy is rampant all over the United States. But soon as you see me stop fighting for what is right, that's the day you might as well call the coroner."

I'm introduced to Gerry, a former steelworker from New York who is dying of lung cancer. He is sitting in an easy chair on a lanai with a view of a lake and a golf course. His wife of fifty-four years and their grown daughter sit nearby, enjoying the gentle tropical breeze. To my surprise, Betsy Anderson was right; The Villages, or at least its hospice, *has* somehow made dying a touch more agreeable.

"I wanted to retire someplace quiet where the children could easily visit," Gerry says.

"It was the best thing they did," his daughter, Erica, adds. "They did their job and now they don't have to worry about us.

They can just enjoy themselves. We can always visit with the grand-kids: they love coming here; they call it a camp for old people."

"It was time to pass the torch," Gerry continues. He looks gaunt and takes short, measured breaths. "We're older and not geared up for the faster lifestyle. You see baby boomers now, bouncing, laughing—that was us when we first came down here in 1995. Now we sit and watch the baby boomers. Then we'll be gone and the baby boomers will be the old ones.

"I loved my time here. I used to play golf six, seven days a week. Where else can you go where you can drive your golf cart everywhere, and dance every night to live entertainment with a drink in your hand? No other place I know of."

Gerry's wife, Alice, expects to stay after he dies, but she's anxious. "I've never lived alone my whole life. I've never filled my car with gas, I never wrote a check, and here I am and I've got to sink or swim. What else am I supposed to do? Move in with my kids? They're working. They've got their own families. What would I do? Clean their house?"

Erica says she contemplates moving to The Villages to be closer to her mother, and to enjoy herself. "I geared my whole life to my children, too. Now they're in their twenties, and it's my time. I just want to work a few more years, and wait until the kids are a little more settled."

Outside Gerry's room, I run into two clowns. One's named Sassy, the other Mopsey. Both have big bright hair and painted faces and wear oversize shoes. They trained with The Villages' clown club and now spend several days a week volunteering at nursing homes and hospices.

When I tell Mopsey about my project, she insists on taking my picture. I hesitate. "Please, please, please!" she begs. "You're my *first* author." Sassy also looks at me with big, pleading clown eyes. I relent. Mopsey aims the camera at me and presses the shutter. A stream of water splashes across my face and drips onto my notebook. The two clowns double over with laughter.

They invite me to sit with them. Sassy exhales deeply and rubs her knees. "We clown around three or four times a week, sometimes more," Sassy says. "That's why I'm sitting; I can barely move. But I believe in this work. My husband died of bone marrow cancer. He was under care for four and a half years and was totally depressed. Sometimes people need a reason to laugh. That's where we come in.

"When my husband died, all my children were gathered in the living room," Sassy continues. "It was so gloomy. I needed to lift the mood, so I said 'OK, which one of you am I going live with?' You should have seen the look on their faces! They were in total shock." Sassy slaps her knees in laughter and wipes away a tear. "The minute I told them it was a joke, everyone relaxed. It worked.

"Look, they've all got their lives, their own problems. And believe me, they have plenty of problems. After a while, I don't even want to hear about them anymore. I've got my own life to lead. And when it comes time to die, they can ship my body north afterward, but I'm going to die in The Villages. This is where my support system is. I have loads of friends here. They say you can't have too many friends, but I don't know; I can't keep up with all of them."

"It's a wonderful place to die," Mopsey adds. "The only way I'm going to leave here is feet first, too."

Although I remain unconvinced that age segregation is either healthy or desirable, I do find my heart opening up to many of the Villagers who are refreshingly unpretentious. I find that some of the older women remind me of my grandmother, who died when I was eighteen. She suffered from Alzheimer's disease, so I really lost her years earlier. And she was my last living grandparent. Perhaps that explains why I enjoy hanging out with people of all ages back home.

I have nothing but fond memories of my maternal grand-mother. Spending the weekend with her in her tiny apartment in downtown Philadelphia was such a treat that it had to be carefully rationed between my two brothers and me so as not to cause fight-ing. The only way to score an extra visit was to be sick, and I hap-pily obliged. Being sick at Grandma's meant homemade chicken soup, fresh brisket sandwiches on miniature slices of bread, and comic books. If my health improved, I was rewarded with a trip to the top of city hall for a view of the city my grandmother loved so much, and weather permitting, bobbing in her little rooftop pool while being fawned over by her "girlfriends."

I'm quite certain that my grandmother would have never lived in a gated age-segregated community like The Villages, even if she had had the money to do so. But that doesn't stop me from seeing a little bit of her in many of the people I meet. And while I suspect that Grandma would have had little use for the likes of Mr. Mid-night and his overt sexuality and hedonism, I find him fun. I resolve to quit sulking, and make some new friends.

The following evening, I attend an affinity club meeting for former residents of my home state, Massachusetts. More than 200 Villagers are gathered around long folding tables in a powder-blue room with fake wainscoting and a fluorescent-lit drop ceiling. The first order of business is inviting new members to come up to the makeshift podium and introduce themselves. Many of the attend-ees speak with heavy Boston accents. Behind them, the club's flag is draped over a hanging picture frame.

"Hi, I'm Annie, and I'm from Agawam," one woman says. "I moved heah one month ago."

"Welcome, Annie!" the crowd says in unison.

"Hi, my name is Nick; and this is my wife, Anita. I was tired of the wintahs so we sold the house and came down heah and we've been in love evah since. My wife still likes to go back to Massachu-setts, so we visit a lot. I went back for a Red Sox game but I couldn't go because I pulled my back that mahning. They lost seven to three. But it was a good visit north anyway."

Next, we are treated to tonight's entertainment: Sheldon's Village Stompers. A handsome silver-haired man steps onto a dance platform on the far side of the room. He's wearing white slacks, a white shirt, and a red bolo tie.

"Good evening, Massachusetts!" Sheldon says.

"Good evening," the crowd responds.

"Back when I started the Stompers in 1992, I was the only clogger in The Villages. All the rest learned it here. My wife and I are from Acton and we're very happy to do a show for our Massachusetts neighbors!"

Six women spill into the room, dressed in red-and-white checked skirts and frilly white blouses. They wear patent leather shoes with metal taps attached to the soles that make a delightful jiggling-clanking sound when they walk. Sheldon turns on a small boom box and "Next to You, Next to Me" flows out of its speakers. The women snap into formation and start a synchronized stomping, like elder Rockettes. Each step sounds like tiny cymbals.

For the next song, "Cluck Old Hen," six men enthusiastically jump onto the dance floor. They are dressed just like Sheldon, who remains beside the portable stereo directing the action. Several of the men have comb-overs that occasionally need readjusting during the performance. The men and women skip around in a sort of square dance.

After they whoop and holler through a few more jigs, they leave the stage, and Sheldon introduces his friend Phil, who plays a medley of polka songs on a pair of short thick wooden sticks called "bones," which rest between his knuckles. Phil flails his knuckles rhythmically, smiling at the audience.

After the performance, the meeting is adjourned and I start chatting with my tablemates. I zero in on a woman who is dressed as if she just walked in from the Boston Common. She wears a turtleneck and a sheer pink cardigan and carries a quilted handbag with a bland preppy pattern. Her name is Carol, and all evening she has looked like a deer in the headlights.

"My heart is still in Boston," she tells me, stating the obvious. "I miss my family. I miss the four seasons. And I miss riding the T into town and walking around." Carol moved to The Villages with her far more enthusiastic husband about three months ago.

"I was in the navy for a lot of years," her husband, Jim, says. "I'm used to moving around." Carol looks down at the table. "I've been looking for a nice place to retire for seven years. Here I can play golf every day. And if something happens to one of us, there are people for us to lean on."

"I miss the snow, the flakes falling down," Carol says.

"Yeah, but she forgets all the slush and shoveling," Jim counters.

"I miss the rain," Carol says. "I'm tired of all this sun, day after day. Everything is the same here. There's nowhere to go. We're in the middle of nowhere. Where's the art museum? Where's the library in Copley Square? Where's the Boston Pops, or the fall foliage? I miss the mix. I miss not seeing any children around. But what I really miss is my family. I miss them terribly."

Jim is quiet. He takes no pleasure in his wife's discomfort. "Look," he says finally. "Let's just give it a while. Try it on for size. You might just end up liking it here. We can fly home as often as you like."

"You promised we could always move back," Carol counters.

"We can buy as many plane tickets as you'd like," Jim responds.

"That wasn't the promise."

"You're right. We can always move back, I suppose."

Carol looks pale. She and Jim excuse themselves.

The other women at my table are a feisty bunch—hard-core Yanks from Boston—with thick accents. Their comments are full of sharp barbs. "You find that a lot of people miss their families," a woman named Ellen tells me. Her short hair is smartly styled, and she wears a touch of lipstick. "It's the husbands. They drag their wives down here for the golf. But the women miss their families. The men—it's like they don't care as much. They'd rather visit them. That's the generation you've got here: the men make the decisions and the women follow them. I run across it all the time. Ninety percent of the men love it here, as if they've died and gone to heaven. But the women—that's another matter. I'm single. I'm a free woman. I make my own decisions."

A woman named Paula cuts in. "You make lots of acquaintances here, but not a lot of close friends. Everybody's too busy running around the golf courses. Me? I love my house. When we took the trolley tour, the woman said, 'We don't sell houses; we sell a lifestyle.' Well, I wanted a new house, not a lifestyle. I never had a new house. I like to cook, to clean. People think I'm crazy because I like ironing. Nobody around here even cooks. When you talk to someone about meeting for dinner, the first question they ask is, 'Which restaurant?' I guess it all depends on where you're from and what you're used to. Everybody here is from somewhere else. Florida is such a transient state."

"This is an excellent place for singles," Ellen says. "I don't care if I never go back north again. There's an excellent support system for single women here."

In addition to belonging to the Massachusetts Club, the Irish-American Club, and the Explorers' Club and volunteering as a docent at a regional museum, Ellen is a founding member of the Sociable Singles Club. But the purpose of this club is not to meet men; it's to provide a venue for single women to meet and make friends.

"Men?" Ellen asks. "I've already been married once. And that was enough. The men here are all letches anyway." Divorced after twenty-seven years of marriage, Ellen now lives with her brother, a Korean War veteran diagnosed with posttraumatic stress disorder who rarely leaves the house. "It's only men that truly retire," she says. "I took care of my husband, I took care of my kids, I took care of my mother when she got sick, and now I take care of my brother. It's time I took care of myself."

Ellen's cousin Pat introduces herself. She's a petite woman who never married. She has lived all her life with one of her sisters, and still does: they share a home in The Villages. "As a single woman, I feel safe and secure here," Pat says. "I don't feel threatened like I did back in Boston. Back home, I'd be stuck in the house, scared. Here I can go down to the square by myself, listen to the music, see people dancing, go home, and I feel like I did something—and it didn't cost me a dime."

"Living down here is affordable," another woman—Debbie—says. "Up north, I couldn't afford to go out. I'd probably be living in an insulated garage or something, counting pennies. Here I can have my own apartment. It's tiny, but it's a home."

Like most northeastern "blue staters," these women are solid Democrats, although they now live in a community where Republicans outnumber them two to one. They have few kind words for Gary Morse and his staunchly conservative politics. "This place lost a lot of its charm when Harold died," Paula says. "It's kind of like when Walt Disney died and Eisner took over. Morse is too greedy. He cares more about money than people. You read his newspaper and you'd think everything is hunky-dory in Iraq and Bush is a genius."

"This place is a dictatorship," Debbie says. "But you know what? If I won the lottery, I'd still live here. I'd just travel more and maybe buy a house on the Cape."

I ask the women for their views on age segregation. "I like kids," Debbie says. "But I don't want to live with them. After four hours with them in the pool, crying, yelling, throwing tantrums—well, it's nice to know that I can relax without them."

"Children don't fit the lifestyle we've got in The Villages," Pat says. "You can't mix the two. It's either one or the other, but not both. If this place was multigenerational, there'd be a lot more crime. We'd have drug busts, wild parties, loud stereos, auto accidents. It wouldn't be the same. We'd be shoved to the side. And afraid."

Although the night is still young, the women all drive home. I head to Katie Belle's. There's a short line outside; an elderly bouncer slowly checks for resident IDs and guest passes with a flashlight and magnifying glass. Three seniors from out of town wait in front of me. The first in line has an awkward comb-over and wears heavy gold chains around his neck and wrists. The next one has a mop of white hair and an unusually prominent Adam's apple and wears a Jimmy Buffet T-shirt. He rocks back and forth impatiently in his shorts and two-toned loafers. The third guy wears a Hawaiian shirt tucked into a pair of jeans pulled up over his belly button. They're agitated at the bouncer's delay and say as much, as if they're spoiling for a fight. By now, most of the bouncers know me, so I just wave and walk right in.

Inside, Mr. Midnight's holding court at the bar, telling friends about his day trip to the beach to meet an Internet friend. "It was a great day," he says. "We swam, ate lunch, smoked some marijuana, and then jumped in bed. She had new tits. Just bought 'em, and they were beautiful. Top-notch. You know what else? She's pierced down there. I'd never seen that before. Right there, under the hood." He pauses to order another low-carb beer. "It's nice to get off campus once in a while."

I grab a drink and listen to the band play Fleetwood Mac's "Don't Stop Thinking about Tomorrow" and another perennial favorite in The Village, "Mustang Sally." About 100 residents line-dance in unison, and the balconies are packed with spectators cheering them on. I watch in amusement as a few younger people struggle to keep in rhythm with the quick-dancing seniors. A woman who seems to be in her late seventies leaves the dance floor swinging her hips and pumping the air with her fist. The contrast with my hometown's senior center couldn't be any starker.

Suddenly, somebody grabs my notebook out of my hands. "What are you writing about, cutie?" asks an attractive middle-aged woman in jeans and a silky red blouse. "What do I get if I give you your notebook back, hmmm?" She grabs me by the arm, pulls me closer, and then reaches down and gives me a soft playful slap on the butt. Her hand lingers at the base of my thigh. "I need another drink," she announces. "How about you?"

I have difficultly responding. Feeling like a prude is a new experience for me, and her seizure of my notebook does not amuse me. I know she's only playing, but the notes inside cannot be replaced. Nevertheless, I walk to the bar and return with two margaritas. She looks me in the eyes and asks what brings me to The Villages. "Research," I answer.

She pauses and then starts to tell me her story. Her name is Jean, and she moved to The Villages six years ago from Wisconsin, where she worked as telephone operator. She looks as if she is in her late fifties and is actually quite pretty. She then returns to the business at hand. "I'm *so* horny," she says, drawing even closer. She rests an elbow on my shoulder and gently tousles my hair. "I gotta use it before I lose it!"

Jean senses my bewilderment and awkwardly pulls back several inches from my groin. "I just hope I meet a guy, somebody to be with," she says soberly. "But maybe it's just not meant to be." She quietly hands me my notebook.

Back at the Andersons' house, Dave is in the lanai, smoking a pipe and working on a large-print crossword puzzle. He puts down his pencil and invites me to join him for a friendly chat, which is something I'm finding myself increasingly looking forward to. He loves to hear about my day, and I enjoy listening to his thoughtful insights. I make myself a sandwich and pop down on a chair across from him.

"People were searching for a place where they could feel comfortable with peers their own age," he tells me. "This place prospers because it provides that. When everyone is retired, boundaries fall away and guys from the assembly line find themselves hanging out with executives. Everybody here is from someplace else; it's what you have in common that brought you here in the first place. All these people were searching for community. And now they've found it.

"A lot of our friends here find their kids don't call them, let alone visit. At some point in life, you become independent of family, or family becomes independent of you. Your friends become your *chosen* family.

"To my mother's generation, it was very important to leave money to your children, even if that meant doing without. But this generation doesn't have the same closeness to their children. It's a social revolution: we're no longer dependent on them to take care of us. We can take care of ourselves, and have fun doing it.

"Besides, what's the alternative? Moving to be near your kids? What happens when your son-in-law gets a promotion and that means yet another move? Do you really think they're going to stay behind and say no to the promotion?"

The following week, Ellen calls and invites me to play cards with her women friends that evening. I accept, and then ask what she's been up to. She excitedly tells me about a night out she had at the Savannah Center for twelve dollars, listening to a medley of show tunes. "I go to that show every year," she says. "Everybody raves about it. It's like seeing a real Broadway show, but cheaper."

I ask her how her friends from the Massachusetts Club are doing. "We get together a lot," she says. "We're always doing something. Just the other night we got together for spaghetti and eggplant

Parmesan, and we had strawberry pie for desert. It was a very nice evening. And on Monday, we went to hear a polka band. That was fun, too."

I'm looking forward to my own fun today. I've decided to forgo a gathering of golf cart hot rodders and play bingo for the first time since elementary school. Silly as it may sound, I'm really looking forward to it, and have planned my day around it. I cheerfully drive into Spanish Springs for a quick lunch before game time.

As I sit eating a sandwich at an outdoor table, I notice a woman on the sidewalk staring at me. She's wearing jeans, a pink T-shirt, sneakers with sequins, and a snazzy purple cap resting at an angle over her white hair. "Hey, Andrew!" she says, waving her hand excitedly. "I betcha you don't recognize me without my makeup!" She's right, and it takes me a moment before I realize it's Sassy without her clown getup. I'm happy to see her, and invite her to join me for a cup of coffee. She says she wants to tell me her story. I've been bombarded with unsolicited biographies, but I really like Sassy and I'm curious about her tale.

"I've been widowed for five years," Sassy informs me. "I don't want somebody else. I haven't dated since I was seventeen, and I'm not about to start. I was raised Catholic and that don't go away easy.

"After my husband died, I was desperate to share things, even little things. I'd call a friend just to say that I found my keys or paid such and such a bill. But I'd rather bite a cyanide pill than live with any of my kids, God bless them all.

"Being single was really, really hard at first. After forty-five years of doing everything together, I was suddenly cast off. I feel gypped that we can't share these years. He missed the birth of our first great-grandchild, and he loved kids.

"We were best friends. He always said that he should be the first to go because he couldn't live without me. Well, he got his wish. He thought I could cope better with being alone. I hate to say it, but he was probably right. But I'm *angry*. It wasn't supposed to happen this way. He wasn't supposed to die of cancer." Sassy shows me her necklace: hanging from a gold chain is her wedding ring wrapped around her husband's. Her misfortune, though a common occurrence at a place like The Villages, is nevertheless starting to make me weepy. I look at the simple yet poignant necklace and my eyes moisten. She looks at me with sad resignation and continues her narrative.

"I'd take my husband back in a heartbeat. The men around here are so different than he was. I always have to tell them to keep their hands to themselves. They're always trying to touch something, cop a feel. I'm a nurse, and I can tell you, that that's the last thing to go. I have a ninety-year-old patient and I can't shower him without somebody accompanying me. Can you imagine?

"Finding love again at my age would just complicate things," Sassy continues. "I've led a full life. I don't feel I need to ask for more. I don't want to be greedy. It takes years to build a good relationship and I only have so many left. Who would want me, anyway?"

Sassy and I finish our coffee and walk slowly down the sidewalk, pausing to look at window displays. "There's a lot of sadness here," she says, placing a palm over her heart. "But I'm not going to let it take over. I'm going to fill up my time until it's my time. That's why I like clowning. It beats sitting at home and crying.

"My husband wasn't the only one to go. I've buried so many of my friends that I need to make new ones on a regular basis. I just buried my best friend who I'd known since 1959. I'm getting really good at saying good-bye."

After this story, I feel sheepish informing Sassy that I need to go because I'm late for bingo. But she just smiles and walks me to my car, where she gives me a big hug. "Thank you for taking the time to listen to an old lady's story," she says.

The bingo game is held in one of the larger rooms at the recreation center. The parking lot is filled with cars and golf carts. Inside, nobody shows the slightest interest in helping me find a seat.

Bingo, I learn, attracts a tough crowd. Social niceties quickly give way to acerbic moodiness as soon as the bingo balls start bouncing. The vast majority of participants are female, but they are not about to coddle me like grandmothers.

I evenually find a seat beside a hunched-over woman with cat's-eye glasses studded with rhinestones. She wears a sweater to ward off the air-conditioning, which whips around the room like a nor'easter. Her name is Dotty, and she introduces herself without looking up. "Bingo's about the only thing left that I can still do," she says when I sit down. "I'm too old to do anything else fun."

A bingo lieutenant walks over and sells me a pile of bingo sheets for five dollars. He asks me if I need a magic marker for dabbing. Dotty flicks one down the table at me like an old penny. "Save your money," she advises, adding tersely, "You owe me one."

A woman at a table next to ours shouts, "Bingo!" She wins fifteen dollars. Everyone at the table is encouraged to touch her winnings. "That's lucky money," Dotty tells me, then kisses her talisman, a little porcelain puppy. The first winner of the game is also presented with a paper crown, and is referred to as the "bingo queen."

The man on the stage calls out a new game. It's hard to imagine that a game as seemingly simple as bingo could be challenging, but I find decoding the announcer's jargon beyond my ability. A slew of numbers are called. I dab as quickly as I can but I can't seem to get the hang of all the variations of the game, each with its own different pattern on the bingo sheets. I have no idea what Lazy L, the Chair, or the particularly enigmatic Doo-dad means. Why can't I just dab at all my numbers?

A woman across the table offers to be my Rosetta stone. Her name is Marianne. She lives in an age-segregated community in Arizona, but she's here visiting her ailing mother. "Am I winning yet?" I ask. She points out that one measly G-50 stands between me and a crisp Ben Franklin. Another number is called and a woman across the room yells out, "Bingo!" loudly enough to make me jump.

"My mother had a lot of friends here, but at some point after her stroke, she just gave up," Marianne tells me. "Friends can only help out so much. Then it's time for family. Who else is going to talk with her doctor and make sure she's getting the right treatment?"

The announcer calls out I-17, and we hastily scan our cards.

"My husband and I like living in our gated community," Marianne continues. "We're proud of it. We've finally made it."

"N-34."

Dotty curses, scrunches her face, and clears the phlegm in her throat. She turns toward me and finally looks me in the eye. She's pissed. "Are you here to talk or to play?" She looks at my bingo card. "C'mon, that's the wrong pattern. Fix it!"

Countless bingo games later, I'm bored and exhausted, and my nerves are frayed. I haven't won a single dollar and my mood has noticeably darkened. A bingo monitor politely asks me not to crumple up and throw my losing bingo sheets against the wall. I stare him down. My eyes are bleary, my leg is shaking like a sewing machine, and I want to tell ornery Dotty to shove her lucky porcelain puppy up you know where. I look at the time display on my cell phone: I've been playing for three hours. The room is littered with stained coffee cups and stale popcorn. Marianne left an hour ago.

The next game is for the jackpot. The room is absolutely silent. I can hear the Ping-Pong balls bouncing on the stage all the way at the far end of the room. Moments later, some jerk yells, "Bingo!" The crowd groans and heads for the bathrooms.

Outside, I stretch my legs and breathe in the scent of orange blossoms before driving to yet another recreation center, where Ellen and her friends are gathered to play their weekly card game, called "Hand and Foot." The room is packed with people seated around long folding tables. There is little socializing between the tables, but the affable participants evidently prefer the hum of a large room to private play at home.

Sitting at Ellen's table are her cousins Pat and Eunice. The two sisters have lived together since their early twenties; Pat is retired, but Eunice works at a nearby pharmacy. Debbie from the Massachusetts Club is also there, as are two friends named Connie and Roberta.

"I miss my grandkids," Roberta says. "But they're getting older. When they're young they want you around. But when they're teens, you don't exist."

"With these new phones you don't miss a thing anyway," Connie says. "My grandson hit a home run the other night and my daughter called me from the bleachers. They can even take a picture with the phone. I'm not missing out on anything."

I ask the women if any of them are lonely. "No, no, no," they say, practically in unison. "There are too many of us to hang around with for any of us to be lonely," Ellen says.

Eunice's job at the pharmacy gives her a firsthand look at the habits of senior singles on the prowl. "You should see all the guys coming in to buy condoms, lubricated jelly, and massage oil," she says. "And the women buy the wrinkle creams. Believe me, those creams don't work."

"The single men strut around Spanish Springs like a bunch of Don Juans," Ellen says. "And the women are all over them. I've got a friend who has a guy living with her. She gets mad because we don't call her anymore when we go to the movies. But why should we call her? She's got a *guy* living with her.

"I knew this one guy whose girlfriend threw him out," Ellen continues. "He asked me if I could put him up. I asked him if he had a car. He said, 'Yes.' I said, 'Good, go sleep in it.'" The women all laugh.

I excuse myself to use the bathroom. An older man at the urinal next to me, wearing pressed jeans and a purple polo shirt, grunts and holds his breath as he rocks back and forth in his loafers. "Prostate," he says with a grimace. "It's killing me."

Back at the table, the women are still talking about men. "Take a look around," Connie says. "There's nothing here of interest. Take a look and tell me if I'm being harsh."

The man with the purple polo shirt and the enlarged prostate strolls up to a table of women across from us. His unevenly dyed shoulder-length hair is combed back and topped with a pair of aviator sunglasses. He leans against a chair and casually sweeps a hand through his hair. "Hey, ladies," he says. "Don't you all look pretty tonight?"

The women at the table greet him warmly. Ellen and her friends are clearly disgusted. They pause in the game just to watch, horrified. Ellen sticks her fingers in her throat and pretends to gag. "Barf," she says. "What a zero."

I decide not to tell Ellen that a far more adept romancer—Mr. Midnight—has invited me to spend a week at his den of iniquity, to research the Village's single life from inside the mother ship.

12

Chasing the Elephant

To GAIN A CLEARER UNDERSTANDING OF THE TREND TOWARD AGE SEG-regation, I return to Phoenix to attend a "50+ Housing Symposium" sponsored by the National Association of Homebuilders. Several months after my first visits to Youngtown and Sun City, I once again find myself touring age-segregated communities in the desert, but this time on a large air-conditioned bus packed with developers and their employees chattering away excitedly about "boomers"—the generation born after World War II when the GIs came home and got down to the long-delayed business of making whoopee. According to demographers, they kept at it for another eighteen years.

Today, roughly 78 million of these boomer babies are still living. It's a giant generational bulge moving inexorably from middle age to retirement. Right now one American in eight is a senior citizen. In twenty years, the boomers will swell that proportion to one in five. The ratio represents an unparalleled business opportunity, and one that will probably skew commerce toward the needs and wants of senior citizens in coming years.

I hear a woman behind me chatting excitedly to her seatmate, "I was building for sixty-two-plus, but they just keep getting younger. Now I'm marketing to people in their forties and fifties."

A man across the aisle points out the window as we drive by a cemetery. "Hey, we just passed an 'inactive adult community,'" he says loudly, and gets a chorus of chuckles. "I guess you could call that 'aging in place.'"

My own seatmate, Laurel, is working on Albuquerque's first age-segregated community, which, she says, is selling like hotcakes. "A lot of the realtors were like, 'Gosh, it's about time,'" Laurel tells me. "We sold thirty lots before we even completed our model homes and clubhouse. That's very unusual."

The fifty-five-plus housing in her development is part of a larger planned community designed for all ages. "A certain market segment doesn't want to deal with kids," Laurel says. "People say they feel 'younger' or 'ageless' when they are surrounded by people their own age. I hear that in focus groups."

Focus groups helped the national developer for whom she works decide to pursue age-restricted housing rather than age-targeted housing. Age-targeted housing is merely suggestive of age exclusivity: instead of playgrounds, there are dog parks and walking trails; and homes have fewer bedrooms. "You just have to design it in such a way that people with 2.3 kids won't be interested," Laurel says. "We chose age-restricted because it differentiates us in our market, and we wanted to make sure our message was clear. A lot of people in the focus groups said they like to see their grandkids but they'd also like to see them go home at the end of the week. They don't want to be designated babysitters; they want to lead their own lives."

We continue west from Phoenix into the flat, expansive West Valley, passing strip mall after strip mall, McDonald's after McDonald's, and countless housing developments, most of which are bordered by concrete privacy walls. "This all used to be agricultural land," the bus driver informs us over the loudspeaker. Aside from water issues, building in the desert is pretty easy, he says. "All you do is scrape the dirt and start pouring foundations."

Our first stop is an "affordable" age-segregated community called Sundance. When it is built out, it will consist of 1,000 homes on 800 acres. According to our handout, the residents' average age is 62.5, their average income is $70,000, forty-percent are still employed, and the major "draw states" are Arizona, California, Washington, and Illinois. The most popular floor plan is 1,800 square feet, with upgraded kitchen cabinets and two small master bedrooms located on opposite sides of the house. The two bedrooms are a favorite feature for wives whose husbands snore.

Our caravan of three buses pulls over and we pile into the sales office, an attractive building that I am told will eventually be discarded to make room for another home. We gather around a diorama the size of a pool table in the center of the room. "These lots over here all border the golf course," a salesman explains. "Those homes pay a onetime $2,000 premium for that privilege."

Though golf courses are often considered prestigious and can help a developer sell homes, they're also money pits, the salesman explains. "To keep residents' amenities fees down, the developer continues to own the golf course even after build-out, unless, of course, he's lucky enough to sell it.

"If the monthly fees get too high, you risk hitting the 'fear factor,'" the salesman continues. "Retired folks are sensitive to monthly expenditures. The vast majority of people don't golf and only thirty or forty percent use the recreation center. They don't want to pay big association fees. It's a competitive market, and the key is to position yourself properly so you can compete. We've positioned ourselves to capture people that are particularly sensitive to price points."

The decision not to gate the community also helps keep monthly fees low. Gates mean a larger staff and more street maintenance. Another way to keep down costs is to buy land in the middle of nowhere because it's cheaper; that is exactly what this developer has done. There's a lonely stretch of interstate nearby, but not much else, at least not yet.

The 15,000-square-foot recreation center houses an exercise room, six pool tables, a card room that seats sixteen, and a "library" with several dozen books. Outside there are two small pools, neither of which is big enough for swimming laps. An activities board lists a book club, a diabetes club, and a training class for people who want a concealed handgun permit.

Down a hall, I find three women in a windowless crafts room contentedly soldering stained-glass butterflies and other knick-knacks. "My husband and I have met so many people who told us they always wanted to work with stained glass," one woman tells me. "Now they have the time. In two months we've taught thirty people how to do it."

The crafts rooms are also used for sewing, quilting, and scrap-booking. To keep costs down, there are no specialized rooms for pottery, woodworking, or metalworking. "They didn't put any sinks in the crafts rooms," one woman complains. "And windows. Windows would be nice, too." I look around the room. She's right; it's just a fluorescent-lit box with tables and chairs. "We have too many tennis courts," another woman says. "People our age like to play pickle ball, not tennis."

I walk to the end of the hallway and leave through a side door. The blinding desert sun greets me, as do a row of empty tennis courts. In the distance I see a green golf course surrounded by vacant desert. When the wind blows, I can taste the dusty brown dirt.

Back inside, I run into a developer from Mexico who is also attending the conference. He is contemplating bringing age-segregated housing across the border—but for American expatriates in Baja. A lot of Mexican families tend to live together as a matter of tradition and economic necessity, he explains. "I don't think this housing would be very popular with my own people."

Pebble Creek, the next community we visit, outside the town of Goodyear, is decidedly more upscale. Gushing fountains and impeccably green lawns greet us as we drive down the long entrance driveway. The developer expects to build out to 6,250 homes on 2,400 acres. The statistics are similar to those for Sundance, with the exception of the average preretirement income, which is around $200,000. More than half of the residents are still employed in some capacity; many commute to Phoenix during the day and relax at night in their gated resort community. Pebble Creek aims a certain portion of its properties (necessarily less than twenty percent, so as to remain legally age-segregated) at people over forty. Of the dozen or so floor plans, one has a second floor. With two luxurious club-houses with a combined total of nearly 100,000 square feet, Pebble Creek is clearly designed for those who have "arrived." The $1,200 annual amenity fee is about triple that of Sun City.

The caravan stops outside the larger of the two clubhouses, named Tuscany Falls. Inside, a gas fireplace big enough to swing a cat in greets visitors. The fireplace mantel is ten feet off the ground and about the length of a small room. Around the corner in one direction is a large, attractive theater with rows of plush seats descending toward a stage.

Nearby, I find a handsomely appointed library with 1,000 or so books. I browse the collection and find *The Life and Works of Lord Byron, The Writings of Jonathan Swift,* and a book about Italian Renaissance painters. I'm impressed by the worldly and eclectic nature of the collection. Because I am an occasional fan of the romantics, I reach over and select the works of Byron. When I pull on the spine, the whole row of books pops out and falls to the floor with the gentle bounce of weightless Styrofoam. Curious, I reach for another book. It's handsomely bound in real leather and contains actual printed pages. Regretfully, it is written in Swedish.

A developer with a background in carpentry inspects the construction of the lounge next door. The giant antique wooden beams are actually a combination of embossed plastic and stained pine, he concludes. He then walks over to an entryway to inspect the doors and quickly announces his verdict: "The only way you could make a more flimsy door is to use love beads." He steps over to the bar. "Now, that's a nice piece of granite. They saved the quality material for the stuff you can actually touch and feel." He points to the shelves behind the bar, which have an eighth-inch veneer of oak over plywood. "I guess you could say the veneer's 'authentic,'" he concludes.

I ask an Australian who was on the bus with me if age-segregated communities are popular in his part of the world. "They're growing in popularity," he says. "Our cultures are actually very similar, except we don't do all this fantasyland in the middle of the desert sort of thing. You Americans like everything to be fake."

Next we drive to our third and final destination, Corte Bella, which is across the street from Sun City West and is one of the Del Webb Corporation's newest offerings—an "active adult country club community" for the affluent. Someone on the bus tells me that the company didn't know what else to do with this remote property. It takes several miles of driving down an awkward access road, which skirts Sun City West on one side and a flood wash on the other, just to get to the front gate.

Inside, there are three ritzy clubhouses: one for fitness, one for socializing, and one for golfers. There's no hint of shuffleboard or horseshoes, but there are plenty of tennis courts. The literature states that Corte Bella is designed in a "Santa Barbara style," and that the housing development is "How a Country Club Should Feel . . . downright friendly, a quality you don't often find at country clubs. You will at this one, the country club where everyone belongs."

With just one country club restaurant and no retailers other than a small pro shop, I can't help wondering what the residents do all day in this exclusive wonderland. The marketing material seemingly anticipates my hesitation: "Every second of your day counts. That doesn't mean you have to fill them all up."

We leave the clubhouse and explore a street of large, richly appointed model homes. The neighborhood is eerily silent, except for cheery music piped out of rocks placed beside cacti. Several homes have exercise rooms, which are really just bedrooms outfitted with treadmills and stationary bikes. These luxuries strike me as yet another way to isolate oneself—even from immediate neighbors.

One model home forgoes the exercise equipment, opting instead to deck out the small guest room for a hypothetical homecoming. There's a chalkboard with "Welcome Home, Boys!" in big, enthusiastic lettering, and twin beds pushed against the wall with cheerful signs above that say "Mike" and "Chris." There's an assortment of college pennants, as well as a baseball mitt and a football. This room is slightly larger than the second walk-in closet in the master bedroom at the other end of the house.

I run into two bankers from Switzerland looking for investment opportunities. "I don't see how this could work in Europe," one of them tells me. "Europeans want to be close to a city, drinking the culture. Here the residents are in the middle of nowhere."

His partner, Dietrich, agrees. "Why would anyone over fifty-five want to live in an environment without people of all ages?" he asks. "Family life is still important in Europe. I don't understand this attraction to age restriction. It's a bit of a ghetto, no?"

Even if the concept were popular in Europe, there are too many other hurdles, Dietrich adds. "We don't have this kind of cheap empty desert to build on, and our land-use policies are much more restrictive. And these homes; they're so cheaply built, like they would never stand up to the weather. We couldn't get away with that, either. The costs for a European version would be prohibitive."

Later that afternoon, I wander around the conference's exposition room, which is filled with dozens of vendors and hundreds of attendees. The booths run the gamut from architects who specialize in age-segregated housing to people who sell handicap-accessible bathroom fixtures and others who analyze market data ("We help you capture boomers"). Much of the networking takes place in front of several seafood buffets and adjoining makeshift bars used to celebrate the opening of the conference. The majority of attendees are small regional builders who, as one industry expert tells me, know how to build houses but not communities. They are here to learn from the bigger players in the age-segregated marketplace.

"Active adult" housing is the fastest-growing sector of the housing market, and these folks want to know how they can grab a piece of the pie. The Homebuilders Association formed the 50+ Housing Council about six years ago. It was originally named the Seniors Housing Council; but boomers don't identify with, or particularly like, the term "senior"—hence the name change. About thirty developers attended the first conference; this year there are more than 800.

American municipalities are as eager to attract age-segregated housing complexes as developers are eager to build them. States, counties, and cities are competing fiercely for retirees. Zoning laws are hastily being amended and density restrictions lifted in a bid to attract age-segregated housing. Why? Although families with children generally consume more, many of today's seniors nonetheless have plenty of money to spend. A good number of Villagers, for example, outfit their new homes with all new furnishings, electronics, and appliances. They're like free-spending tourists who bring their life savings with them and never leave.

And retirees generally don't commit crimes, so they are less of a burden on police services; they tend not to drive as much, so they put less stress on a town's roads; and their housing developments usually care for their own landscaping, reducing hassles for the public works department.

Best of all, they don't use the schools. Any municipal accountant will tell you that residential housing generally loses money because schooling kids costs a lot of money and local property taxes don't come close to bringing in enough revenue. That's why most municipalities bend over backward to attract businesses: a business pays a lot in taxes but doesn't burden the system with more children. Seniors can be viewed in much the same light.

The next morning, the man introducing the conference's keynote speaker revs up the audience with some pleasing statistics. "The elderly are the fastest-growing segment today," he says. "For the next twenty years, boomers will be turning into seniors at the rate of 10,000 a day. In ten years alone, they will represent nearly 80 million consumers. And in a few short years, half of all American housing will be owned by someone over fifty." One can almost hear a cash register going cha-ching.

Next up is the keynote speaker, a renowned expert in generational marketing. His presentation is unusually entertaining, but also sobering. Marketing to the new crop of seniors will be anything but easy, he says, and he suggests that the communities we visited yesterday on the bus tour will soon be "dinosaurs."

The audience is silent; some of the listeners look perplexed and deflated. Nobody can predict exactly what the baby boomers will want, but what they won't want is another Sun City, he says, adding that his research shows that boomers don't like giant "one size fits all" planned communities. "They're used to specialized services and products that meet their unique needs and convictions," he continues. "And most of them don't want to move far away from their families or live in the sunbelt. They want a more 'authentic' lifestyle experience."

In broad strokes, he relates the following attributes about the boomers and the vastly different generations that preceded them.

Members of the "GI generation" (born 1901–1924) and the "silent (or Eisenhower) generation" (1925–1942) generally didn't question authority but rather obeyed it. They held low-risk jobs that supplied steady paychecks. Retirement for them represented an opportunity to finally take it easy and relax after a lifetime of toil. They prefer group activities to individual pursuits. They like communal hobbies; and when they travel, they often do so in large groups. These are the folks who have enthusiastically populated retirement communities modeled on Sun City.

By comparison, he continues, the boomers are risk takers searching for purpose. Whereas Sun Citians flocked to hear Lawrence Welk perform old favorites at the Sun Bowl, boomers were camped out in the rain at Woodstock listening to Jimi Hendrix reinterpret "The Star-Spangled Banner." They're the generation of LSD, the Pill, Watergate, and protests against the Vietnam War. "They are active, adventurous, and individualistic, and you're more likely to find them mountain biking, surfing, and sipping espresso at sixty-five than playing shuffleboard, clog-hopping, and square dancing.

Given their penchant for rebellion, he says, boomers are unlikely to embrace their parents' vision of retirement, just as they rejected their parents' definition of adolescence. They don't like rules, let alone the sorts of rules and regulations that rigidly define acceptable behavior at a planned retirement community like Sun City.

He continues: The vast majority of boomers (some surveys indicate seventy-five percent) don't plan on retiring. Many find meaning ("a mission") in their work; others haven't saved up enough for retirement, preferring to earn and spend as they go. Others are fearful that they will be financially sandwiched between paying for their children's education and paying for their aging parents' medical bills. After a decade or two of fun in the sun, many retirees return home to rely on their boomer children to help care for them as their health fails.

Perhaps most important, boomers have no intention of growing older. Boomers typically list eighty-five as the age when they will finally consider themselves "old." Not surprisingly, that's two years longer than actuaries predict many of them will live. They may just get their wish after all, the speaker says.

Anyone who thinks that they can put up a cookie-cutter age-restricted community and walk away with a tidy profit is kidding himself, the presenter cautions. "The future of boomer retirement housing is wholly uncharted and full of potential pitfalls," he says, "but we had better be ready, because the surge of boomers is just around the corner."

The speaker ends his presentation with a question: How many people in the audience are baby boomers? The auditorium is a sea of raised hands.

I see a lot of stunned attendees stumble out of the auditorium into the painfully bright Arizona sunshine. "Wow, it's a lot more complicated than I thought," I hear one woman say. "I thought I knew my market," another woman remarks. "Now I have to rethink my niche."

I happen upon the Australian from yesterday's bus tour. "You got to wonder what's going to happen to all these giant Club Med–like communities that don't appeal to boomers," he says.

Looking for answers, I approach an architect from Washington, D.C., named Neal, whom I met at the exposition. "Look, I'm fifty-three, but I feel like eighteen," he tells me. "I have lots of energy and I'm just figuring things out. I play tennis with my friends and Rollerblade with my daughter. You can't tell a boomer like me that a place like Sun City is a place that I will want to retire to. I live three blocks from the National Gallery, one block from the metro; Kennedy Center is just down the street. And I'm going to keep on working. I *like* what I do. I like the challenge. It's rewarding. I'm going to age my own way—and at home. This is what makes sense to me."

The crowd soon splits up as people make their way to a variety of seminars. By early afternoon, the shock of the morning's presentation appears to be subsiding, and the participants I speak with tell me that they are feeling a bit more grounded. They remain confident that age-restricted housing will continue to be the hottest housing sector for years to come, for a number of reasons.

Boomers may say they don't like today's age-segregated housing, but who can be sure they'll stay true to these convictions in fifteen years? It's a generation full of contradictions. Many boomers took drugs to think outside the box, but now give their kids Ritalin to ensure that the kids remain inside it. Women who once burned their bras now pay handsomely for expensive brassieres and plastic surgery. Many of the folks who ran around naked at Woodstock ended up espousing traditional family values and voting for Ronald Reagan. Other boomers never rebelled to begin with and don't fit into these stereotypes.

The fact is that nobody knows what the boomers want. They're like a tsunami (some call it an "age wave") rolling over the housing industry; and trying to predict what they will want is like trying to predict the weather twenty years from now. There is no magic formula: the boomers are simply too diverse and too hard to pin down.

But given their staggering numbers, even if a development appeals to only a small minority, that market segment can still represent several million people and billions of dollars. As one attendee told me, "People are always asking me what they should build for the boomers. I tell them, 'Everything.' There are enough boomers to support just about any business model."

How many boomers will opt for age-segregated housing is anybody's guess. One implausibly optimistic consultant at the conference suggests that seventy percent of boomers will seek a life secluded from children. Another study proposes that fifty percent will opt for such housing. Others consider the gold standard to be Del Webb's research, which suggests that twenty-five percent of boomers will actively seek age-segregated housing. A more conservative estimate of fifteen percent is also bandied about, but even that low figure still represents 12 million Boomers—or at least one in twenty-five Americans.

If Sun City is to be shunned, then just what will these communities look like? Research indicates that the vast majority of boomers are emotionally closer to their children than previous generations, and consequently, they don't want to move more than 150 miles from them, or move to another state. And with so many expected to continue working, employment is another factor in choosing a locale.

Rather than expecting boomers to relocate to leisurevilles, developers are bringing Sun Cities to them, albeit on a much smaller scale. In 1995, nearly eighty percent of all age-segregated communities were built in the traditional sunbelt. Ten years later, sixty percent of them are located in northern states, such as Michigan and Massachusetts. This trend is accelerating, even though there are many challenges associated with constructing Sun Cities near Chicago or New York City: a dearth of large tracts of land; the high cost of whatever dirt remains; and more restrictive zoning.

Consequently, age-segregated communities are shrinking in size, and often include attached townhouses and apartments. Whereas the original Sun City has upwards of 40,000 residents, newer communities generally have fewer than 1,000. That figure is down from an average of about 3,500 just a decade ago. But by most estimates, boomers who opt for age-segregated housing prefer smaller, more intimate communities anyway.

This means that children will probably live nearby, but gates and age-segregation policies will keep them from intruding onto the grounds of these smaller housing projects. Active adults can thus venture into the age-integrated "melting pot" for work, shopping, and other activities, but breathe a sigh of relief at day's end when they then return home and the security gates close tightly behind them.

A sizable number of boomers also like city life. That is why developers of age-segregated housing are turning their attention to urban "infill" projects, such as converting old hotels and office buildings into age-segregated luxury lofts, with elevators, shared gym facilities, and concierge services. These apartment buildings become child-free zones in the midst of a bustling cityscape, much like the smaller age-segregated housing units near traditional suburban housing and strip malls.

But if the trend is to live closer to home in more "authentic" communities, then why bother moving to an age-segregated community at all? Why not just stay put in a traditional neighborhood?

The answer is the amenities. People want swimming pools, tennis courts, and clubhouses; and traditional housing developments typically don't offer such perks. Boomers also want low- or no-maintenance housing. They don't want to mow, plow, or paint. They want a place where they can lock the door and leave for a month. And when they're not traveling, they want to be able to come home after work to a peaceful child-free resort community where friendships with peers are easy to form. Some want a childless environment; others put up with it to reap the other benefits. But they all want an easier, more convenient way of life.

Amenities can come in many flavors. Easy access to Manhattan can be considered an amenity; so can access to walking trails, medical facilities, a college offering special classes, an outlet mall, or for that matter the Atlantic Ocean. Golf courses are expensive to build and maintain, and they take up valuable real estate. By comparison, train service for easy access to museums and the symphony doesn't cost residents a dime in monthly maintenance fees.

The nation's housing developers are betting heavily on these strategies. Pulte's Del Webb division has been building age-segregated housing at the rate of 25,000 units a year. It already has more than 100 communities in various stages of planning and construction in fifty-two real estate markets scattered across the country, most of them near large metropolitan centers outside the traditional sunbelt.

"All we know is that our business keeps growing year after year," one of Del Webb's top executives tells me. "It's a demographics-driven business and the floodgates are about to open. I like the odds."

The trick, I realize, is to seduce aging boomers into believing that they need to move to an age-segregated community. To learn how, I attend an afternoon seminar about selling and marketing these communities. A grizzled veteran of the industry named Bill, and his more reserved colleague, don't mince words.

"The biggest challenge is getting folks to move at all," Bill says. "These folks don't need a new house. Our job is to convince them that they *want* a new house. It's a matter of upping what I call the 'hate factor'—getting them to resent their current home enough to motivate them to pack up and clean out forty years of junk.

"We have to create the image that their current house is 'old,' that too many things need fixing, like the plumbing and electrical work. Let them know how much an electrician costs today. Ask them if they really want to keep mowing their own lawn. Why cut grass when you can play golf?"

His colleague cuts in. "You reach a point when you want to get rid of all the men in your life," she says. "The plumber, the pool man, the lawn man. People want a house without maintenance issues."

Bill continues, "Are they going to go through all the expense and trouble to remodel an old house from the 1970s, or are they going to buy a new house where they can have it all and more?" Bill continues. "Granite countertops, stainless-steel appliances, high ceilings, Jacuzzi tubs—they see their friends with them, even their adult kids, and they want them too. This is their chance to loosen control and buy whatever they've always wanted but couldn't afford, because they were too busy paying for their kids' braces and school. Walk them through your design center. Tell them they won't need the expense of an interior decorator, because the builder will do everything for them. You're selling them a lifestyle—and this is where it begins."

Many new homes are coming with "universal design" features that help people preserve mobility and dignity as their health declines, Bill explains. Wider hallways, floor lighting, showers without steps, and first-floor master suites: these all make aging in place more convenient. "But for God's sake, don't mention aging in place!" Bill warns. "Tell them that it'll make life easier when their parents visit. Nobody wants to be reminded that his or her body is deteriorating. Call them 'lifestyle features' for 'easy living.' Speak of them as 'luxury' components and 'upgrades.'

"The words you use are important," Bill continues. "Don't call your development 'age-restricted,' 'senior,' or even 'retirement' housing. That's a no-no in our business. These folks aren't seniors, and they're not retired either."

Bill's not thrilled with the other recent euphemisms either—active adult, fifty-five plus, fifty-five and better—but if push comes to shove, "make sure you at least say age-*qualified* instead of age-restricted. The fact is, I don't like any of this emphasis on age or restrictions. We're selling an *ageless* lifestyle, and the lifestyle should be the tagline. Fifty-five-plus? It'll be gone in three years. You won't hear it again." Peel away all the distracting fancy terms and it still looks like bigotry to me, but "age segregation" is a term I cautiously avoid among boosters.

"But why would someone choose 'age-qualified' housing in particular?" I ask. "Why wouldn't people choose a regular community with amenities?"

"They like seeing kids play—they like seeing happiness," Bill responds. "But what they don't like is kids on top of them. They don't want somebody else's grandkids peeing in the pool. Kids can be messy."

Bill returns to his marketing presentation. "When it comes to publicizing a future community, make each construction milestone an event worthy of a party. This demographic loves to party. They've been partying all their lives. Make the groundbreaking an event. Make the completion of the first model homes an event. Show them a house being framed. Take them on a 'muddy-shoe tour.' And make sure you create a sense of urgency. There's no better way to do that than increasing the price a notch."

Given all the talk of boomers demanding flexible housing options and flexible communities, a branch of housing called the continuing care retirement community (CCRC) takes a hit at the conference.

The CCRCs offer several housing alternatives that represent a progression of care. As people age, they can move from independent-living housing to assisted-living quarters or to a traditional nursing home environment. It's the ultimate in one-stop shopping for the inevitable. But whereas previous generations may be interested in such prudent predictability, boomers will supposedly scorn such attempts at easy surrender.

A feisty Texan in her mid-twenties tells me she is having none of this marketing nonsense. She manages a CCRC for her father, and over lunch she shakes her head at all these fancy consultants and their prognostications about the next generation.

"Look, people are getting older every day and they can't help it," she says. "Boomers might *think* they know what they want—until they trip and fall and break a hip. It's a fact of life. There's no pill or cream out there that's going to keep them from aging."

She points to the several hundred conference participants attending the luncheon. "All these people, they're not going to move into an active adult community. They're still working and traveling. They've got kids, and so do their peers. They're going to keep working and living at home. If they have enough money, they may move to where their kids are.

"Who are all these folks building active adult communities for? I don't know. If you ask *them* if they're going to move into an active adult community, you're going to hear a hesitant 'yes' and then an honest 'no.' The older senior is the one who's moving, not the younger one, and they don't want some big new house. My ninety-year-old resident doesn't want a home; she wants to rent an apartment. And where else is an older couple going to go when one of them is sick? This way, they can always live near one another.

"I'm like Wal-Mart: I want the masses. Our facility is completely full. We don't have any models to show people, because we

sold them all. We have a waiting list for 510 units, and all I'm showing people are copies of floor plans I made at Kinko's. We don't market and we don't advertise.

"Time's on our side; they'll come to us eventually. And once
they do, they just move around our campus, like on a Monopoly
board. Best part is—we own the land and the hotels."

Before I fly out, I spend the day with a good friend, Stuart, at his
"amenity-rich" apartment complex, located in a dusty and otherwise undeveloped "neighborhood" in nearby Tempe. The closest
neighbor is a Starbucks several blocks up a multilane avenue without a sidewalk. To get to Stuart's apartment, I have to pass through
two sets of gates before I reach his locked front door.

Once I am there, he walks me down to the pool and hot tub
for a dip. There's a sizable workout room with high-end equipment,
as well as a small theater. There are rules posted everywhere governing behavior.

"I could have lived in a more traditional so-called 'neighborhood,'" Stuart tells me. "But this is so convenient. There are
so many amenities. I never have to leave." My friend is in his late
thirties.

Interestingly, neither of us had ever heard the word "amenities" while we were growing up, at least not in this context. It was
never a buzzword. At best, the term was a euphemism for a collection of public toilets.

The pool is inundated with attractive and scantily clad college
kids who have chosen to live off campus. They're running around,
yelling, and generally annoying me on my day off. Worse yet, I feel
dumpy in comparison with their sleek bodies. I turn to my friend:
"Don't you think it'd be a lot nicer if everyone at the pool were over
thirty? It'd be a lot quieter and we'd all probably have a whole lot
more in common."

Stuart mulls this over and glances at the half-naked coeds splashing in the pool. "You've been in Florida *far* too long," he says.

With a head full of prognostications about the boomers, I head back to The Villages for a reality check. Naturally, my first stop is The Villages' Baby Boomer Club, which happens to be giving a sock hop in one of the recreation centers.

The room is filled with young retirees alternating between the dance floor and a make-your-own sundae station. Most of the women have tied their hair up in playful ponytails and wear their jeans rolled halfway up their calves, revealing brightly colored socks and sneakers. Their clean-cut husbands, dressed in patterned short-sleeved button-downs and cardigans, more closely resemble Richie Cunningham from *Happy Days* than they do Marlon Brando.

A banner with the group's logo hangs from a wall. It shows the word "Boomer" surrounded by a jagged circle exploding with energy. The industry experts in Phoenix tell me the boomers won't gravitate toward plantation-size retirement communities in the middle of nowhere, but the Boomers Club is already one of the biggest at The Villages.

The music alternates between favorites from the 1950s and rock standards like Lynyrd Skynyrd's hard-driving "Sweet Home Alabama." At some point the disc jockey plays the Rolling Stones' "Brown Sugar" and many of the boomers jump excitedly into neat rows and start line-dancing to Mick Jagger's lusty portrayal of sexually exploited African-American slave girls.

I introduce myself to a man so well groomed that he resembles Pat Boone. His name is Craig, and he's campaigning to be the club's next vice president. The music is too loud for us to carry on a conversation, so we step into the hallway. I ask him what it's like to live in The Villages as a younger retiree.

"People are always asking me if I'm old enough to live in The Villages," Craig tells me. "It's fun not to be the old guy anymore. Back home I was always cast in musicals as the king or the father figure. Here I can be the kid in the group. I'm only fifty-six, but I knew the time was right to settle somewhere like this. And I'm not alone; my age group is starting to arrive. It's very exciting. I can't wait to invite them to our boomer bowling nights and pool parties. I could sit here all day and list all the fun things we do."

Craig's wife finds us in the hallway. The dance is over, and she's visibly upset. "Gosh, I'd better go," he tells me. His wife's frown remains. "We've already missed the last dance," she says, walking away.

Back inside, I walk up to the disc jockey as he packs his equipment away. "I'm the music guy," he says by way of introduction. "I DJ parties, and there are a lot of parties down here. Seems like there's one every day. I have more friends here than I've had all my life. People are always dropping by my house out of the blue. They just drive on over in their golf carts, and before you know it, it's a party. We like to say that parties 'break out' in our neighborhood." He pushes his bifocals farther up his nose.

"The boomers are coming down here in droves just like everyone else. This place is growing like hotcakes. If they have a house available, they call you from a waiting list and give you three hours to decide. Pretty soon The Villages is going to be the fifty-first state."

The growing age gap between Villagers becomes clearer to me as I drop in on a few more activities. The next day I'm intrigued by a listing for a club with the unusual name "Harmonitones." I arrive to find a dozen retirees sitting in a semicircle, blowing into different-sized harmonicas. Hearing aids abound, and one guy is attached to an oxygen tank. A bandleader taps his baton and leads them in "Moonlight and Roses," and then "It's a Small World" and "Fly Me to the Moon."

I am reminded of my first-grade recorder class, where we used to play "Hot Cross Buns" in unison. As with us, there are no Bob Dylans here yet, but the group is still proud of its progress. "That's good stuff!" the man with the oxygen tank says after club members play "Hello, Dolly." "Did that bring back any memories?" the bandleader asks. "Heck, let's play that one again!"

Next, it's "Sentimental Journey." Between takes, a guy in a Yankees cap complains that he'd play better if his wife would just let him practice in the house. The other men nod in agreement. The bandleader smiles and gently taps his baton. "What do you say we give the 'Pennsylvania Polka' another try?"

In a nearby room a group of Villagers are learning to line dance. The instructor calls out the steps. "OK. Rock step, coaster step, turn hold and heel, point, point, sailor shuffle, sailor shuffle, sway, sway, cross-turn counter-step."

That night, I head over to the Bistro, a new hangout a few blocks down from Katie Belle's. I arrive to find Mr. Midnight's foul-mouthed friend Frank sitting on a stool nursing a beer. His eyes are bloodshot. "I just got back from a cruise," he says. "It didn't feel any different. The only thing that changed was the location. I'm not even sure why I went. We *live* on a fucking cruise ship."

Frank asks me what I learned in Phoenix. I tell him about the experts' dim outlook for the future of mega-developments like The Villages.

A boisterous Brit joins the conversation uninvited. "Poppycock," he says. "I've traveled the whole world and this is the best place in it! I just turned sixty and everyone like me is going to move here."

Frank can't resist. "Hey, Andy," he says to me. "Why'd ya bother flying to Phoenix to listen to a bunch of experts when you got an opinionated asshole right here?"

13

An Idiot's Farewell

MR. MIDNIGHT GRACIOUSLY INVITES ME TO SPEND MY LAST WEEK AT his den of iniquity in order to, as he says, "live the life." Intrigued, I accept, and trade the dependable comforts of Dave and Betsy's place for the vagaries of bachelor living.

To further get into the swing of things, I finally rent a golf cart at a dealership in downtown Sumter Landing. I've resisted renting one until now because my travels have frequently taken me beyond the borders of Gary Morse's "golf cart nation." But according to a state transportation study, as many as ninety percent of all daily trips made by Villagers remain within The Villages—and that doesn't even take golf carts into account. If it did, the number would be closer to ninety-nine percent. It's not unusual for Villagers to go weeks without leaving their all-inclusive community.

After looking around the glitzy showroom, I choose a worn rental in a dull shade of cream from the back parking lot. It's the sort of clunker you'd expect to see on a public golf course, and it even comes with a clip on the steering wheel for a scorecard and two stubby pencils. My humble ride is a far cry from the pimped-out leisure chariots with their supersize aluminum wheels, chrome grills, and burled dashboards that I see many seniors tooling around in.

Golf carts were introduced on a grand scale in the early 1950s. Lazy golfers immersed in a car-crazed culture weren't the only reason. Golf carts sped up the game so that more paying customers could be cycled through a golf course. Perhaps it was the introduction of the Pope-Mobile or the Queen Mum's royal golf cart that spurred interest in taking golf carts off the golf course. They are now ubiquitous in many gated communities. The Villages' own golf cart dealership, which displays its models just like automobiles, sells a few thousand golf carts a year. There are several private dealerships off campus that seem to be doing a swift business as well. The vast majority of Villagers own a golf cart in addition to a car and many homes even have separate five-eighths-scale mini-garages to house them. It's not the fastest means of travel, but when you live in a retirement community, what's the rush?

Half an hour and many miles later, I pull into the driveway with the Playboy bunny ears. Mr. Midnight shows me to my room, a tiny but pleasant sunporch with a leaky inflatable mattress. His friend Harry is also visiting this week, he tells me; otherwise, I'd be staying in the formal guest room. He hands me several clean towels and tells me I can use the bathroom in the hallway.

On the bathroom counter are all sorts of hotel-sized soaps and shampoos as well as a sign that instructs guests to ring the front desk if they have any additional requests. Like Betsy, Mr. Midnight also has Mardi Gras beads on display; his hang from the showerhead. When I ask him how the celebration compares with the real thing, Mr. Midnight says there's one distinct difference: "Here we give the ladies beads for *not* showing us their breasts."

When Mr. Midnight sees my golf cart, he asks me how it runs. "I don't think the rentals go too fast," he says, putting on his sunglasses and adjusting his flip-flops. I challenge him to a drag race. We line up at the edge of the driveway and Mr. Midnight counts to three. Sensing trouble, I lead-foot it on "two."

My cart accelerates smoothly at first, but then the engine hesitates as if to say, "Hey, not so fast, buddy." As we careen around the block, Mr. Midnight keeps gaining on me. I gun the engine, swerve to and fro, and try to cut him off on a tight turn. But it's hopeless; Mr. Midnight wins by more than three cart-lengths.

"Don't worry about it," he says. "I must have had the wind on my back."

I hop into his cart, and we drive to a nearby pool. Along the way we see an ambulance speed by with lights flashing. "Looks like another tee time has opened up," Mr. Midnight says.

We make a quick pit stop at the neighborhood mailbox gazebo. "I have to pick up my Viagra," he says, and soon returns with a brown package. "It's not that I need it, mind you. It's an enhancement, like whipped cream and nuts on a sundae. If it's a special night, I might take 100 milligrams. If it's one of my regular honeys, I'll probably pop a fifty. Friendship only goes so far."

When we arrive at the pool, Mr. Midnight pauses and carefully scans the crowd, which is mostly female. "Not bad," he says. "Not bad at all." Despite copious warnings, Mr. Midnight is addicted to sunbathing. He sprawls out on a lounge chair and scoffs at the mention of sunscreen. He then glances through his mail, which contains his financial statements.

"I'm not greedy," he says, putting his mail away. "All I care about is getting my money's worth. I mean, look at all we have here." He points to a collection of shapely younger visitors sitting along the pool's edge, their long legs dangling lazily in the water. He sighs, and readjusts himself on the lounge chair.

I ask him if he wants to read the newspaper after I'm finished with it. "Nah," he says. "The news doesn't really interest me. I guess I wish the world was a better place, but I somehow feel distant from it."

Early in the evening, we head to the Bistro in Spanish Springs and sidle up to the bar. I spot an older couple dancing slowly in a tight embrace. "That's 'the Prosecutor' with his new girl, Holly,"

Mr. Midnight explains. "He's in love. I've never seen the guy so happy. It's like he's a new man. You can't pry those two apart. It's truly sad, but it's a fact: for some people life is better when they're in love."

An hour or so later, I head out back, behind the bar's small patio, where all the guys go to pee. The bar has only one toilet for men, and few can hold their bladder long enough for the wait. Frankly, after a few beers, I can't either.

When I emerge from the bushes a few moments later, I'm embarrassed to find a couple sitting down at a nearby table and toasting themselves with glasses of wine. It's the ebullient Prosecutor and his attractive new girlfriend.

When he sees my notebook, he waves me over and introduces me to Holly. His smile is so genial, and his red Hawaiian shirt so casual, that I wonder how he got such a belligerent nickname. "This is the most remarkable woman I've met in the six decades of my life," he tells me warmly. "I never thought I'd find someone like her. You can write that down!"

He points to Holly's lantern-lit shadow on the outdoor wall. "Look at that profile. Isn't it the most stunning thing you've ever seen?" Holly blushes and takes another sip of wine. "I thought it was too late for me," the Prosecutor continues. "But something continues to burn within the human breast."

A man walks outside and catches the tail end of the Prosecutor's pleasing homily. He lights up a cigarette, and then flashes a kindly smile at the doting couple. "Ain't love swell?" he says.

"You're a smoker," the Prosecutor snaps back. "Obviously you don't have any love; at least not for yourself."

I look at Holly, and then at the man with the cigarette. We're all too stunned to say much. The man awkwardly extinguishes his cigarette and hastily walks back inside.

"You see, we know what love is," the Prosecutor continues. "We're *in* love." He takes a sip of wine and slowly savors it. "This place can be a real meat market, but Holly is different from the rest. She understands that real love is different, and that women must be subservient to men, because that's the way God intended it to be. That should be the first question a man asks in any relationship: 'Will you respect me as your leader?' Every ship needs a captain."

Holly looks at me and clears her throat. "I think there can be more than one approach," she manages.

"Sounds a bit like a dictatorship," I blurt out.

"That's because it is," the Prosecutor responds. "Men are meant to lead and women are meant to follow. That's what it says in the Bible. Or haven't you read it?" He takes another sip of wine. "Are you married? If you are, your marriage won't survive. I can guarantee that. But I'm here to tell you that you can find love again, even at my age."

I excuse myself and walk back inside, where I recount my bizarre encounter to Mr. Midnight. "Why don't you ask the Prosecutor whether he goes down on Holly," he advises. "Tell him you're writing a book and you're looking for the one guy in The Villages who refused to pleasure a woman. That son of a bitch is one squeamish lover. As for Holly, I could help her get over the heartbreak."

I leave the bar early, and hurry down to Sumter Landing in my golf cart to catch the last showing of the remake of *King Kong*. The theater, despite its enormous screen and stadium seating, is crowded, so I pick a seat high up in the back row. After the movie, I stick around for the screen credits to gather my thoughts, and ponder the sad fate of the colossal gorilla. When I finally stand up to leave, the lights are on and theater is empty.

As I exit the row, I'm surprised to see that the wall behind me isn't really the curtained panel I distinctly remember when I first sat down, but rather a two-way mirror concealing a luxury skybox. The lights are on inside and I spot an older man with white hair surrounded by what I assume to be grandchildren. For a short moment our eyes lock and I feel goose bumps form on the back of my neck: I'm staring at the elusive Gary Morse and he's staring right back at me through half an inch of soundproof glass.

Can this really be happening? I stand there like an idiot, my face close enough to the glass for my breath to leave a circle of moisture. Should I knock on the window and wave hello? I've fantasized for weeks about interviewing Morse, but not like this. This is too weird. Frankly, I'd given up on ever meeting him. I had located Morse's private home, his eating club, and even his airplane hanger, but I never caught a glimpse of him.

Did he know I was digging around in his business? Was he keeping tabs on me? Given his abundant wealth, did he even care? Apparently not: Morse quickly loses interest in my gaze and exits through a door leading to a hidden corridor, trailed by a small coterie of rambunctious children.

I rush outside. It's after 11 PM, and Sumter Landing is deserted. The only sound I hear is Frank Sinatra's "Fly Me to the Moon" merrily wafting from the lampposts to an audience of one—me. I figure that Morse must have a hidden exit, so I run to the back of the building where the dumpsters are located. I find nothing but unmarked doors, all of which are locked. I wait a few moments and run back to the marquee. Ten minutes later, there is still no sign of Morse.

I jog down the street and look for signs of life at Morse's private eating club, which, unbeknownst to residents, is hidden above a popular Italian restaurant. I run up an unmarked staircase at the back, only to find the club door locked and its windows dark. Resigned, I walk back to my golf cart, but I soon notice, across the parking lot, a lone SUV with its lights on, idling. Curious, I walk toward it. The driver puts the car in gear and slowly drives off. I watch the red taillights grow smaller as the SUV heads toward the big white spot in middle of the map.

I'm left wondering what I might have asked him, if given the chance. In some ways, Lester is right—the story of The Villages' is really about the residents: why they've chosen to live here, and what they make of it. But Morse is the one who created this kingdom of leisure that will one day be home to 110,000 retirees. Is the wizard pleased with his creation? Does he have second thoughts about his impact on the region, let alone the end result of the lifestyle he is selling? And why does he keep such a tight rein over his residents and the region as a whole? Does he consider such measures necessary to protect his investment? Or is he simply monopolizing local politics and the media because he can? After all, The Villages isn't a charity; it's a business. If there's one thing I feel reasonably certain about Morse, it's this: he has an uncanny ability to provide people with what they want, and make a fortune doing so.

I toss on a sweater and drive my cart back to the house with the bunny ears. Mr. Midnight is still out, most likely at Crazy Gringos with the usual suspects. I sit down at his computer to check my e-mail, but I'm distracted by an instant message query in the form of a purple and pink cat with long lashes winking repeatedly in the middle of the screen. "Hey, Mr. Midnight. Are you there? My kitty's purring for you."

A few days later, the ground collapses beneath a house in the Andersons' village, while a utility company is digging in the area. The collapse causes the house to shift dramatically, and a gas line springs a leak. There's no explosion, but the place looks like a disaster zone. The flashing emergency lights and yellow crime scene tape look acutely out of place. Neighbors do their best to simply ignore the mess as they go about their daily business. When I ask Dave about the sinkhole, he expresses little concern. "I'm sure they'll patch it up soon enough," he says.

The lead story in the next day's *Daily Sun* is decidedly upbeat: "Study Reveals People Living Longer." Farther down the page is a short article addressing the neighborhood calamity. The reporter extensively quotes a utility foreman on the job, who explains in excruciatingly technical detail how his crew executed the dig to exacting standards consistent with industry regulations.

I read the story two more times, but still can't figure out what happened. Nowhere in the article is it explained how or why the ground collapsed. I recognize the byline; it's by Kim, the reporter I met at The Villages' government orientation class. I call her cell phone.

"It was a spontaneous sinkhole," Kim tells me flatly. "It had nothing to do with the digging. I tried putting it in the story, but my editor deleted it. When I complained, he told me to stop bulldogging the story. The Villages doesn't want to admit sinkholes exist, because they're related to the aquifer, and that scares them. So, we're not allowed to mention them."

By now, my own "Village vision" dims my concern over the incident and its outrageous yet predictable manipulation. I'll be leaving shortly, and after weeks of hustling around from morning to night, I want to relax and try *living* like a Villager.

And so here I am. The sun is shining, the gentle breeze smells sweet, and I have a golf cart to tool around in. If the sinkhole doesn't affect me directly, then why should I care? I have my own concerns back home to worry about. Sinkholes aside, life in The Villages is relaxing, pleasant, and comfortably predictable. I spend my last days lounging at the pool with Mr. Midnight, going to the movies with Sassy, and lingering over lunches at outdoor tables in sun-splashed Spanish Springs.

Waking up on the little sunporch, I face few bigger decisions than which friend to visit during the day and where to go out at night. Sometimes, the decision isn't even that difficult—friends often come calling at Mr. Midnight's. It's not unusual to wake up from a lunchtime nap and see a caravan of golf carts turning into the driveway.

"Hey, is Midnight around?" a friend named Danny shouts across the yard one day. He's wearing an open shirt, a big floppy straw hat, and a stripe of zinc oxide down his sunburned nose. His attractive young wife sits beside him and waves pleasantly. Another three friends pop open beers and wait in a second golf cart decked out to look like a fire engine—it even has miniature ladders. I squint into the sunlight and explain to Danny that Mr. Midnight's probably at the pool scouting bikinis and popping Viagra.

I hear a shuffling behind me and turn around to see Harry, Mr. Midnight's best friend from back home, who is visiting for several days. To his credit—as I mentioned earlier—he has been assigned the coveted formal guest room reserved for non-female A-list visitors. Harry, like me, is hungover. He reminds me of a college freshman the morning after a blowout party, but half a century older. His beer belly is sagging over a pair of polka-dot boxers and his skinny legs.

"Hey, Harry!" Danny calls out. "Some night, eh? Welcome to 'the lifestyle'! Sure beats shoveling snow, don't you think?" Harry belches and nods.

"Hey, why don't you and Andy join us for a few beers at the pool?" Danny asks. "You could use the sun. You look like a plucked chicken." Harry stares down at his pale legs and knobby knees. Four aspirins later, Harry and I hop into my cart and join the caravan.

One day I peel off from Mr. Midnight and his crew while they hack their way through a few holes of golf. I don't play golf, and I've already soaked up a bit too much sun, let alone beer, so I resolve to visit Wendy Marie, who spends most days cocooned indoors.

On the way over, I get lost yet again. After all this time driving around The Villages, I still find that its sprawling suburban layout frustrates my otherwise adequate navigation skills.

I pull over and wave down an approaching golf cart. Its lone occupant is an African-American man in his mid-sixties, one of the very few I've seen since arriving. I ask him for directions, and then inquire about The Villages' black community. He tells me there are about 250 African-Americans living in the development.

"We're here for the same reason white people are: we enjoy the amenities," he tells me. "I came here because I'm accomplished and I can afford to. I've proved everything I wanted to prove. I excelled in a white man's world. I climbed the corporate ladder. Now it's my time to relax. I don't cut my own grass or do anything else I can pay someone else to do."

When I arrive at Wendy Marie's house, she's giving a tour to a realtor. "I'm thinking of selling," Wendy Marie says. "But I still don't have any concrete plans. I don't know where to go."

I take a look around the house. It's small and tidy. Nothing about it betrays the fact that the woman next to me has a penis under her skirt, except a small collection of pickle-ball trophies on which her name appears as Donald. After the realtor leaves, Wendy Marie prepares tea and we sit in her mint-colored living room to drink it. I compliment her on her appearance.

"I just had a visit to the Hair Club," she says. "I'm actually balding a bit, so they cement hair to my head. I figure in my situation, good hair is an absolute necessity."

I ask how her plans are progressing for the big operation.

"I'm going to Thailand in October," Wendy Marie responds. "They have a really good program there. And it costs a whole lot less." I caution that perhaps price shouldn't be the most important consideration: does she really want to cut corners when cutting off her penis?

"Oh, they know what they're doing," she says. "Thailand is like the sex change capital of the world." Wendy Marie begins to describe the procedure in painfully graphic detail, but then stops.

"I don't really want the operation," she says. "The only reason I'm doing it is so I have a shot at a relationship. Not too many people would want me in my present condition, and I want to love and be loved.

"But even after the operation, I'll probably still be lonely here. They say it's better to start fresh somewhere. But where? I have no place to go."

I ask Wendy Marie if she has heard of a new retirement community for lesbians, gays, bisexuals, and transsexuals in the Santa Fe area, or about plans for others around the country. She hasn't. We go to her computer and get online using an old-fashioned dial-up modem. "Have you thought about getting broadband?" I ask. "What's the rush?" she responds. "I'm retired. I've got plenty of time."

When I find the community's home page, she grows excited. "Print it out! Print it out!" she fairly yells. "Maybe there *is* a place for me."

But once she looks at the information about prices, her enthusiasm quickly deflates. "I can't afford it. The only money I earn is from my military pension, and from dog sitting. And that money is going toward my operation in Thailand."

"Maybe there's a way," I say, trying to pierce the gloom.

"Maybe," Wendy Marie softly replies. "Maybe."

For dinner, I'm invited to a potluck meal at Ellen's Sociable Singles club. Ellen tells me not to bother bringing anything, but I'm embarrassed when I arrive empty-handed and everybody else is unwrapping platters of food. Most of the women have brought casseroles. The few men who attend mostly bring pizza and dough-nuts, except a guy named Woodrow, who brings a poached salmon with homemade cilantro relish. "It's amazing what you can do with a microwave," he says.

Another man brings chocolate-covered jelly rings with a clearance sticker still displayed on the cellophane-wrapped box. His name is Hugh, and he tells me he's lonely. "I would love to meet someone," Hugh says. "My wife died nine years ago. There's nobody in the house but me."

"Have you met anyone at these meetings?" I ask.

"Nobody has chased me yet—and I don't run too fast," Hugh responds. "One day the right one will come along. I'm still hopeful."

Before we can eat, we have to recite the Pledge of Allegiance and listen to several club announcements. Ellen delivers the club's financial report. "We have $1,123.67 in the bank," she says. Next, she pitches a day trip: a river cruise. "It only costs fifteen dollars, and soup and salad bar are included," she says. "We need a minimum of eighteen people to sign up, and so far we only have eleven." Ellen then notes that only seven members showed up for a recent scavenger hunt. "That was disappointing," she says.

Each table is called up to the buffet at random. Mine is next to last. When I scoop up the meager remains of a lifeless chicken noodle casserole, a woman behind me gives me the evil eye. "That was *my* casserole," she snaps. "And now you've finished it before I even got a taste. That's the last time I'm making that dish." She slams the metal serving spoon against the Pyrex dish and bitterly pushes the now empty casserole aside.

I stare down at the cold noodles and one lonesome chunk of poultry splayed across the center of my paper plate. I don't know what to say. What can I say? I didn't even bring something to offer as compensation. Ellen jumps in and tries to defuse the situation. "That's *good* if it's gone," she says cheerfully. "It means that everybody liked it!"

The sharp-tongued woman who brought the chicken noodle casserole ignores her. She looks around the buffet table and motions at the rest of the food. "What is this crap? It's all pasta. My dish had *chicken* in it."

Back at the table, Ellen leans forward and whispers in my ear. "No wonder she's single!" Then she imitates the woman. "Everyone ate my green beans! I got none to bring home. Poor me! No green beans!"

The following night, Dave and Betsy Anderson invite me over for a going-away dinner. I soak in the simple comforts of their tidy home, careful to not walk on the white carpet. Betsy prepares a tasty meat loaf, and after dinner we spend an hour or so chatting easily on the lanai.

When I ask if they have any plans to travel, Dave responds, "Not at all. We're in no rush. It's like we have all the time in the world. When the mood strikes, we'll just hop in the car and go. But take a trip? I can't think of a reason."

"I'm already on vacation," Betsy says. "The comfort level here is wonderful."

Betsy points out a neighbor's latest bit of handiwork—an outdoor light that illuminates a backyard palm tree. "Isn't that nice?" she asks. "It took him most of the morning to put it up."

"A lot of these folks feel a need to keep 'doing,'" Dave says. He gestures in the direction of various neighbors. "This guy over here lays tiles to keep busy. That one over there helps people file their taxes. He really likes to crunch numbers.

"That's what some people need. I don't have that one. I'm happy with who I am. I don't need to keep 'doing.' Some days if I feel especially ambitious I might put up a shelf or fix a light, but most days I don't. On the golf course, I'm competing against myself, not others."

"Leisure certainly has its benefits," I say.

"The Villages isn't about leisure," Dave responds. "It's about opportunity—the opportunity to pursue one's real interests."

"What I want is peace and quiet," Betsy says. "I don't want

to join clubs and get involved in anything right now. We wanted to shed our obligations when we came here, not increase them. But that will change. Before we moved, I did a lot of volunteer work and I enjoyed it. At some point I'll probably volunteer here as well."

"Back home, the future I could see was very limited in terms of my golf game," Dave tells me. "There was just one golf course and it didn't really have enough variation to make me a better player. My golf game has improved a lot here, and I've met some nice people. In six months, I've talked more with my neighbors here than in fourteen years back home." As a former neighbor who enjoyed chatting with Dave regularly, I'm not sure how to respond. But I do know that I am grateful for their hospitality.

After dinner, I pop over to Katie Belle's, and then to the Bistro for a last beer. Inside, a graying keyboardist dressed in a black shirt, sunglasses, and a cowboy hat is playing a medley of Johnny Cash songs. I run into Harry, Mr. Midnight's friend who's visiting for the week. I ask him if he's thinking about moving to The Villages.

"I could never leave my kids," Harry says. "No. No. No. Exclamation point! No. My kids are too important to me. Moving down here would be like abandoning them. I don't care what anybody else here says. That's just how I see it."

Harry orders another vodka cranberry. "Besides, I couldn't take this 365 days a year," he says. "My liver would explode." I couldn't agree more. Back home I rarely drink more than a few glasses of wine or beer a week. I'm surprised—and exhausted—by how much partying I've done here at The Villages.

Mr. Midnight strolls in and goes to the bar, then shakes his head in disgust. He's as close to pissed off as I've ever seen him. Apparently, one of his old flames from back home had the audacity to buy a house down the street from him in the very same village.

"I told her, 'That's it, the party's over.' She knew the rules."

Harry can't resist. "Are you *ever* going to fall in love?" he asks his friend.

"I don't fall in love," Mr. Midnight responds. "I don't have that emotion."

"I wouldn't want to die alone," Harry says.

"I'm *not* alone," Mr. Midnight responds, growing agitated.

"I'd rather be in an argument than be alone," Harry continues. "Jesus Christ. Get a dog."

Mr. Midnight loses all interest in the conversation. He swills his beer, takes a look around the bar, and gets up to leave. "I'm beat," he says. "I only came here for a quick walk-through, to see if anybody really needed me tonight. I'm headed home to fall asleep in front of the TV like a normal old person. I need to rest up. I got another lady coming in this weekend. You should see this one. Legs up to here."

He walks to the door but turns around before exiting. "Right down the street, in the same village," he says, nodding his head in disbelief. "Can you imagine that?"

The next morning on my way out of town, I decide to attend my last club activity. I choose a breakfast hosted by the so-called "Village Idiots." On my drive over, I take a last swing through Spanish Springs. I watch as songbirds hop around the "fountain of youth" and a retired couple mosey along the sidewalk hand in hand. Katie Belle's and the Bistro are silent, but Starbucks is filled with early birds, their golf carts neatly parked outside. A radio announcer's soporific voice flows gently forth from a lamppost. "Good morning, folks," he says. "It's another beautiful day in The Villages."

There's also a crowd at the bakery where I conducted many of my interviews. The sun creeps across the outdoor tables filled with customers reading the *Daily Sun*. I notice that the breakfast crowd has grown considerably since the nearby sales office wised up and quit serving free doughnuts and coffee.

Outside town, I look over and see a dozen men sitting in lawn chairs on the banks of an artificial pond, maneuvering remote-controlled sailboats. One man wears a skipper's hat. Some ducks paddle past the boats, hop ashore, and promptly fall asleep in the sun.

The Village Idiots' breakfast is held on the back patio of one of The Villages' many country clubs. I arrive to find two dozen Villagers dressed in pajamas and silly hats. I ask a woman wearing a flowerpot on her head if she could direct me to the club's president. "Who's the head idiot?" she asks. "Idiots don't have heads! But you might want to speak to Bob; he's a *real* idiot!"

Bob wears a name tag that says "Boob," and a button that says, "It takes a Village to raise an idiot." He's wrapped in a bathrobe, has green furry slippers on his feet, and wears a giant dunce cap. When I try to introduce myself, Boob stares at me with a look of exaggerated bewilderment that is practically frozen to his face for the next two or three minutes, making me increasingly uncomfortable. Frustrated, I look around. I'm greeted by blank stares. I am indeed surrounded by a bunch of idiots.

A kindly woman finally invites me to sit at her table. "I'm probably the oldest idiot," she tells me proudly. "My name is Ruth, and I'm ninety." She wears purple satin pajamas and childish barrettes in her hair. "We have so much fun together. We're always doing stupid things!"

Boob joins our conversation. "I just thought it up one day," he says. "Every village needs an idiot, don't you think? There are no dues, no roll calls, and no minutes. We have absolutely no redeeming social value whatsoever. We're a 'dis-organization.' Only idiots can join. If your intelligence increases, you're put on probation."

The club meets once a month for breakfast, giving its members a chance to shake the lead out and act silly. "If you retire early and just sit around, you die early," Boob tells me.

Partway through breakfast, Boob clinks his glass and stands up. "A toast," he declares, then raises a triangle of crispy buttered rye bread and promptly eats it.

"What an idiot!" Ruth shouts in delight.

14

Cat's in the Cradle

"We all have a lot more in common than it seems."
—Fortune cookie

BEHIND ALL THE GATED AGE-RESTRICTED LEISURE, ERSATZ ARCHITEC-tural nostalgia, and nightly hanky-panky, what I saw in The Villages is a concerted effort by a segment of older Americans to find com-munity—something that in today's turbulent world can be hard to chance upon, particularly for the elderly. Many Villagers simply don't care if they live in an autocratic fantasyland founded on a policy of segregation; they just want a place to call home, a geritopia where they can be comfortable among their peers.

Most of the Villagers I met were blissful—thankful that such a place existed and that they had been lucky enough to find it. Retire-ment can be a stressful stage of life. There's no script to follow for the decades between giving up work and reaching advanced old age. Private developers such as Webb and Morse are filling that void for some people, peddling a glamorized vision of serene, financially predicable leisure living in segregated resort-like communities. It's a powerful vision that has proved to be very appealing to a sizable segment of aging Americans.

Much of life's unpleasantness is erased in such a community. You don't have to worry about boom boxes interrupting your sleep, or about tripping over a tricycle as you walk down your driveway, or about skyrocketing local property taxes. Nor do you have to worry about potentially volatile encounters with people who are significantly different from yourself. Real life is filled with friction; these communities attempt to remove the source of some of that friction—mainly children, troublesome neighbors, and the underclass.

And residents don't have to grow old alone and afraid—a cheerless fate by any measure. Some of our cities and towns provide senior citizens with enough targeted services and built-in social networks, as well as conveniences accessible to pedestrians and by public transportation, but many don't. Nor do many communities provide seniors with a critical sense of personal safety.

And the alternative to an artificial "downtown" is often worse: what's a retiree supposed to do in the car-dependent suburbs, where so many Americans now live, often with no family nearby? Twenty years ago the average American drove 12,000 miles a year. Today that number is 21,000 miles. Not only is suburban sprawl antithetical to aging in place; it's not a lot of fun to grow old in.

By contrast, for many seniors The Villages is fun because it's a community specifically designed for them. When you drive up to The Villages' security checkpoints, you are leaving behind a culture that worships—and caters to—youth. Certain ground rules are different in The Villages. The music is gentler; it's "lights out" earlier, and social interaction is overall less belligerent and competitive. Residents can pass mostly worry-free days comfortably playing tennis and golf, and not have to fight for a court or tee time with a fast-paced younger crowd. And they never have to be lonely again, because it's so easy to find friends with similar interests.

The relative dearth of younger people and real-life concerns frees up these seniors. To younger folks, they may be old fogies, but to each other they're just peers. An older man with thinning hair, paunchy midsection, and bad knees can buy a woman a drink and not get heckled. A gray-haired woman succumbing to gravity's pull can dance the night away, swim at the pool, and be a cheerleader with pom-poms without feeling self-conscious or foolish. Best yet, women feel safe enough to drive downtown in a golf cart at night to meet friends for drinks and live music at the town square, and then drive home alone in the dark.

What better place to park one's parents than a leisureville? It's safe; everything—even the hospital—is acessible by golf cart; and there are educational and recreational activities galore. For older family members, it can be a vacation from depression and loneliness. And for younger generations, it's a ticket away from worry. That's a beautiful thing.

But as history has shown us, utopian movements are much like balloons—they either burst or slowly deflate. People tend to rebel against rigid programming, even if that programming is centered on their own leisure. The developers I met at the housing conference in Phoenix expect such rebellion when enough boomers come of age and reject the Sun City model. And yet these developers are supremely confident that small tweaks to this "senior playpen" paradigm are all that it will take to entice another generation to buy their product.

But it's not just a matter of smaller and more intimate communities placed closer to urban areas. It's something more basic: something's rotten at the core of these leisurevilles. While it's not for me to say seniors shouldn't enjoy themselves, the reality behind age segregation is another matter. No clever euphemism can hide the fact that these communities are based on a selfish and fraudulent premise—the exclusion of children and families. And no amount of volunteerism and continuing education courses—however admirable or enriching—can compensate for the high societal price of this exclusionary lifestyle.

To be sure, our elders have special needs, which are all too often sadly ignored by our youth-centered society. Age restrictions can be appropriate (if not redundant) for institutions designed to address these needs, such as specialty care facilities or vitally needed low-income senior housing.

But housing for senior citizens is one thing; "adult" housing is another. Just what "special needs" do today's wealthy middle-aged boomers have? Not only do they represent the least marginalized generation in human history; they're not even old. Developers are merely exploiting a legal loophole.

If The Villages is any indication, the so-called special needs include, among other things, alcohol-saturated faux downtowns and an opportunity to play golf on a different course every day of the month. People in the prime of life—they are called "active adults" for a reason—don't need nursing stations and communal cafeterias so much as tennis courts, lap pools, and espresso bars. So why are we providing these "seniors" with a legally codified right to keep the rest of society at bay?

Clearly, our federal government shouldn't be in the business of endorsing discrimination against young families. The Fair Housing Act was originally intended to protect Americans from bigotry, not promote it. It's been well over two hundred years since we shamefully designated blacks as three-fifths human. Are young children—and their parents —any less than whole? Do we really want to promote communities where birth certificates are scrutinized at points of entry? Congress needs to reexamine this legislation and either eliminate age discrimination altogether or, at the very least, periodically raise the qualifying age as time and science progress. But given the strength of the retirement housing lobby, a swift legislative remedy is unlikely. I suspect that deteriorating market conditions for such housing, rather than a concern for the civil rights of families with children, will drive change.

Simply raising the qualifying age still leaves me feeling uneasy. Age-targeted housing in "naturally occurring retirement communities" seems like a far fairer compromise. Cities and small towns are a natural fit for seniors who can no longer drive. They also encourage a mingling of ages. Promoting age-targeted housing and facilities —as well as a sense of safety—in these locations strikes me as a worthy pursuit. Such a setup worked for my grandmother; why shouldn't it work for me?

But until we establish a coherent vision for addressing the needs of our senior citizens, private developers-cum-social engineers will continue to exploit this lack of cultural consensus. As one industry consultant heartily assured me, the lid to Pandora's box is already wide open.

"Age-restricted housing is out of the embryo stage and it's here to stay," he said. "It's the housing sector's sweet spot." He then proudly shared with me his new term for age segregation: "Age-preferred. It just sounds nicer."

Half a century after Ben Schleifer realized his modest vision for Youngtown, retirement has become more than a life stage—it's become big business. But do we really want to encourage private developers concerned solely with their bottom line to toy with something as critical as our nation's social fabric?

The Villages and age-segregated communities like it represent the coming together of a number of cultural trends emerging from the muddle of modern America life: geographic and financial withdrawal, "enhanced reality," and the endless pursuit of leisure. Taken individually, each trend is niggling but points to a mounting desire for escapism. When the trends are lumped together, the result is worrisome.

A society that embraces secession and escapism is clearly not a society addressing its problems and planning for a better future. Nor is it a society concerned with sustainability. Sun City and its guiding philosophy are about as disposable as its aging housing stock and the strip malls that surround it. Children represent the future, and a community without them is as doomed as the celibate Shakers.

The Villages is probably not far behind—perhaps a few decades. The architecture may present a historical facade, but nothing there is built to last—not even age segregation, which may be abandoned one day out of desperation, in a last-ditch attempt to add vitality and population long after the Morse family has disbanded its advertising and sales departments and left the scene with its fortune. The Villages' form of government guarantees that amenities fees will be collected, but it doesn't guarantee that there will be people to collect them from. I suspect it won't be such an attractive destination once the homes start to deteriorate and the vast majority of residents are shuffling by on walkers. At some point even Mr. Midnight will have to admit defeat as nature takes its course.

The people living in age-segregated housing are still a small minority of Americans, but that's unlikely to remain the case. In 2004, ground was broken for 100 age-segregated developments; ten years earlier, that figure was fifteen. There is no firm number for how many of these communities exist, but industry experts estimate that there are more than 1,500, of various sizes, either completed or under construction.

What will happen when there are thousands of these segregated communities across America, housing millions of aging secessionists? What happens to the rest of us—those left behind who don't qualify in terms of age or finances? For that matter, what happens to American society in general, and our municipalities in particular, when a critical mass of mature Americans form self-contained private cities and disengage from the general population? Experience shows that these privately owned quasi-governmental entities often resent paying local taxes for schools as well as for municipal services that they prefer to perform for themselves. And they are potent voting blocs that can swing elections addressing these issues.

Our national mythology extols the concept of the melting pot. We are supposed to work together and strive to assimilate into a commonality called citizenship. Our national motto, displayed on the back of the dollar bill, is E Pluribus Unum—out of many, one. But as an increasing number of Americans secede into niche communities, we risk further loosening the ties that bind our nation together.

The lesson of Sun City couldn't be any clearer: segregation reduces social contact and leads to a willful forgetting of commonalities, which can further deteriorate into generational resentment. Many Sun Citians have lost sight of the fact that they live within a larger age-integrated community that also has special needs, such as schools.

For me, Sun City's de-annexation from the local school district was the proverbial canary in the coalmine. Two decades later, Villagers living in the Lake County portion of their gated community voted down an additional halfpenny sales tax that would have helped fund local schools. The measure failed countywide by a two-to-one margin, but Villagers defeated it by nearly four to one. Three years later, a similar measure easily passed countywide, but Villagers still voted against it in alarming numbers.

Two of the biggest special-interest groups vying for funds in Florida state government are retirees and young families. Evidently, the seniors are more than holding their own: Florida law stipulates that retirement communities are exempt from paying new-housing impact fees designed to help fund school districts. Because this burden is spread across fewer taxpayers, families with children must now pay higher impact fees to make up the difference.

Seniors emphatically insist that they needn't contribute, because their housing has no direct impact on school systems. But as we have seen, these senior communities need employees, and those employees have children who need schooling. Besides, whatever happened to the idea—perhaps naive—that we're all in this together, that we have an obligation to the generations that come after us? What if everybody drops out after getting his or her own needs met? When do things start to fall apart?

Retirees move for a variety of reasons including weather, family, and finances. Many seek a lower cost of living—a prudent consideration for those on fixed incomes and limited resources, particularly in an age of seemingly skyrocketing municipal expenses. More often than not, local taxes are a factor; in effect, these seniors go "tax shopping."

Many are picking communities on the basis of how little they can get away with when it comes to paying into local coffers. These retirees are abandoning the communities that once paid for and nurtured them and their families; few have much interest in investing in their new community and its children. Otherwise, they wouldn't be shopping around for lower taxes.

I think of my grandmother, who retired on Social Security and a meager pension. Contributing money to Philadelphia's crumbling inner-city school system must have been daunting, but I don't remember her ever complaining about it. To her, it was just something you did; something that had to be factored into the cost of living in a real community, a community she cared about.

When I first learned of school system de-annexations, I was reminded of Harry Chapin's melancholic song "Cat's in the Cradle," in which an inattentive father ignores his son, and eventually the son grows up and rejects him. An aging generation that chooses gated secession and de-annexation may ultimately pay a similar price when the next generation inherits the purse strings and starts playing tit for tat.

It remains to be seen how generous this excluded generation will be after a lifetime of peering through the gates at sybaritic seniors. How eager will the new generation be to throw its elders a financial life preserver after being treated as a nuisance and thought of as little more than an expensive "invoice" burdening local taxes? Will it pull the plug on Social Security, pensions, Medicare, and Medicaid when funding for these programs requires too much sacrifice? Who wants to foot the bill for millions of hedonistic young seniors living in gated geritopias? And with an estimated 72 million Americans over sixty-five by 2030, younger Americans will be asked to pay for a whopper of a tab. The Boomers lived large and subsequent generations are

Andrew D. Blechman

inheriting nearly ten trillion dollars in national debt as well as entitlement programs on the verge of bankruptcy.

Social Security calls itself a compact between generations; but
can you maintain such a compact without continued contact? One
wonders if up to thirty days of fun-filled visits will be enough to bond
the generations, or if the good works of some volunteers in The Villages will be enough to foster goodwill.

I often think about the youngster in Lady Lake with a history
of being harassed for skateboarding in the Spanish Springs "Town
Square." How will he and his friends—and thousands of future teenagers—look on this generation of aging Villagers? Will they resent
them, or will they merely count the years until they too can live inside the gates? The message many of these Villagers and their compatriots around the country are sending to subsequent generations
is that success is defined by secession and perpetual self-gratification.
I spoke to countless Villagers who complained that they had "done
their share" and were "tired of giving back." But what exactly have
they given? Blessed to be born into one of the richest generations in
the history of the world, they've led a life that most people can only
dream of. Such good fortune wasn't a matter of luck: it was given to
them by previous generations who made untold sacrifices through
two world wars and a devastating depression.

Taking a sabbatical after retirement from our grueling modern
workaday life is one thing, but a thirty-year vacation is another. Promotional materials for age-segregated communities would have us
believe that "life" is really a matter of "lifestyle"—a marketing concept that can be tweaked. But at what point do convenience and leisure bring us diminishing returns? At what point do conveniences
make life too easy, so that it becomes insipid and uninspiring? More
often then not, enrichment requires struggle and effort.

Surely today's retirees have something more to pass on to us
than a love of golf and a perceived entitlement to lock themselves

away in leisurevilles. That's not citizenship; that's secession. It's a form of surrender, an acknowledgement of societal failure.

America is a country that celebrates liberty and individual autonomy, anyone with enough resources is free to secede. But imagine the opposite of disengagement—millions of retirees reengaging and actively working to leave behind an admirable legacy. Today's retirees are among the best-educated people in the world. Never before have so many people had so much knowledge and so much time to impart it. They undoubtedly have wisdom to share with us. It's no secret that strong ties between the generations lead to stronger communities and greater hope for the future.

It's equally important that we as a nation once again recognize the importance our elders, whom we often treat less than admirably. Another way of saying that a society is youth-centered is that it ignores its elders. A recent survey found that fewer than half of all American communities have begun to address the needs of our rapidly increasing elder population. It's time we began discussing things as basic as senior-friendly crosswalks, adult day care, and job retraining so that a skilled generation of workers has more options than being a greeter at Wal-Mart.

Worse yet, elder abuse remains a sad reality: an estimated 5 million seniors suffer from mistreatment by younger generations. Even the millionaire philanthropist and fabled socialite Brooke Astor was allegedly among their number. The stereotype of senior citizens forced by poverty and neglect to eat cat food or live in decrepit nursing homes is at times not far from the truth.

In a society that places less and less emphasis on cultural and institutional traditions, it's worth remembering that seniors are our link with the past. They are our institutional memory, our repository of experience, and perhaps our greatest natural resource. A program in Massachusetts understands this and pairs seniors with foster children, an arrangement that facilitates both interaction and volunteerism, which is of benefit to both generations. And a promising multistate initiative, called the Experience Corps, encourages people over fifty-five to remain involved in their communities by tutoring and mentoring elementary school children.

The days when a "hoary head" was considered a "crown of gold" may be long gone—we are far more likely to dye our hair at the slightest sign of natural maturity than don a powered wig as a symbol of wisdom and authority—but that doesn't mean our elders have any less to teach us.

It's to be hoped we will take an interest in them, and they will take an interest in us. This should be of concern to all of us, because one day—if we're lucky—we'll all be old.

I took some time to readjust to my less convenient life back home. Although it was already spring, I still found myself occasionally trudging through wet snow to shovel my driveway and brush off my car. As the days grew longer, I spent countless hours prepping the lawn against crabgrass, pruning the hedges, and nurturing new plantings. Somewhere along the way, the lessons of Sun City took root; I gave up the fight to preserve my lawn's artificial monoculture, and opted to scatter clover and wild thyme.

To me, the gardening was hard work, but I took great pleasure in sitting on my patio and surveying my modest accomplishments. I missed seeing Dave mowing his lawn at picture-perfect angles, or strapping on his leaf blower (and outsize safety goggles and headphones) for spring cleanup. And I missed Betsy applauding as I skateboarded shakily past their old house.

But I've become friendly with our new neighbors: a single mom and her charming teenage daughter. What they lack in gardening know-how they make up for with tasty impromptu dinners. Another neighbor, one of my close friends, impresses me with his desire to hang out with younger folks like myself. In his sixties and retired, he regularly invites me over for home-brewed beer and slow-cooked barbecue ribs. He loves to entertain my toddler daughter with his comedic antics, and my daughter adores him in return. Despite his age, he keeps current with the hip-hop music scene so that he can continue being a disc jockey for middle school dances—a favorite pastime.

Our town, thankfully, remains happily age-integrated for the most part, with strong bonds continuing to keep the generations close. Elected town officials range in age from the mid-thirties to the mid-seventies; and people of all ages routinely mingle on the sidewalks or at our new community center. When the operator of a local cinema butted heads with a sometimes less than endearing crew of teenagers loitering in his downtown parking lot, and attempted to repel them with a device that produces a painfully high-pitched noise heard only by younger ears, most people agreed that he had crossed the line. Neighboring merchants unanimously condemned the action and petitioned the town to outlaw the device. "We feel that young people are welcome members of our community and we enjoy the vitality that they bring to our town," they wrote. Similarly, many of my peers and I enjoy hanging out with older residents. They are entertaining, and there's a lot to learn from them.

I can't help thinking that the Andersons left something wonderful behind: an authentic community with a rich history. Since moving, they've missed seeing our previously fractured neighborhood pull together mightily to fight the proposed firehouse—and win. Our fellow citizens finally concluded that saving an extra three dollars a month in property taxes wasn't worth giving up our children's green space. A better site was chosen—one that the fire chief actually preferred—and construction has already begun. The senior center remains as is. The town's older citizens are generally a thrifty bunch, and few of them have voiced a desire for a bigger, fancier building. But we do have a newly renovated and enlarged library that is finally wheelchair accessible. Funding for the project was a contentious issue. It was rejected at first, but enough residents—both young and old—banded together and approved it the second time around.

The glow of victory in our neighborhood may be fading, but the park remains and our cohesion persists. Now, I can't walk ten yards without bumping into a neighbor that I know. And we all help keep an eye on the aging seniors in our neighborhood (especially when it snows) and on one another's children, doing our best to keep them all out of harm's way.

My wife and I live on a corner lot, and in the warm weather it's not unusual for half a dozen neighbors to stroll by my backyard and stay for a glass of wine or a bowl of ice cream. To me, the whimsical happenstances in a traditional community—the accidental crossings—give life its vibrancy. My patio's often filled with three generations of neighbors at a time: the adults yapping away while the children run around the yard and swing on the hammock. If it sounds idyllic, that's because it is. Community is precious, and I plan on soaking up as much of it as I can. It fills me with hope.

That said, in some ways Gary Lester was right. I sometimes wish our neighborhood and town had better planning. If they did, I wouldn't have had to dedicate so much time and anxiety to campaigning for our community green. And like any parent, I worry about the safety of our daughter, occasionally allowing myself to dream of the reduced traffic and the sense of security that a gated community provides.

But when push comes to shove, I'm not interested in the Faustian bargain that living in a controlled community demands. I love my town, warts and all, and take comfort in the knowledge that no entertainment specialist designed our downtown; nor can it be bought, sold, or traded like a stock certificate.

As any parent knows, kids can be trying, and it's true that generational peers tend to gravitate toward one another, but I still can't bear the thought of living in community without children. I find such a fate, improbable though it may be, heartbreaking. As it is, I can hardly stand it when my wife and daughter leave town to visit relatives and the house echoes with loneliness instead of our daughter's youthful wonderment and laughter. One day she will necessarily leave the nest, but if we're fortunate, she'll choose to live nearby and our garden will once again be filled with a new generation of lively youngsters.

Epilogue

"[They] longed to stay forever, browsing on that native bloom, forgetful of their homeland."

—The Odyssey

DEVELOPERS SELLING AGE SEGREGATION CONTINUE TO BULLDOZE their way across the country, catering to an aging public eager to have the easy life. To my chagrin, several of my friends' parents are moving into age-segregated communities. My friends aren't sure what to make of their parents' decision, but most of them confess a sense of unease and bewilderment, as well as some relief. My own parents are now living in an age-targeted housing development, not because they dread young families but because, much like their new neighbors, they enjoy the amenities, which include easy access to New York City, and the speedy sense of community that living with one's peers provides.

There are already 150 age-segregated communities in my state alone, with proposals for nearly 200 more. Many municipalities have incorporated "vasectomy zoning" ordinances with provisions (such as higher density limits but restrictions on the number of bedrooms) that encourage the creation of retirement communities and accord them preferential treatment, even though there is a critical need for affordable family housing. Some even mandate that a certain percentage of new construction be in the form of "adult" housing, particularly if local school buildings are already at capacity.

Every week I read news accounts from surrounding areas about these and other proposed developments, helplessly monitoring the

233

trend as it inches closer to our bucolic hamlet. The developments are perceived as a form of tax relief, and most communities can't embrace them quickly enough. There's never any discussion about the larger societal costs of building childproof leisurevilles. Nor is there any attempt to distinguish between adult playgrounds and much-needed care facilities and affordable senior housing. The utter lack of public debate at the local or national level about age-segregated housing continues to surprise me. Press reports of Donald Trump's entry into the market with an age-segregated community north of New York City made much of the fact that he is a baby boomer, but never questioned the premise behind such real estate developments.

As was predicted by the Mexican developer I met in Phoenix, the movement has now spilled south of the border, where an age-segregated community for American expatriates is expected to be up and running in Baja before the end of the decade. Now you can spend the rest of your life at an all-inclusive beachfront resort. Similar communities are establishing beachheads in additional warm weather locales, such as Spain and Panama.

In a twist on modern planned communities, quasi-governments, and America's long history of religious utopias, the founder of Dominos Pizza is now financing a new for-profit Catholic-themed community in Florida named Ave Maria. It will feature both age-integrated and age-segregated neighborhoods, thus giving dedicated pro-lifers the choice of living with children or keeping them at bay. One wonders how the "pizza pope" will govern his private theocracy, and how residents will respond to his occasional edicts. He says he is following God's will. Before construction had even begun, he expressed his opposition to the sale of condoms and other contraceptives at future on-site pharmacies, and to the offering of X-rated premium channels by cable television providers.

The lesbian-gay-bisexual-transgender communities will soon be coming online as well, with Billie Jean King workout rooms and drag cabarets, much to my gay brother's delight. He says these marginalized populations are seceding for their own safety—and sanity. "We're terrified, understandably, of ending up in an ordinary retirement place, where a heterosexual lifestyle and sensibility could be 'imposed' upon us," he tells me. "Many of us would be misfits, and a lot of us would die of boredom."

I suspect that as a dedicated New Yorker, he'd be less than thrilled by the canned environment in such a community, gay or straight. But many in the industry expect so-called "affinity communities" to gain in popularity with retirees. New entrants might include artists, environmentalists, athletes, and "new age" devotees. Regardless of the infinite ways to self-segregate, all these groups have one basic commonality—a desire to live without children.

The housing market, once rocket-propelled, is taking a plunge, so the industry is bracing for a cyclical slowdown. Some of the midsize players have already declared bankruptcy—often leaving behind thinly populated "communities" with only partially realized clubhouses, pools, and "neighborhoods." Many of the bigger developers have begun to reduce their staffs and cancel some planned projects. This is a possible preview of what could happen when all such communities outlive the boomers.

For now, developers are working hard to sell the product, but regardless of how beautiful the weather is in North Carolina or some such place, it's hard to persuade people to buy a new home if they can't sell their present one. I've been offered reduced financing, unsolicited advice on how to sell my existing home (plants help), and three years of free heat and electricity if I buy a new home. And in keeping with the perceived fascination retirees have with the *Guinness Book of World Records,* I have also been invited to participate in a contest involving stacking golf balls.

My favorite marketing ploy was a folksy letter from a senior sales executive named Mike, questioning the importance of a softening in the housing market. "It's not a good time to buy real estate?"

he asks. He then quotes a happy customer: "Mike, if we waited until someone else told us it was a good time to buy something, we could be waiting the rest of our *lives!*" Mike writes that this "prophetic" comment "floored" him.

Meanwhile, the spotlight remains on the self-obsessed boomers, wrinkles and all. They helped manufacture the cult of youth in the first place, and owing to their sheer numbers they're in no fear of age bias and marginalization as they grow older. The business world is already devising products and services to cater to them and the trillions of dollars they have to spend. This will soon change the way nearly all consumer products—such as cars and houses—are designed. And so, as books move to larger type, homes exclude stairs, and cosmetics models proudly display gravity's inevitable toll, it's possible that our current cultural obsession with youth might graduate to at least middle age.

Given my own age, I can still only guess what it's really like to be old, and I can't say I look forward to old age. The daily newspaper feature "Fifty Years Ago Today" brings back no memories, and probably won't bring any for another two decades or so. Indeed, I have difficulty imaging my own retirement, or how I will navigate it, and even thinking about it makes me rather uneasy. I'm still too busy climbing up the mountain to know what the other side looks like; such worries remain abstractions that I'd rather not dwell on yet.

I miss my friends in The Villages and keep in contact with a number of them. Few of them are actually old—many of them are younger than my parents—and so they're doing just fine. My wet-blanket prognostications seem to have little effect on them; they're too busy having fun.

The Andersons are happy to report that they have a new golf routine. Instead of playing on an eighteen-hole championship golf course, they now play two nine-hole executive courses and bring along a picnic lunch to eat between tee times. "It's a great way to split up the game," Betsy informs me. "It's even more relaxing."

A year and a half after moving to The Villages, Dave writes to tell me that they have finally ventured out for a cruise around the Caribbean. "While most folks were frantically searching for sun and relaxation—actually wearing themselves out in their quest—we knew ours was just an extension of our life in the Villages, minus the golf," he explains. "In some ways we felt like Peter Pan and Wendy. I guess the decadence of the experience was wonderful (didn't Adam eat the apple?), but when superimposed on the dire poverty of the islands it makes me wonder, and a little sad."

Mr. Midnight continues to write to me about what he describes as his life of Riley, and always lets me know that there's a room available for me. For a short while, it appeared as if his Teflon facade was cracking. He met an airline stewardess in her mid-forties whose job necessitated accommodating Mr. Midnight's "three-day rule." "She's wonderful," he writes. "I think I could actually fall for her. And her schedule's perfect: I still need my space."

I remained dubious and he chided me for having so little faith in him. A few weeks later, my suspicions were confirmed. "She wants to get married," he wrote tersely. "She is history. She knew the rules."

At age sixty-five, Wendy Marie is no longer half a man. She had the surgery in Thailand as planned. The recovery was daunting and weeks later landed her in the Villages Regional Medical Center. But she is happy to report that her Florida driver's license now has "F" for female. She still contemplates leaving The Villages, but has no idea where she'll feel comfortable; and after $100,000 worth of surgeries, finances remain a very real concern. "The older you get, the tougher it is to figure out what you want to do with the rest of your life," she explains.

I'm told that Kat continues to show her mouse tattoo to startled acquaintances at Katie Belle's, and that the Prosecutor is still the captain of Holly's ship. Ellen and her friends are as sharp as ever and continue to meet weekly for dinner and cards.

I've kept in touch with Pete Wahl, who runs the central districts. Every now and then I contact him for basic information about the sprawling metropolis he runs. He's fond of reminding me that by law he's required to provide *access* to information and no more. When I ask him roughly how many golf courses The Villages intends to build, he replies: "I do not and have never worked for The Villages, which is a private corporation, to whose information I have no right of access."

After two decades of marriage, Elton Mayer's second wife died. "I'm no longer looking for love," Elton told me by phone from his little home in The Village of Orange Blossom Gardens. "I'm just looking to survive and perhaps enjoy my remaining days." He tells me he has fallen a few times lately, and one of his retired daughters is contemplating moving to The Villages to keep an eye on him. "But I still eat what I want, and take a nap when I want, no matter what time of day it is. I go anyplace I want to go in my golf cart, and I play golf once a week!"

There are occasional reminders of how cruel the real world can be. Several months after my last visit, Sassy the clown sends me a rather disturbing e-mail: two residents of The Villages (a husband and wife) were shot at point-blank range. The wife died instantly, but the husband, who ran outside to plead for help dressed only in his underwear, survived.

This incident had the makings of stereotypically brutal crime that seemingly justified a life of secession. The couple's somewhat estranged adult daughter had invited three young men to her parents' home. These men shot the parents, stole some jewelry, and then fled, allegedly taking the daughter as a hostage. The culprits were angry youths right out of central casting, and the daughter had a history of substance abuse and reckless behavior. Once captured, the men snarled at the camera, and one demanded "the best lawyer in Florida." The daughter maintained her innocence, but her father took out a restraining order, effectively banning her from her mother's funeral.

Sassy described the sordid crime as a parable about parenting. "When we seniors reach the retirement portion of our lives, we are not always finished being parents, and we can *never* escape our children. I have had friends in that position or with children who are still struggling to get it together and have lived with them here. You'd think by the time you reach my age the kids would be squared away, or have done themselves in by now. Thank God the worst problem my kids have is to be overweight."

On the lighter side, The Villages was national news once again when a report cited an alarming number of sexually transmitted diseases among residents. The late-night comedy shows had a ball with this rich material.

Meanwhile, The Villages and Gary Morse have continued to tighten their noose on politics in Sumter County. As Election Day approached, the candidates backed by The Villages had amassed a huge amount of campaign funds. As expected, Gary Breeden received favorable coverage in The Villages' media, and Jim Roberts did not. Roberts's ally on the board of commissioners, Joey Chandler, faced an equally difficult primary against a candidate who was backed by The Villages and who worked for a contractor in The Villages.

The Villages' candidates ran a bare-knuckles campaign. Roberts found himself forced to run in the primaries against a shadow candidate—a twenty-one-year-old waitress who never campaigned. Her mom works for a contractor in The Villages. Villagers living in Sumter County were also the target of many so-called "impartial" telephone surveys filled with serious misinformation. A sample question: "Would you still vote for Commissioner Chandler knowing that he raised taxes twenty-two times?" The two candidates responded with a Web site that attempted to address these distortions and others coming from The Villages' media.

Not unexpectedly, Roberts and his colleague lost. They garnered plenty of votes in their own districts, but Villagers now represent a majority of voters in the county, and as seniors, they are more likely to actually vote. I must say that I felt a pang of remorse, even in distant New England.

Goodwill—which is critical to the healthy functioning of a complex interrelated society—has seemingly evaporated. The new board of commissioners is looking into moving the county government from Bushnell to a more "convenient" location beside The Villages in the county's far northeastern corner, because it is the "geographic center of the population." Legal notices have been moved from an old countywide newspaper in Bushnell, which had published them for decades, and which was the low bidder for the contract, to The Villages' *Daily Sun.* County residents must now purchase Morse's heavily biased newspaper if they want to read such announcements. Frustrated by their marginalization, many county residents are hoping to overturn "One Sumter" or even split the county in two.

The board is also questioning the wisdom of building a park for families in the southern end of the county. "The one thing that's missing in these parks is children," a commissioner said. He didn't mention that many of the parks are dilapidated and uninviting. The board will probably sell two-thirds of the south county parcel and ask volunteer groups to construct park facilities. And now the board wants to prohibit nonresidents of The Villages from using certain gated roads within the development, regardless of the fact that residents of the county are paying to maintain them.

The board is also moving to reduce the fees Villagers pay the county for emergency services. There's no talk, however, about the one financial issue that should be of real concern to Villages: the hundreds of millions of dollars in debt they are saddled with—an amount that is likely to rise as the community builds out.

New homes, golf courses, and recreation centers continue to

pop up seemingly overnight as the development bulldozes its way across Sumter County. The Villages has finally released information whose existence it continually refused to confirm: plans for a third "town center." It will be named Brownwood, after the Morse family's tourism complex in Michigan, which once included Gary's failed steak house. Business in Spanish Springs appears to be brisk, but Sumter Landing continues to struggle commercially, with stores and restaurants coming and going. One wonders what effect the addition of Brownwood will have. Home sales are also slowing. Some newer residents complain that they are living in virtual ghost villages.

Morse's own Villages chamber of commerce, where I bought a map on my first day in town, has closed after "achieving its goal"— whatever that means. Meanwhile, supersize strip malls continue to sprout up all over the place.

The Villages is finally beginning to comprehensively address the concerns of residents who are actually old. A seven-story enclosed assisted living and continuing care facility is under construction across the street from the recently expanded hospital. Plans call for 250 living units, with their own pools, spas, and covered parking for golf carts. The Morse family continues to wrangle with the state over how much more development local aquifers can withstand; the water district is considering temporary water restrictions, especially in light of the continuing drought.

Rich Lambrecht of CDD 4 and Joe Gorman of the Property Owners Association continue their relentless pursuit of fairness and equity for all Villagers. Lately they've had some successes. Rich got The Villages to pay the lion's share for fixing the sinkhole on the Nancy Lopez golf course, and to assume a liability for eighteen other retention ponds. Rich was much relieved: "With two or three sinkholes a year we had a big issue on our hands," he said.

Joe's relentless crusade for fair representation led to another concession by Morse: The Villages agreed to let residents in the older

241

of the two central districts vote on whether they want to elect representatives to the central district government or leave it in Morse's hands. However, most of the big decisions have already been made in this central district, and so far there are no plans for a similar emancipation of the newer Sumter Landing central district.

The nonbinding resolution passed narrowly, but its future remains uncertain. Democracy is messy, and many Villagers prefer the convenience of government by contract. Concern over outsiders using The Villages' pools seems to get more attention from residents, particularly after one Villager's wallet was stolen. Other Villagers have complained about contractors who use clubhouse bathrooms, and about the increasing number of children who arrive without guest passes.

Villagers may be able to exclude young families and the poor, but Mother Nature still plays by her own rules, sometimes to frightening effect. In February, a powerful tornado came through central Florida and hopped across newer construction in the Sumter County area of The Villages. Hundreds of homes were damaged or destroyed, a country club near the Andersons' is no more, and an untold number of golf carts were tossed around like discarded Jolly Ranchers. Although neighboring communities reported more than a dozen fatalities, there were none in The Villages.

Although many of my friends were shaken by the tragedy, life in The Villages hardly skipped a beat. The deadly tornado interfered with plans for a chili cook-off the next day; but as Sassy reported, somewhat surprised, Spanish Springs was still filled with suntanned seniors happily strolling about as if the tornado had never happened. And the severe weather did little to dampen Mr. Midnight's lusty enthusiasm.

"We escaped with no damage," he wrote to me a day later. "We have plenty of food and water. Please send Viagra."

Afterword

For much of the time I was writing *Leisureville,* I had the uncanny sensation that I was chronicling the last days of Rome. After the book was published in hardcover, Villagers continued to live generally blissful lives in their gated geritopia, a place one resident described to me as a "private Walden Pond with all of the amenities." They were more interested in uncovering Mr. Midnight for defaming their "wholesome" way of life than in debating the merits of their segregated lifestyle. But reality has a way of intruding eventually, and Villagers got hit hard.

As with many Americans, their retirement investments were squeezed by the global credit crisis. The bust in the real estate bubble also struck a blow—The Villages population may have topped Daytona Beach, but its growth has finally begun to slow. Not surprisingly, America is receiving a reprieve from the onslaught of new age-segregated communities as more and more builders are forced into bankruptcy. Nobody tracks the number of stalled or sacked projects, but as a spokesman for the National Association of Home Builders conceded, "It's big." Some developers are even tossing out age requirements in a bid to attract a larger pool of applicants. As reported in *The Wall Street Journal,* some communities are merely *lowering* age requirements, even though such actions are against federal laws. I'm told that state and federal authorities are looking into the matter. A sign of the times was this year's 50+ Housing Symposium, which, aside from reduced registration fees, included seminars on "financing

243

strategies to stay alive in today's market" and "sales—gone are the days of taking orders."

The Villages faces another challenge, more treacherous than sapped 401ks and an increase in foreclosures: the IRS. In early 2009, after conducting a year-long investigation, the IRS released a preliminary report concluding that $64 million worth of tax-free bonds that the Villages Center Community District sold in 2003 should be taxed. These bonds, which paid for only $11 million of actual properties— the remaining $53 million was for amenity-fee contracts—apparently violated a number of the requirements for tax-free bonds. Perhaps most importantly, the report questioned the entire structure of The Villages government. The agency wrote that the Morse family's business enterprise and the central district were "almost indistinguishable" and that Morse's perpetual ownership of the Central Districts "effectively perverts" the legal intent of Chapter 190, which "allows the developer to engage in unchecked self-dealing . . . with absolutely no oversight," and effectively "disenfranchises" residents.

It would be difficult to imagine a more damning indictment of The Villages's system of district governance. For Villagers, the implications are frightening. The eventual ruling could extend to $271 million worth of bonds, only $52 million of which paid for tangible property. Tens of millions of dollars of back taxes may be owed, as well as millions of dollars in penalties. How The Villages would pay back such a huge sum of money, or who would be forced to pay for it—Morse or residents— remains unanswered. So far, *The Daily Sun* has managed not to write a single story about the IRS's preliminary findings.

Many of the retirees I interviewed for *Leisureville* complained that they were tired of giving back after paying their "fair share." Given that retirees are by definition on fixed incomes, it's understandable that they might feel the need to pull tighter on their purse strings. But as the United States falls further and further into debt, one wonders how generous younger generations will soon be toward their elders. They are inheriting more than $11 trillion in debt, after all, and the government spent nearly $1 trillion on elderly benefits in 2007 alone, up from $600 billion in 2000. Social Security, Medicare, and Medicaid now represent 35 percent of the federal budget. It's the largest budget expenditure (and that's not even including military or civil servant pensions) and translates into roughly $11,000 for every non-senior household.

The average senior now costs the government nearly $28,000 a year. By comparison, children cost about $4,000 a year. And the demographics aren't getting any prettier. The first Baby Boomers turn sixty-five in 2011, and by 2013, 40 percent of American households will be run by citizens over the age of fifty. If this fiscal train wreck's not a recipe for generational conflict, then I'm not sure what is.

Perhaps the one bright spot on the generational horizon was the image of Marian Robinson—the nation's "First Grandmother" —moving into the White House. At a time when more and more Americans are finding themselves once again living in extended family households due to economic pressures, such an image must certainly have been comforting. By contrast, former President George W. Bush chose to spend his post–White House years in a gated community whose neighborhood covenant excluded non-white residents (servants exempted) until a decade ago.

On a personal note, as Sun City turned fifty this year, I turned forty. While I certainly don't consider myself old, I'm no longer young either. Members of the media often ask me if I would consider living in a Leisurevillesque community one day. I'm happy to report that this is one question I can unequivocally answer: "No, not in this lifetime."

A. B.
Düsseldorf, Germany
2009

Acknowledgments

I'D LIKE TO THANK THE MANY RESIDENTS OF THE VILLAGES WHO let me tag along with them for days (and nights) at a time. I'd particularly like to thank my former neighbors for opening their lives to me, as well as their home. This book would never have come to fruition without their help and generosity. I'd also like to thank Erin Cox, formerly of *The Orlando Sentinel* for acting as my initial Villages tour guide and sounding board, and *The Orlando Sentinel* as a whole for their brilliant investigative work on Chapter 190, The Villages, and Gary Morse. Central Florida should consider itself fortunate to have journalists of this caliber. I'd like to thank the following people for kindly enduring hours of seemingly endless questions: Joe Gorman, Rich Lambrecht, Jim Roberts, Dan Connelly, Mark Fooks, and Edson Allen.

There were a number of people who were instrumental in the writing of this book. I'd like to thank my keen editor, the ever-dapper Jamison Stoltz, Morgan Entrekin, Catherine Drayton, Sid Plotkin, Dr. Gerald Lucas, JHK, my wonderful parents, and of course, Erika and Lillie.

Lastly, I'd like to thank my hometown for being a real community by nurturing its elders and youngsters, demanding participation, and holding fast against the forces of mindless sprawl and other community-destroying trends. May we continue to live in generational harmony for years to come.

For more information regarding the subjects I write about, I highly recommend the following books: *Fortress America* by Edward J. Blakely; *Prime Time* by Marc Freedman; *Geography of Nowhere* by James Howard Kunstler; *Suburban Nation* by Andres Duany, Elizabeth Plater-Zyberk, and Jeff Speck; *Privatopia* by Evan McKenzie; and *I'll Be Short* by Robert B. Reich. There are some groups out there working to promote social reengagement—civicventures.org is one of them. For more information regarding *Leisureville,* please visit www.andrewblechman.com.